IMAGES
of America

KING

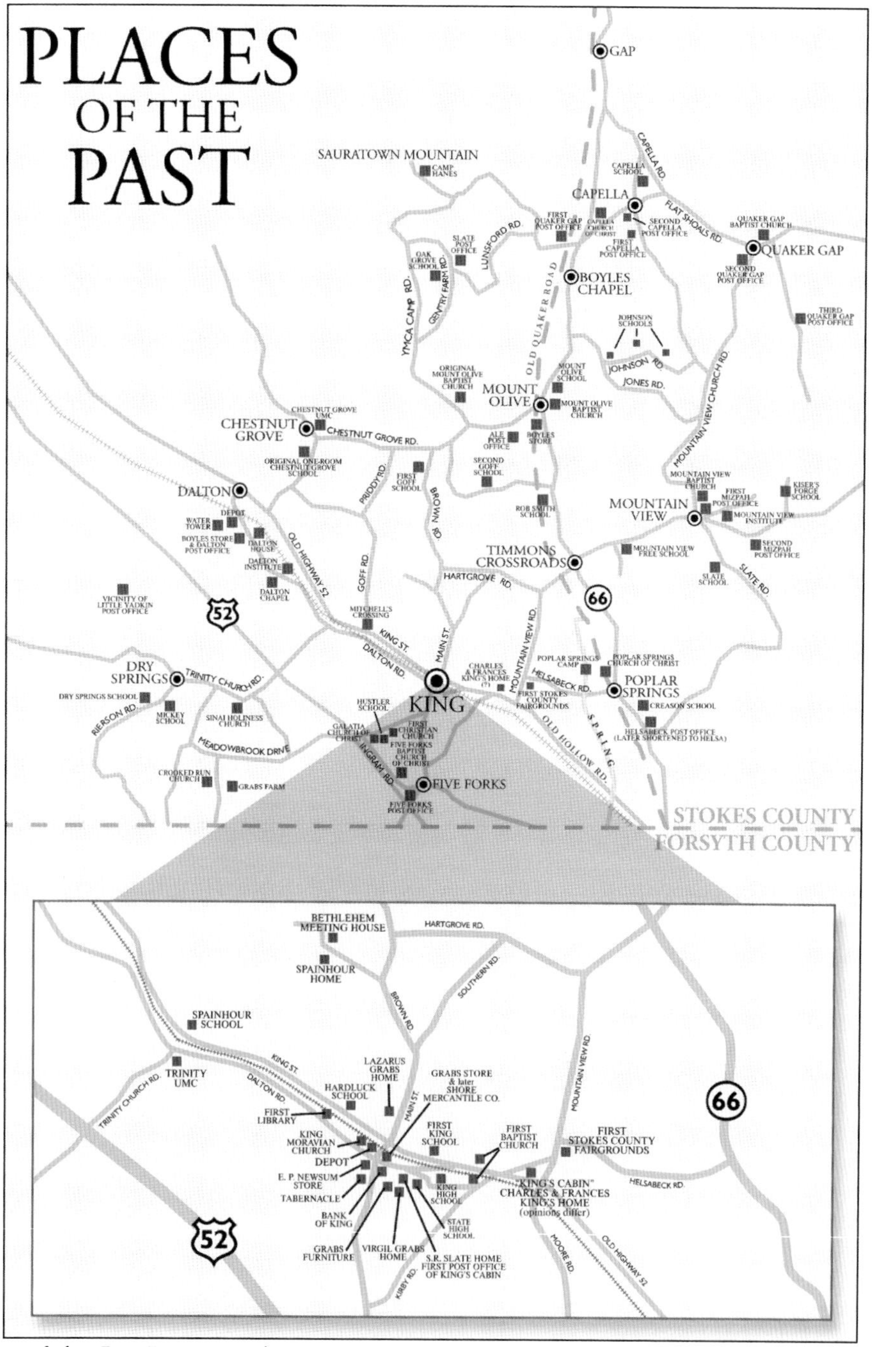

"Places of the Past" gives a glimpse at places in King no longer in existence, including surrounding communities, some of which are starting to fade from current maps or have been erased by progress. (Researched by the author and illustrated by Kenny Meade.)

On the Cover: In June 1970, *Winston-Salem Journal* photographer Frank Jones captured Tony and Jim Horton priming Ed White's early-season tobacco crop in King. (Courtesy of Forsyth County Public Library Photograph Collection.)

IMAGES
of America

KING

Chad Tucker

ARCADIA
PUBLISHING

ISBN 978-0-7385-4222-9

Published by Arcadia Publishing
Charleston, South Carolina

Printed in the United States of America

Library of Congress Catalog Card Number: 2005933194

For all general information contact Arcadia Publishing at:
Telephone 843-853-2070
Fax 843-853-0044
E-mail sales@arcadiapublishing.com
For customer service and orders:
Toll-Free 1-888-313-2665

Visit us on the Internet at www.arcadiapublishing.com

For Jenny,

Always

Contents

ACKNOWLEDGMENTS

This collection of historical images gained strength thanks to many of you who gave of your time, opening your homes and your personal photograph collections to help preserve our past.

In addition to those credited with sharing photographs throughout this collection, my appreciation is extended to: Deanne Moore and the King Chamber of Commerce, Matt Thorpe and the King Fire Department, librarian Molly Rawls of the Forsyth County Public Library Photograph Collection, librarian Steve Massengill of the North Carolina Archives Photograph Collection, Julie Harris of the *Winston-Salem Journal* News Library, Atlantic & Yadkin Valley Railroad researcher David Bott, Eddy McGee and the Stokes County Arts Council, Bob Kahle and YMCA Camp Hanes, Stokes County Historical Society, Max Bennett, Ted Bishop, Rodney Booth, Jim Boyles, Norma Cox, Sonya Cox, Max and Linda Engelhardt, Hughes Gentry, Patsy Ginns, Annie Sue Griffin, Brad Ingram, Margaret Johnston, Terry Kimel, Margaret Phillips McClanahan, Bobby "Crow" McGee, Marty McKinney, Kenny Meade, Clyde Moorefield, Eddy Morphies, Jim Moser, Ralph Moser, Rebecca Rains Moser, Susan Petree, Anne Phillips, Sarah Riddle, Trish Shouse, Mary Beth Sizemore, Sallie Spainhour, Stormy Speaks, and Chris Weaver. I am forever indebted to Lewis Carroll and Peggy Wall, who both worked extensively to locate and research photographs.

Thanks to my mother, Sue Tucker Lawson, whose faith, strong will, and grace for others continues to inspire me. Thanks to my Jenny, whose heart full of love and support made this project a reality.

A sincere thank-you to King historian Robert Carroll, whose knowledge and passion of local history has been a strong cornerstone of King and Stokes County's historical preservation. My greatest reward has been getting to know him over the years. The weekday mornings and Sunday afternoons that he welcomed me into his home quickly passed, but each visit held lessons that will always be cherished.

There is something a man nearing the century mark, such as Robert Carroll, can share with each of us, and for me, nearing three decades of life, it is this: the future is shared by those who helped write the past and paused in the present to preserve a glimpse.

For Robert Carroll's life work, the following pages are dedicated to him.

—Chad Tucker
October 2005

INTRODUCTION

Remember the days of old; consider the generations long past. Ask your father and he will tell you, your elders, and they will explain to you.
—Deuteronomy 32:7

The red clay rolling along the hills that lean toward the waters of the Little Yadkin River first welcomed settlers to this land. Before the land took on names, Native Americans may have spent time here, living along the riverbanks. This same water drew families of European descent to settle here. These founding families claimed a fertile future in the rich red clay.

One of the first to migrate here was Johann Jacob Spaenhauer (Spainhour) from Yorktown, Pennsylvania. He married Anna Catherine Volck (Fulk) in 1773 and the following year built a home along the streams that flow into the Little Yadkin. The land the Spainhours called home and raised 13 children on became the first known village in the area with a school and Lutheran church, which held services in a community building called Bethlehem Meeting House.

The Bethlehem Meeting House was built by John Fulk and may have even been used as a voting precinct. As 1812 records show, Fulk sold two acres of land for four shillings to Frederick Fisces and Adam Fulk, trustees of the Lutheran society called Bethlehem. The purchased land was near the Bethlehem Meeting House. In 1841, the first post office, named Little Yadkin, opened to serve this village. Before the post office, mail came from Germanton, Salem, or Bethania.

The community school, known as Spainhour School, closed in 1868 after being determined unfit for use. The meetinghouse closed soon after, and the village, located one mile north of present-day downtown King in what is today the Country Place neighborhood, slowly passed away. Its existence is only marked by the final resting place of these first settlers between two homes at the end of Shortie Court.

Two years after the school closed, a new Spainhour School opened on the Hollow Road that linked Salem to "The Hollows," today known as Mount Airy. The school was built near present-day Trinity United Methodist Church, which held its first services in the school in 1873. A community began taking shape here with several small businesses, but another village, known as Five Forks, was being born at the intersection of present-day Main Street, Jefferson Church Road, and Ingram Road. When the stagecoach route from Bethania met the intersection, it split into a five-road junction, with one of the roads no longer in existence.

Because Five Forks was a stagecoach stop, it became a strong village of commerce. The Five Forks Primitive Baptist Church began services in 1870 with the Five Forks Post Office opening the following year. Several stores, a tavern, a blacksmith shop, and a private school all opened to serve the village of Five Forks. But the stagecoach village's promise faded when the railroad decided not to lay tracks through Five Forks but instead through the open fields near the Hollow Road, called King's Cabin.

The community of King's Cabin began when several businesses and families saw the economic advantages the railroad could offer and moved closer. For 17 years, the community had been served by the Five Forks Post Office until Samuel Rufus Slate opened a post office in his home in 1888. Slate named the post office King's Cabin after a home on the Hollow Road that had become a landmark reference point in the area. Locals began using it after Charles and Frances King left Stokes County and their log home, owned by Frances's father, in the late 1830s. Some descendants believe Charles and Frances King were Quakers and against slavery, leaving the South for the free North and settling in Illinois. Others believe they left like many families did for open land in the North and West. After they left, residents used it as a landmark in traveling and directions, saying, "We're going over near the Cabin" or "You pass King's Cabin on your way." Charles and Frances King never returned to Stokes County and never knew their former home became the namesake of a town.

King's Cabin bloomed after founding families worked to make it a stop on the railroad. Nick Dalton, who had established the growing town of Dalton north of King's Cabin, wanted the train to only stop in his town, guaranteeing growth and commerce. Dalton gave the railroad two miles of a right-of-way through his property under the condition the railroad would never build a depot between Dalton and Rural Hall. When the people of King's Cabin found out, they built their own depot and sold it to the railroad for $1. The railroad kept their promise, and King's Cabin prospered over Dalton. On July 6, 1891, the community turned over the depot to the railroad, which started shortening the name to King in all its business transactions. Three years later, the postal service ordered that if mail was being delivered by train, the post office must have the same name as the depot to eliminate confusion. On September 26, 1894, King's Cabin became King.

The community grew into an unincorporated town of churches, a school, and businesses. With the first automobile arriving by train in October 1911, new highways followed, including the national highway today known as Old Highway 52 and King Street. With new roads, the town's close proximity to Winston-Salem, and a new four-lane Highway 52 built in the 1960s, King opened its front door to growth, turning farmland into subdivisions and changing its cash crop from tobacco to houses. With growth exploding, community groups like the King Lions Club acted as an unofficial town council, providing services such as a fire department in 1956, a water system in 1966, and a sewer system in 1978. On September 13, 1983, King became an incorporated town, 95 years after the King's Cabin post office opened.

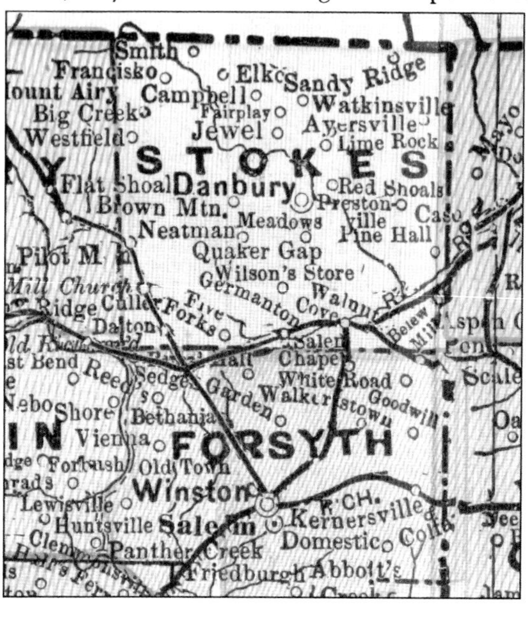

The village of Five Forks, along the stagecoach route, prospered before King and landed a place on this 1899 map commissioned by Congress. Notice other communities such as Dalton and Culler—today known as Pinnacle—are on the map, but King is not.

One

The Way We Were

As long as I can remember I've been interested in history and genealogy. I've always believed your history should be important to you. Especially the children, they need to know where they came from.

—Robert Carroll, King historian

"History is a gallery of pictures in which there are few originals and many copies," wrote political thinker and historian Alexis de Tocqueville. Images captured in photographs give us an open eye to the places of our past. Most of the images in this collection represent the first half of the 20th century. They help tell our story of a period not far past in comparison to the existence of time.

With the opening of each photographer's lens, a moment was captured; an image, a life, and a piece of time were recorded. The times before photography can only be told in words: the moments of courage when those who first came here moved on faith, planted their seeds, and prospered by grace.

The following pages hold more than images of founding families and the places they lived; they hold a spirit of community. This spirit built homes, commerce, schools, a depot, and, in turn, prosperity. This historical summary of King's past captures that spirit in the faces of its first families—our neighbors of the past whose foundation remains our cornerstone.

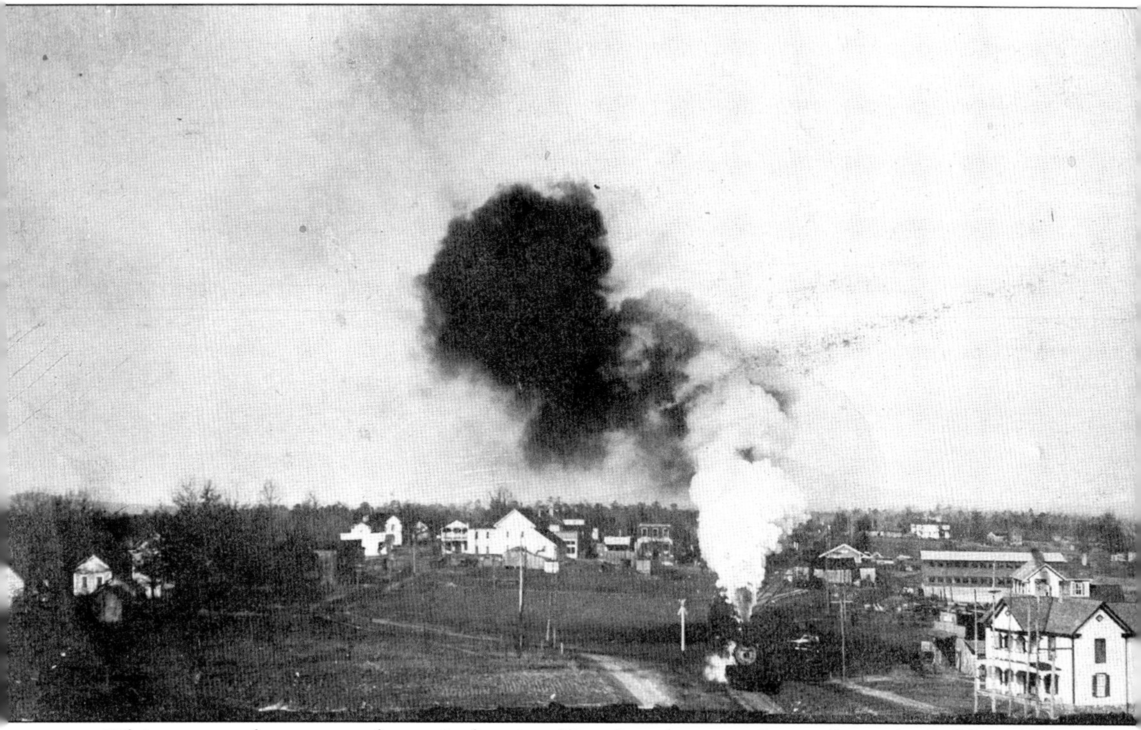

This postcard captures the train leaving King heading southeast from the belfry of State High School around 1911. Present-day downtown is in the distance underneath the train's black smoke. The white house in the foreground was the home of Allen White; his business, Allen's Livery Stable, is seen to the left. The two-story home behind Allen White's would become the home of Obert Rains, the King depot agent for almost 50 years. The large two-story building behind the Rains home was the machine shop and foundry of Virgil Grabs and William Holder, built in 1905. The two-story house above the foundry in the distance was the home of John Squire David Pulliam. Pulliam's home was used as a boardinghouse for schoolteachers. The home was torn down in 1988 to make room for the King Fire Department. To the left of the foundry, the top of the depot can be seen just above a fertilizer shed. Charles White's store can be seen left of the train's white smoke. White sold the building to the Stokes Supply Company the year this photograph was taken. The brick building to the left of White's Store is Soloman Kiger's store, the first brick building built in King. The large white structure is the Shore Mercantile Company, owned by the Grabs family when this photograph was taken. To the left of the Shore Mercantile Company is the Butner Store; W. E. Butner bought the building in 1904 and it stood until 1927, when the King Drug Company was built. E. P. Newsom's store, built in 1908, can be seen left of the Butner Store. The building was moved to make room for a gas station in the 1950s. The dirt road running through town, called Hollow Road, connected Winston-Salem with Mount Airy. Hollow Road became Main Street and then changed to Dalton Road after King incorporated in 1983. Depot Street, which runs horizontally in this photograph from in front of the depot to Hollow Road, became Main Street. (Courtesy of Robert Carroll.)

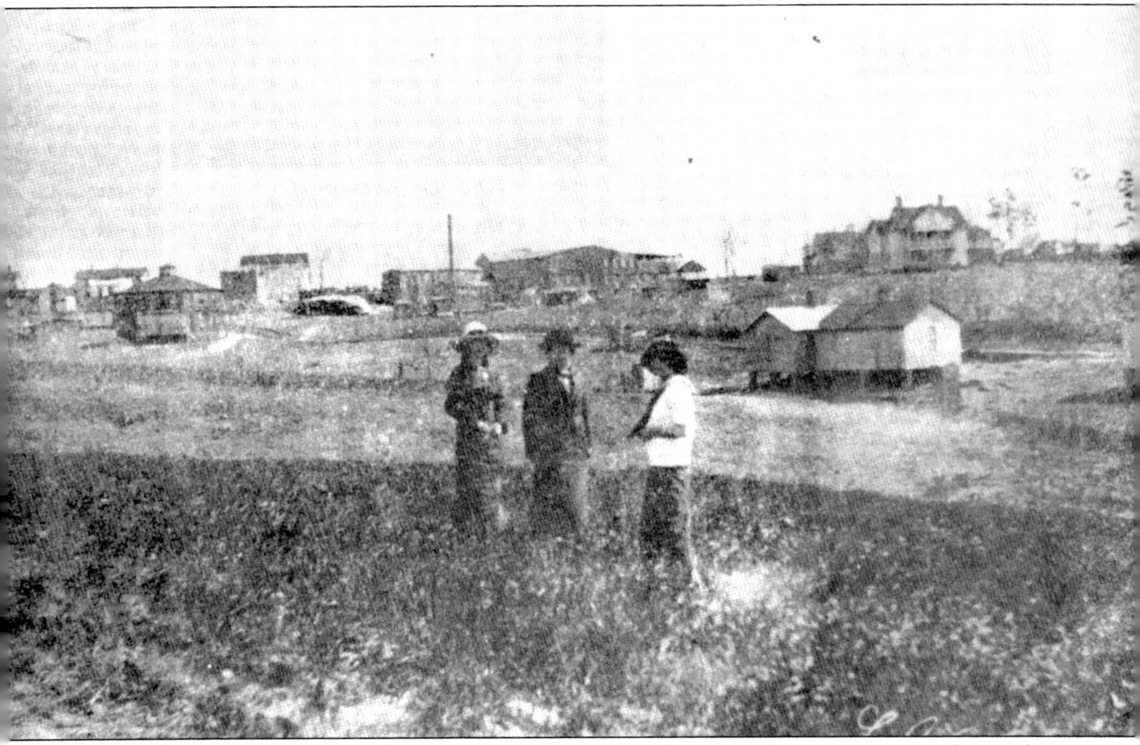

This 1912 photograph of Viola Ingram Spainhour (left), Rena Love Newsome (center), and Naomi Ingram Thompson was taken from a hill southwest of present-day downtown between Pulliam Street and Meadowbrook Drive. At far left is the Tabernacle, an octagonal building completed in 1900. Community leader Virgil Grabs; his brother Lazarus; and father, Lewis, seeing a need for a structure to house community assemblies, sold one acre for $1 to a committee for the construction of the Tabernacle. The building was built across from present-day city hall with a platform for school programs, commencements, preaching services, and elections. All the material was donated, and the Grabs Furniture Manufacturing Company dressed the lumber. The structure had no floor and only wide-dressed planks from the door to the platform for seating. The Tabernacle was used until an auditorium was built at the King High School. Behind the Tabernacle, to the left, the top of the Butner Store can be seen. To the right of the Tabernacle is the Grabs's tenant home. John Love lived in the home when this photograph was taken. About two years after this photograph, the home was replaced with the Bank of King. The Shore Mercantile Company can be seen behind the tenant home. The long two-story building with a smoke stack to its left is the V. T. Grabs Furniture Company. The large two-story home on the hill to the right of the factory was the home of Virgil Grabs and his wife, Alice. Behind Virgil Grabs's home was the home of Samuel Rufus Slate, King's Cabin's first postmaster. The first post office was located in the Slates' home. The small white structures in the foreground of the Virgil Grabs home sat along Depot Street (today South Main Street) and were owned by the Grabses, who used them as tenant homes. (Courtesy of Robert Carroll.)

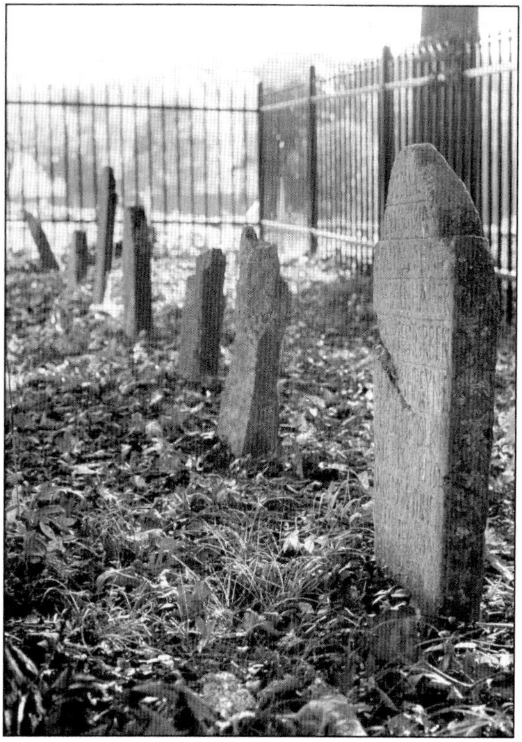

The Spainhour Cemetery, located today between two homes on Shortie Court in the Country Place neighborhood, is all that is left of the first village in the area that would become King. The Bethlehem Meeting House is believed to have been located next to the cemetery.

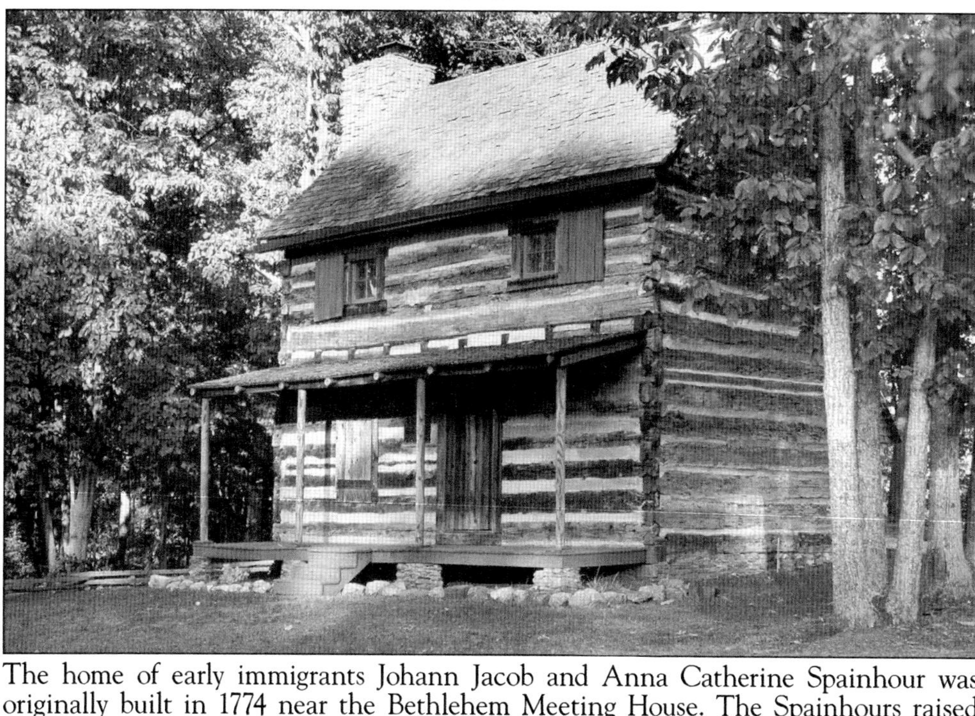

The home of early immigrants Johann Jacob and Anna Catherine Spainhour was originally built in 1774 near the Bethlehem Meeting House. The Spainhours raised 13 children in this two-story cabin made of forest pine logs. In 1997, the home was dismantled from its original site and two years later reconstructed in King's Central Park as a tribute to the courage and commitment of the area's early immigrants.

Charles King and Frances Kiser, in the only known photograph of them together, married in August 1826. Their home, King's Cabin, became the namesake of King, North Carolina. Charles King was born in 1806 near the historic Rock House of Stokes County. While traveling south on Quaker Road (today Highway 66) *c.* 1826, he stopped at Poplar Springs, a well-known rest stop and camp for travelers. Here he met Frances, whose father owned the springs and thousands of surrounding acres. The couple moved into a log home on Frances's father's land on Hollow Road (today East King Street). The Kings later left Stokes County for Illinois, never returning and never knowing the home they left behind, called King's Cabin by locals, would become a reference point in the community and later be used as the name of a town. (Courtesy of Max and Linda Engelhardt.)

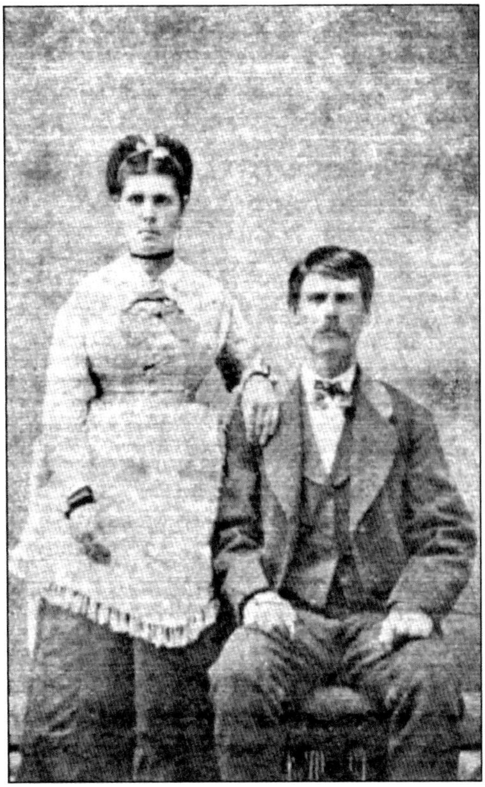

DIED.

KING.—At his residence in this city, Friday morning, August 9th, 1878, after a brief illness, CHARLES KING.

Mr. King was born in Stokes county, North Carolina, December 14th, 1806. He was married August 4th, 1826, to Miss Frances Keyser, who at the age of sixty-seven years, in full health, survives her husband with whom she lived an eventful life of four days more than fifty-two years. They were the parents of twelve children, only two of whom are dead. Two are in North Carolina, two in Indiana, two in Colorado, one in Texas, and three in Illinois, one of whom, Mrs. F. M. Davis, resides in this city. They removed to this State in 1855, settling in Richmond precinct, where the town of Newmansville now is. In 1864 they removed to this city where they have since resided, where he has often held positions of public trust, and as often faithfully discharged his duty. It seemed to be his greatest joy to preach, and he has often traveled from place to place holding revival meetings. As late as last Summer he worked in the cause, holding services at Sand Prairie and near Meredosia. He has long been feeble and suffered much up to the time of his departure. The funeral services were conducted by Rev. J. D. Wyckoff, at the family residence, on Saturday at three o'clock

Records show Charles and Frances King left Stokes County in the late 1830s. Charles's obituary (seen at left), says they last settled in Richmond Precinct, Illinois, in 1855. Some descendants believe Charles and Frances King were of the Quaker faith and against slavery and that they left the South for the free North. Others believe they left like many families of the time heading for open land. They had 12 children; two young sons are presumed to have died after they wandered in the woods of Illinois and never returned. Charles spent his life as a farmer and preacher before he died in 1878 in Beardstown, Illinois. Frances, a homemaker, died the following year on Christmas Day from marasmus. (Courtesy of Max and Linda Engelhardt.)

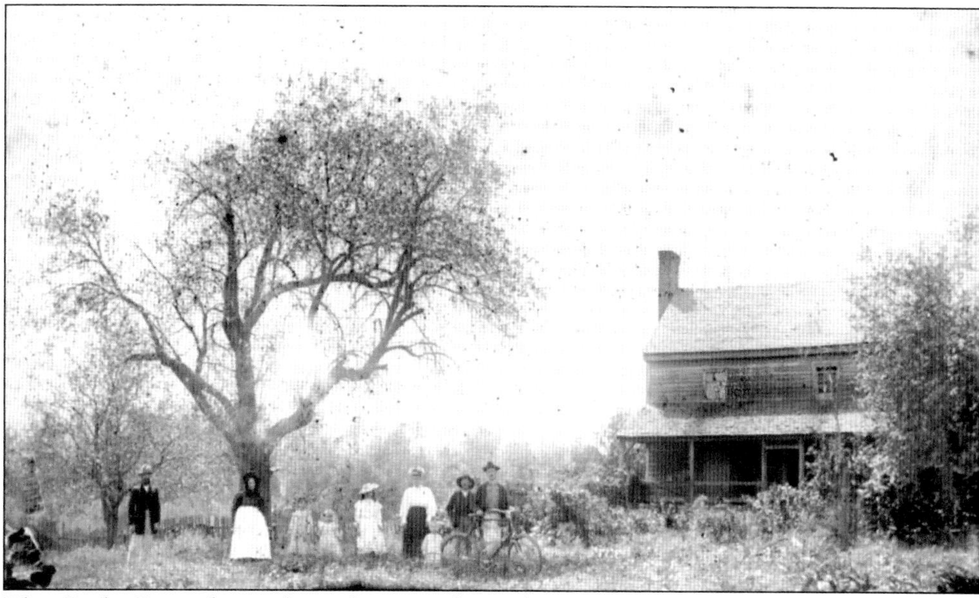

The Grabs Farm, located in what is today "The Farm" neighborhood in King, is seen in 1896. John and Maria "Polly" Grabs bought the farm in 1829 when they moved from Bethania with their daughters—Julina, Pamelia, Felicia—and son, Lewis Edwin Grabs. After John and Polly's deaths, Lewis remained on the family farm, married Harriet Spainhour, and had seven children. His sons Lazarus and Virgil helped lay King's foundation. From left to right are Frank Grabs, Harriet Spainhour Grabs, Grace Grabs, Elsie Grabs, Hattie Grabs, Alice Fulp, Manly Grabs, John Grabs, and Gene Newsome. (Courtesy of Susan Petree.)

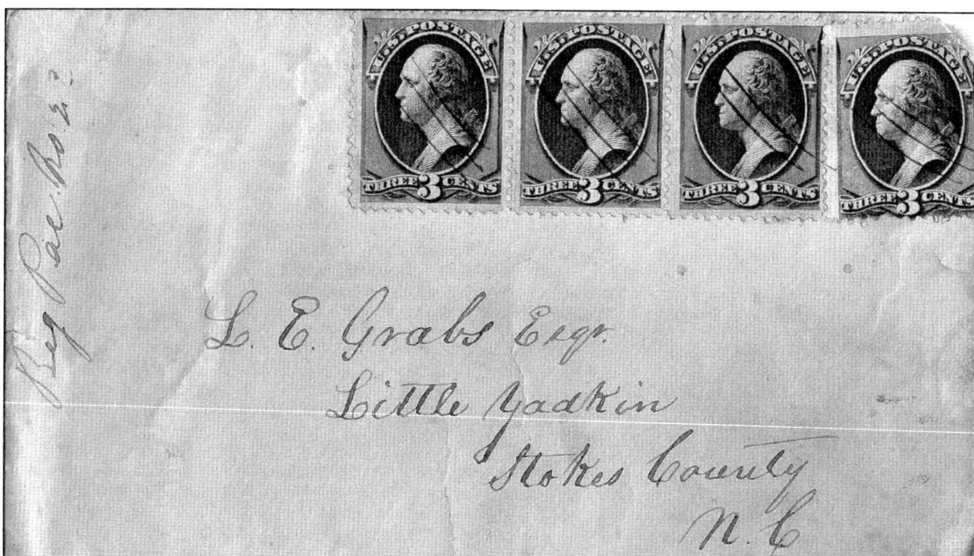

When the Grabs family arrived in 1829, there was no local post office, and the mail, if any, came to the area from Bethania, Salem, or Germanton. The first local post office believed to serve area families was the Little Yadkin Post Office, which opened in 1841. The above letter is addressed to (Lewis Edwin) Grabs of Little Yadkin, Stokes County, North Carolina, about 1860. (Courtesy of Susan Petree.)

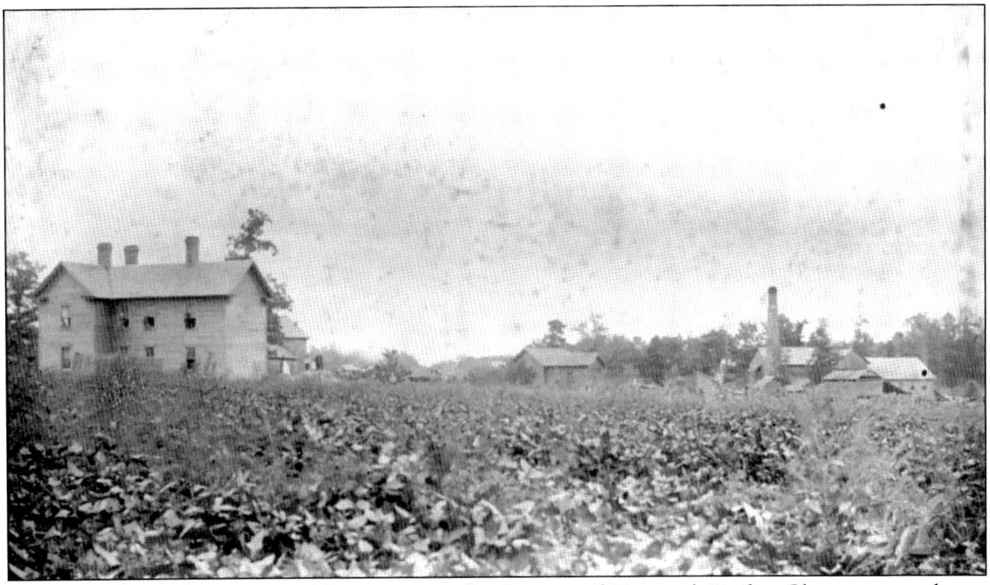

King's Cabin's first post office was in the home of Samuel Rufus Slate, seen above in the far left of this 1897 photograph. The Grabs Furniture Manufacturing Factory and its brick smokestack can be seen in the right of the photograph. The post office opened on March 30, 1888. The King's Cabin community had been receiving their mail first from Little Yadkin until 1871, then from Five Forks for 17 years. With people and businesses leaving the stagecoach route of Five Forks for the railroad tracks at King's Cabin, residents requested their own post office. Samuel Slate named the post office King's Cabin. When the community turned over the depot to the railroad in 1891, the railroad shortened the name to King as a form of abbreviating. The postal service soon after ordered that the depot and post office must have the same name to eliminate confusion. On September 26, 1894, King's Cabin Post Office became King. Below is a letter addressed to (Lewis) Edwin Grabs in Kings Cabin, Stokes County, North Carolina. (Courtesy of Susan Petree.)

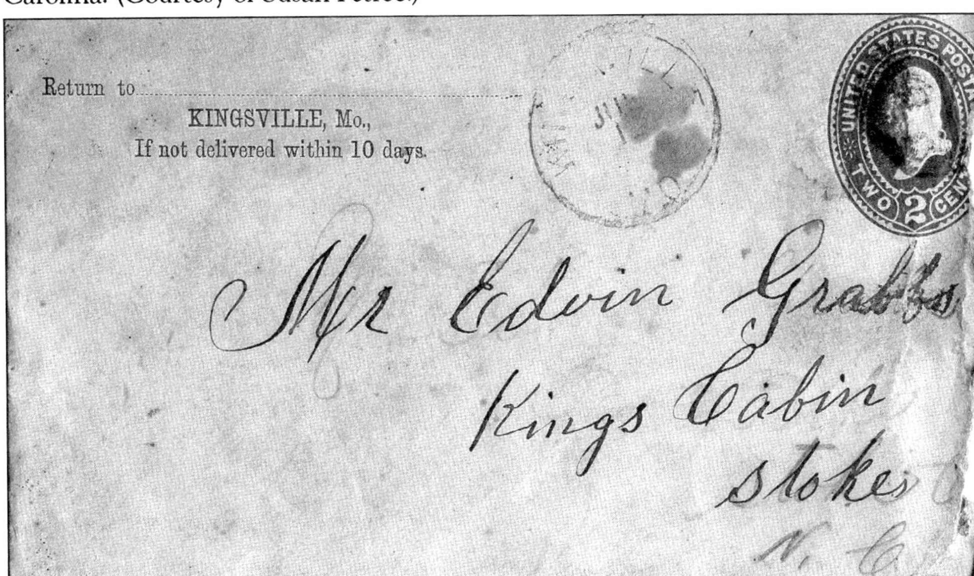

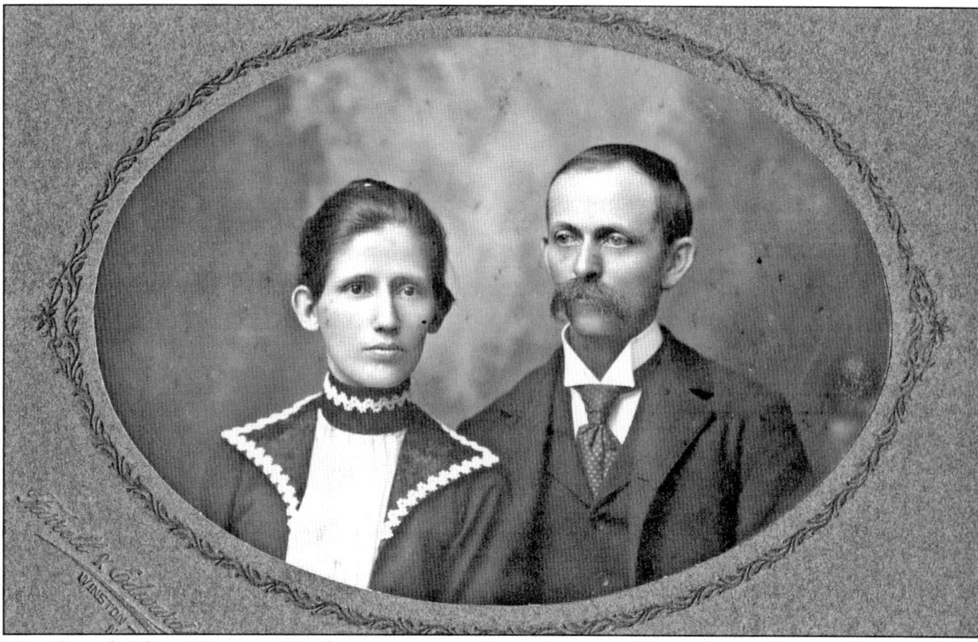

Virgil and Alice Kreeger Grabs are pictured on their wedding day in December 1900. A talented inventor receiving patents on inventions such as pie safes and slat beds, Virgil Grabs is credited with being a leader in helping found King. He promoted building a depot in 1890, building a community building known as the Tabernacle, opening the Bank of King in 1913 with himself as president, pushing for a high school, and helping establish King's first telephone company. Virgil and his wife had no children. Virgil died in 1935, and Alice died in 1950. (Courtesy of Susan Petree.)

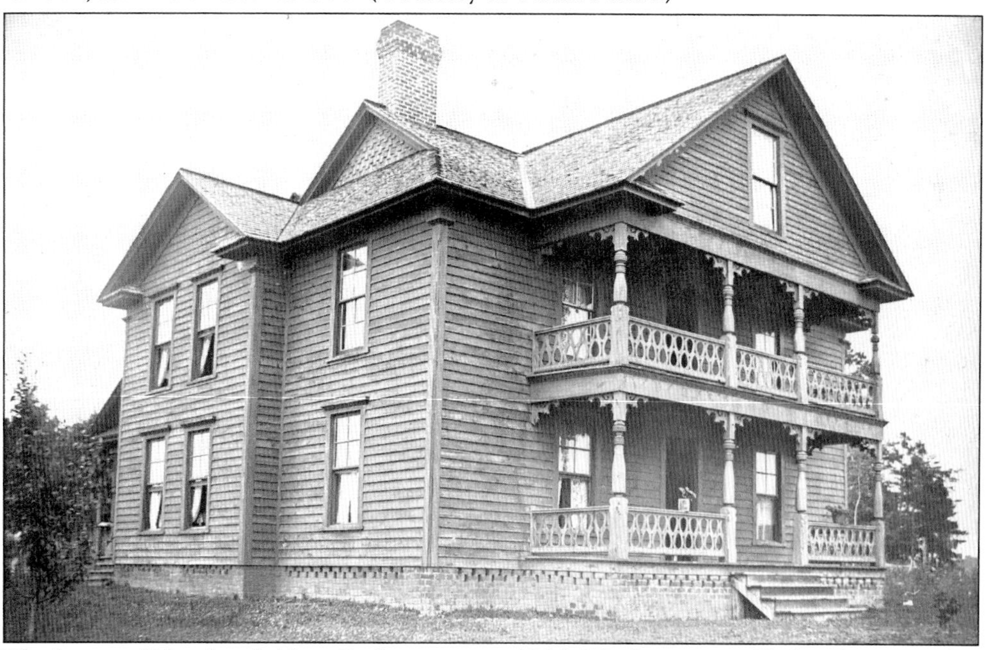

The home of Virgil and Alice Grabs is seen in 1900. The home stood behind present-day King City Hall until the home was burned in the 1960s. (Courtesy of Susan Petree.)

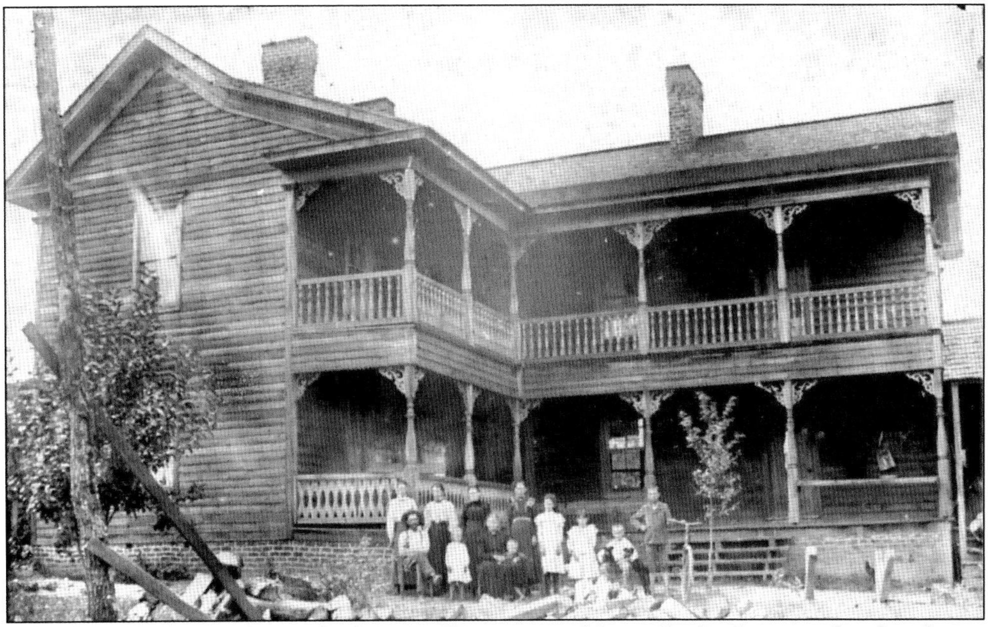

This *c.* 1898 picture shows the home of Lazarus and Jane Grabs. Lazarus first lived in a log house on Brown Road in King, where he ran a water-wheel grain mill. In 1893, he built this home, which still stands today on Bob Rierson Road. Lazarus and Jane Grabs married in 1876 and had nine children. From left to right are Lillian Spainhour (a neighbor), Lazarus Grabs (seated), Lula Grabs, Elsie Grabs, Minnie Grabs, Jane Grabs (seated), Manly Grabs, Girtie Grabs, Hattie Grabs, Grace Grabs, Omnie Grabs with his two dogs, and Baxter Grabs holding his bicycle. (Courtesy of Susan Petree.)

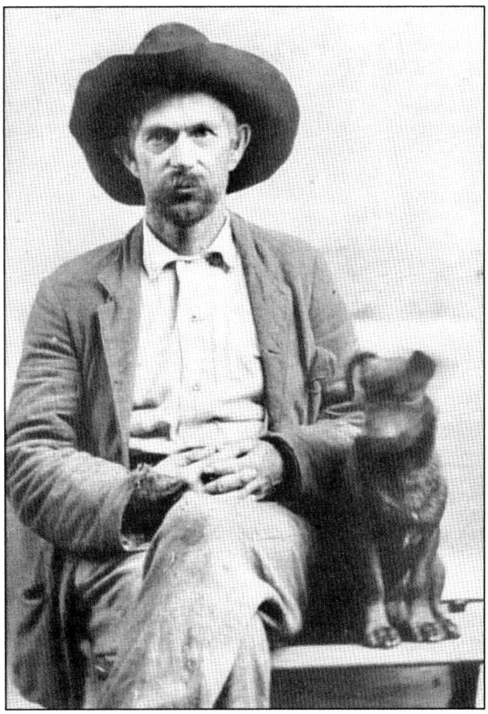

This undated photograph captures Lazarus Grabs with his dog, Money. Lazarus, his brother Virgil, and his father, Lewis Edwin, started L. E. Grabs and Sons Manufacturing Company and were active pioneers of King. Lazarus died in 1938, and his wife, Jane, died in 1945. (Courtesy of Susan Petree.)

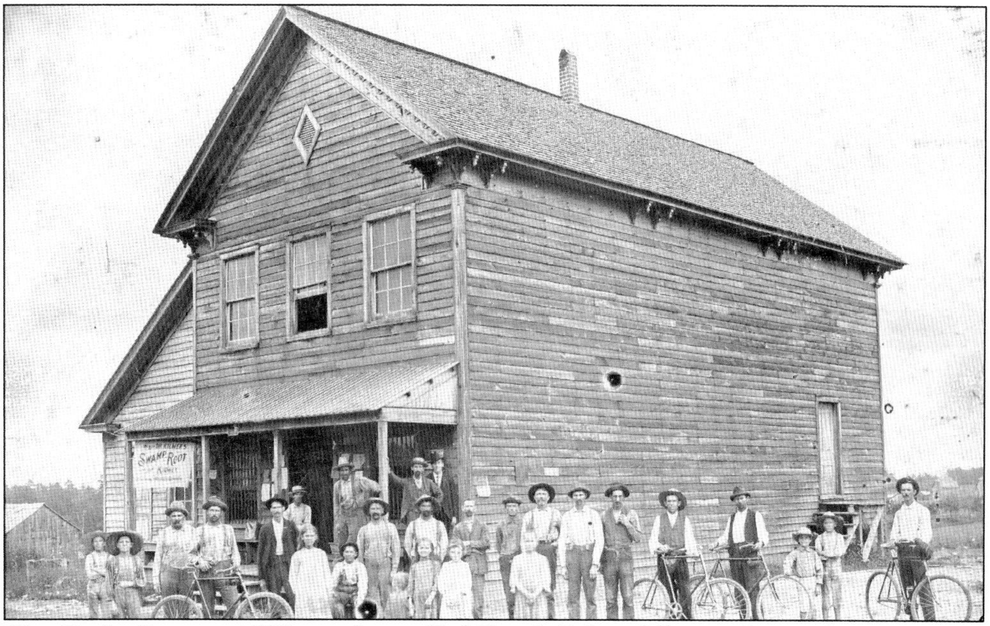

The Grabs Store, *c.* 1897, was first called King's Cabin Alliance Store when it opened in 1890. Lewis Grabs's sons started many projects under the roof of this store, which later turned into a successful business. When King's Cabin became King in 1894, the Grabs family changed the name of their store to L. E. Grabs and Sons. The store remained open until 1910, when the Grabs family leased the building to the Shore Mercantile Company. From left to right are (on the porch) unidentified, Ike Barr, Julius Kreeger, and ? Stewart; (standing below) Ike Barr's unidentified son, Jim Love, John Wes Spainhour, Jim Hutchens, unidentified, Flora Spainhour, Tom Love, John Love, Stacey and Dewey Lane, Bob Love, Grace Grabs, Sam Newsome, Kick Hutchens, Ann Love, Bob Hutchens, Sid Pulliam, John Ransome, Sid Shaub, Virgil Grabs, two children of Ike Barr, and Tom Moser. (Courtesy of Susan Petree.)

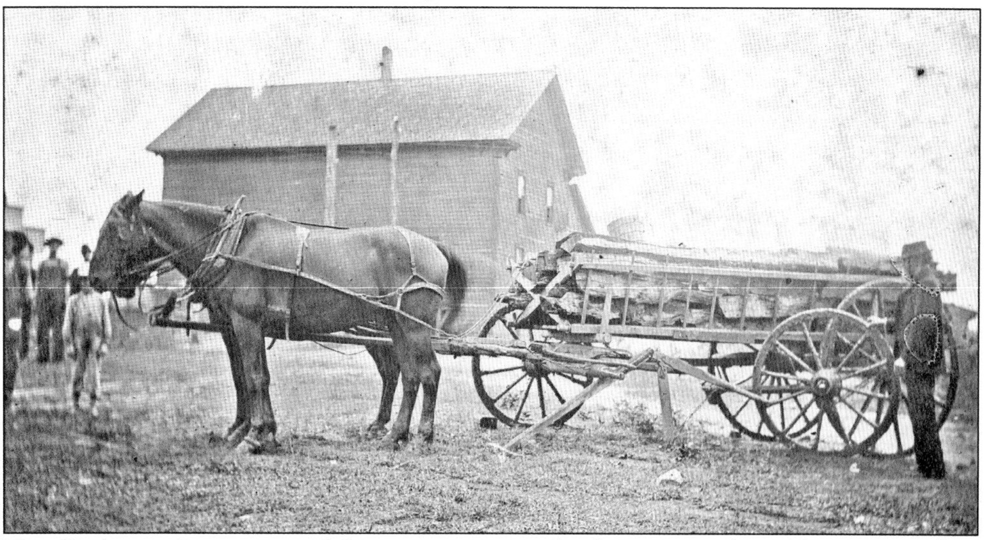

The Grabs sons' invention of the grease wagon wheel is seen in this 1894 picture taken behind the Grabs Store. (Courtesy of Susan Petree.)

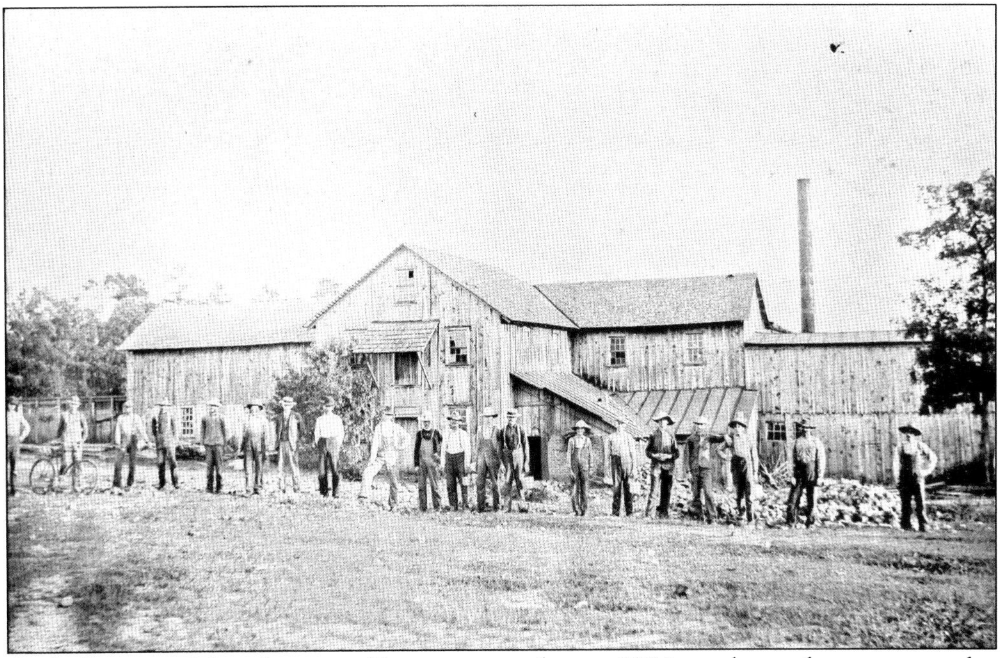

Grabs Furniture Manufacturing Company, seen here *c.* 1904, was located near present-day downtown King and city hall. Owner Virgil Grabs produced his inventions of household furnishings here, including the pie safe and bed railings with wire chips to hold the bed slats in place. The building was torn down in 1926. (Courtesy of Hughes Gentry.)

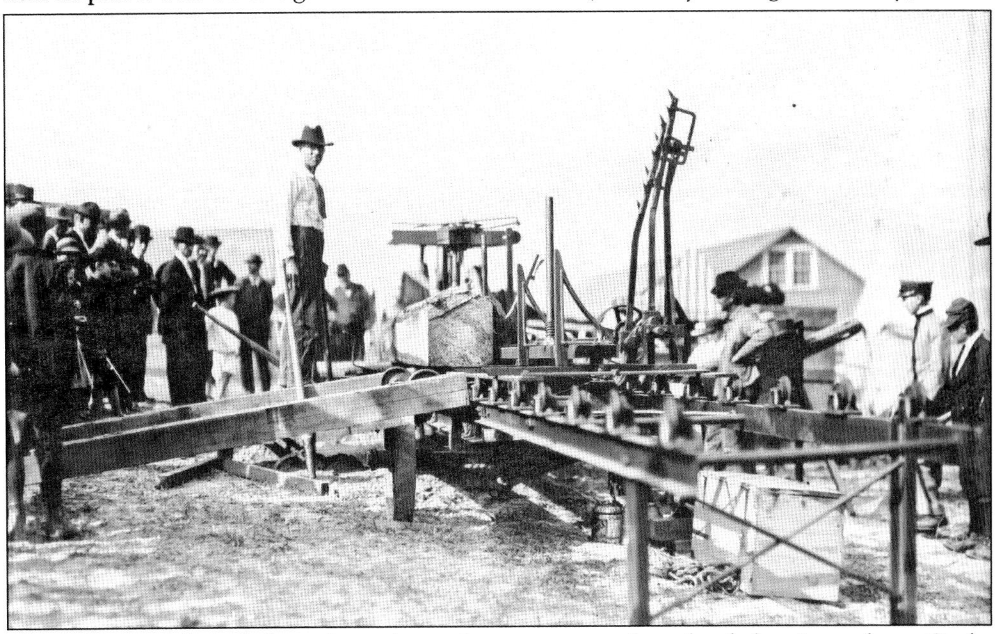

This photograph is believed to show the system used to load furniture from Grabs Furniture Manufacturing Company onto the train at the depot *c.* 1917. The roof of the depot can be seen behind the man standing on the platform. A railroad agent can be seen in the far right, with the Grabs Machine Shop and Foundry behind him. The company shipped furniture up and down the southeast coastal states. (Courtesy of Adeline Kiser.)

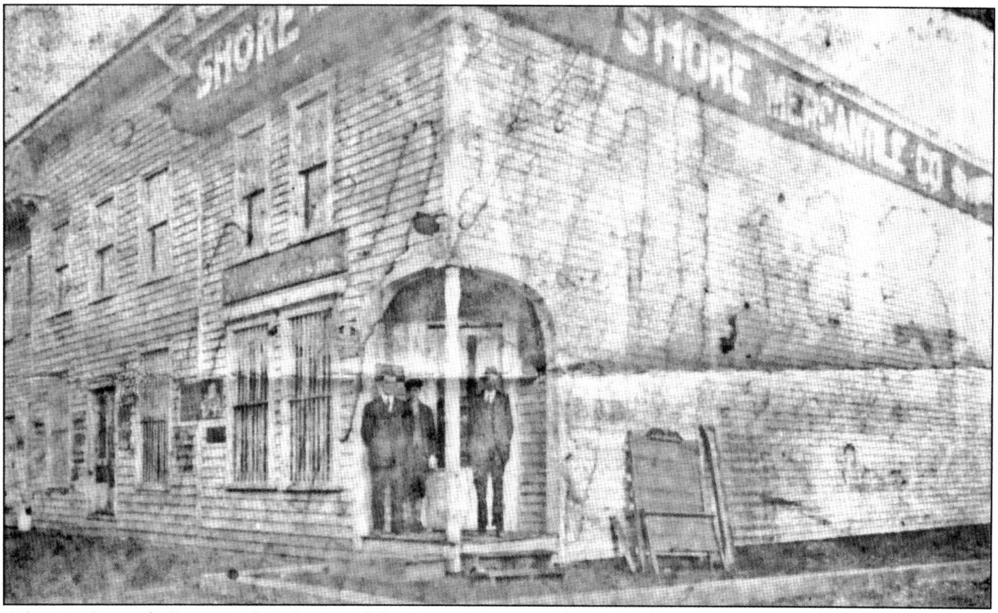

Above from left to right, James Newsom; an unidentified man; and Newsom's brother-in-law, Fred Shore, are seen at the entrance of Shore Mercantile Company *c.* 1911. Newsom and Shore became business partners and opened the store a year earlier, renting the building from the Grabs family, who had operated the Grabs Store here since 1890. In 1912, Calvin Ollie Boyles rented the building from the Grabs family and opened the Boyles Dry Goods Mercantile Company, as seen below. In 1914, Fred Shore re-opened the Shore Mercantile Company here with W. I. Eaton and R. A. Moore as stockholders. The company bought the building from the Grabs family and advertised it as "The Big Store." The store became a landmark in the community for decades, with Fred Shore and later his son, Tink, running the company. The wooden structure was torn down in 1958 to make way for the brick building that houses Terry's Furniture today. Fred Shore died in 1963, and his son, Tink, died in 1982. (Courtesy of Bobby "Crow" McGee.)

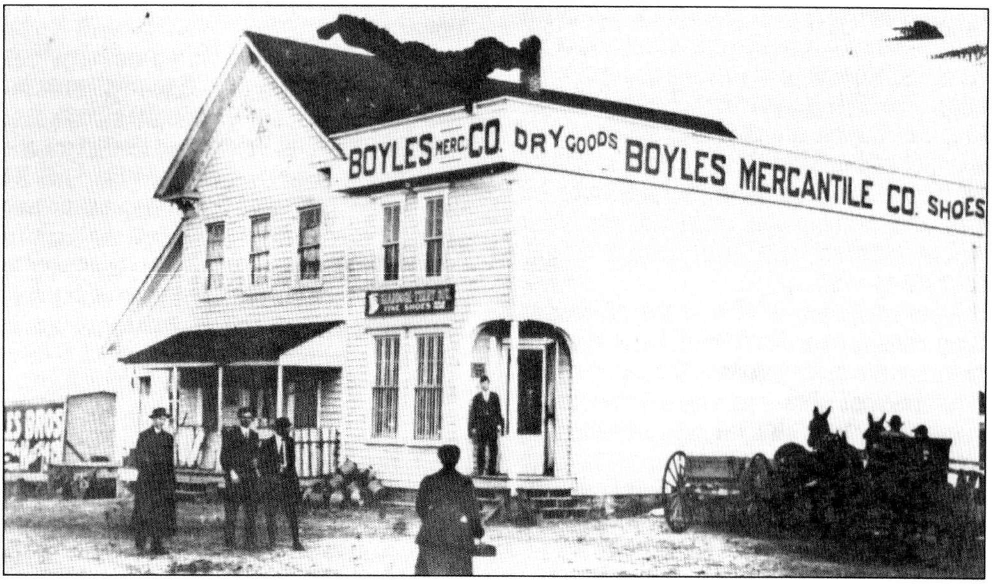

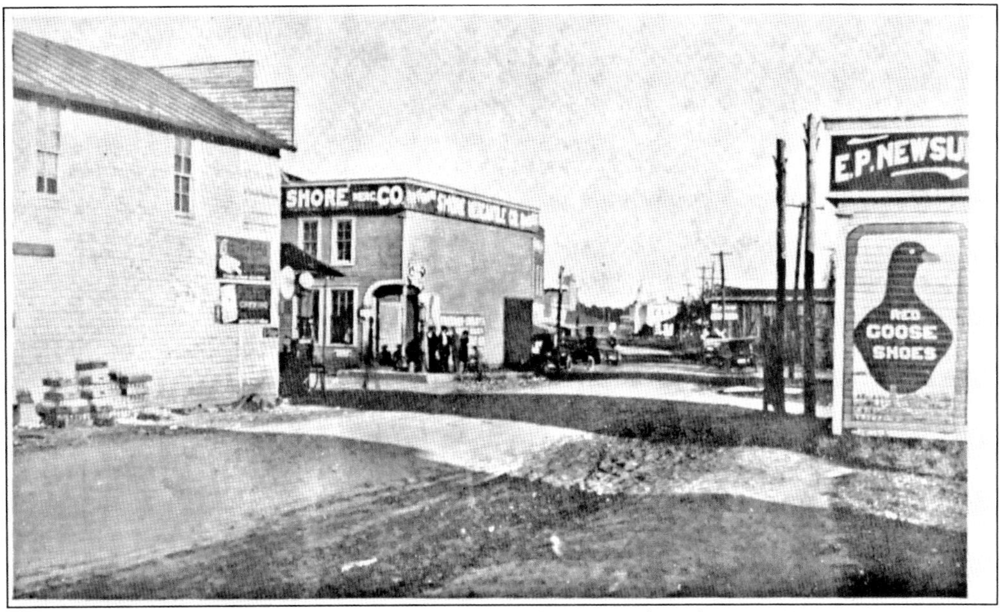

This 1920s postcard shows the present-day Dalton Road and Main Street intersection. The photograph looks east toward the State High School, seen in the distance. The building to the left is the Butner Store, which stood until King Drug Company was built in 1927. Shore Mercantile can be seen with several men standing around the gas pump. The edge of E. P. Newsum Store, with an advertisement for Red Goose Shoes, can be seen at right.

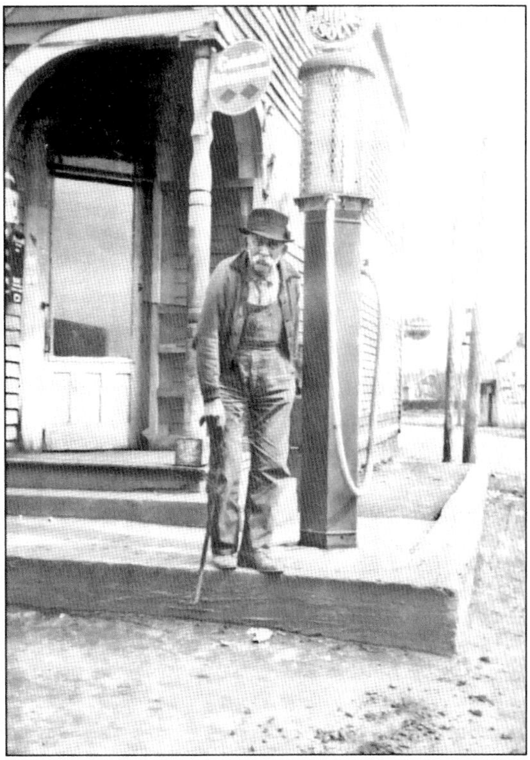

"Tom Frank" Newsom stands in front of Shore Mercantile *c.* 1923. Newsom operated stores at Rockford, Five Forks, Tobaccoville, and King. He operated the post office at Five Forks from 1875 until 1879. Newsom was hired as the King's Cabin postmaster in 1894 to help the post office change its name to King. He married Martha Pulliam in 1877 and they had nine children: Elmer P. (owner and operator of E. P. Newsum Store), Oscar, Martha, Claudia, Charlie, Cladie, Theodore "Fip" (a local historian), Annie, and Paul. (Courtesy of Dorothy Newsom Marshall.)

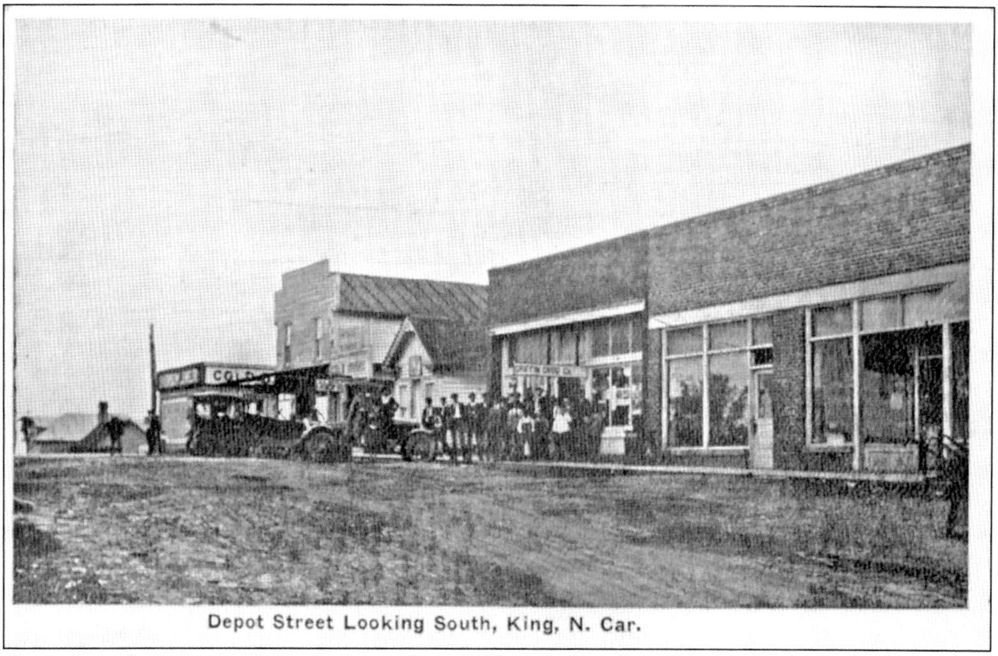

A group of men are captured in this 1920s postcard gathered around Griffin Drug Company on Depot Street (today's Main Street). The photograph was taken from the railroad tracks looking south at downtown King. (Courtesy of Marshall Boyles.)

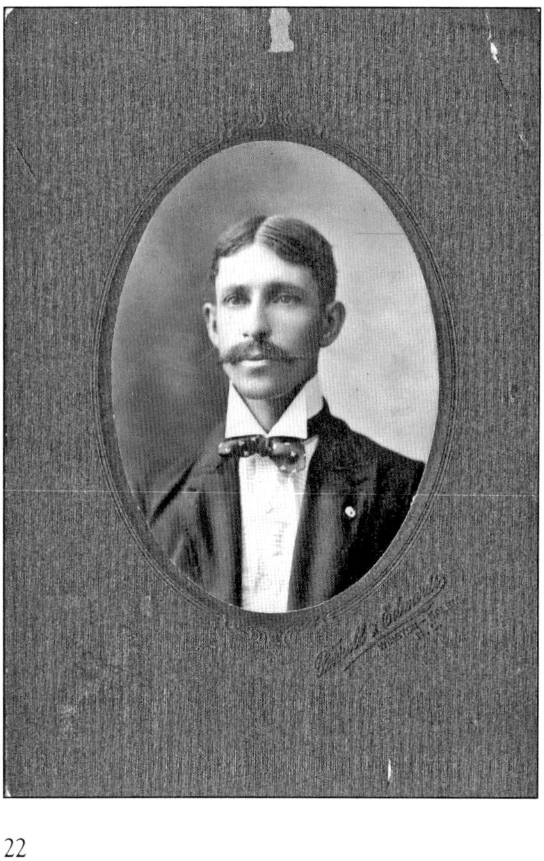

Dr. Ernest Griffin opened the Griffin Drug Company shortly after arriving in King in early 1919 from Farmington, Davie County. Griffin practiced medicine in the drug store with his wife, Blance, a practical nurse, until eight days before his death in 1944. (Courtesy of Annie Sue Griffin.)

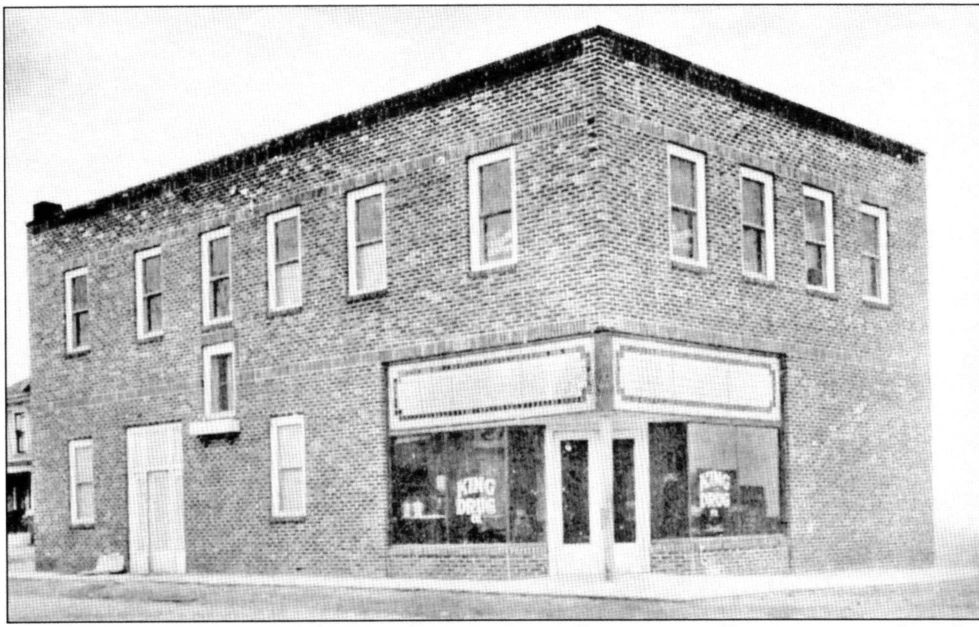

The Stone Building, which houses the King Drug Company in King, is captured in this 1930s postcard. (Courtesy of Adeline Kiser.)

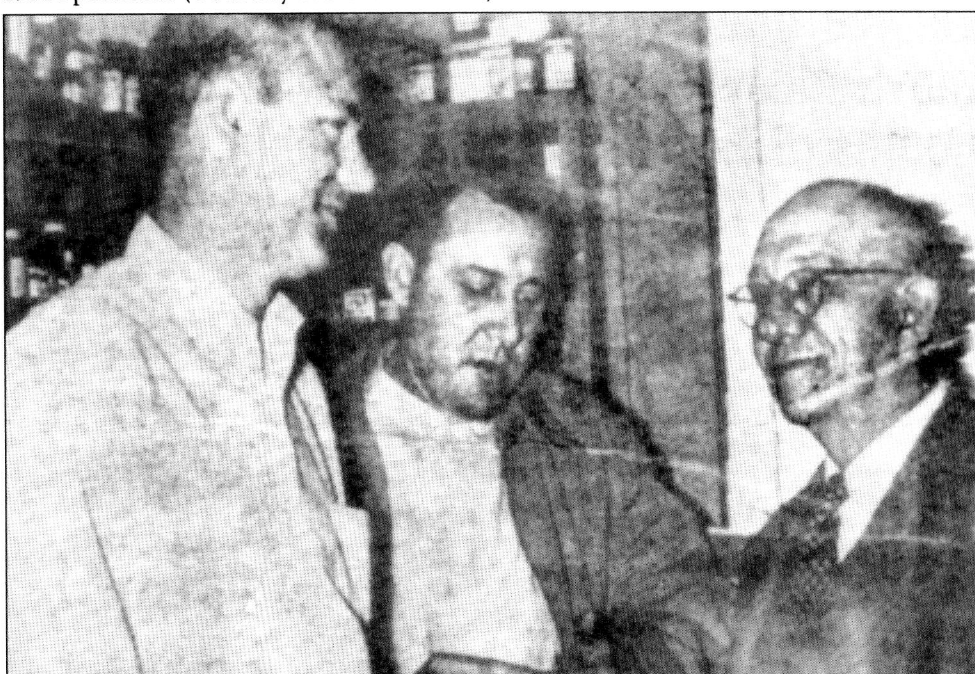

From left to right, pharmacist Richard Stone, Dr. Grady Stone, and Dr. Rupert Helsabeck are pictured inside the King Drug Company. In 1925, Dr. Helsabeck and Dr. Stone bought the Butner Store and property, which had been located here since the early 1890s. Two years later, in 1927, they replaced the two-story wooden structure with a brick building that housed King Drug Company. (Courtesy of Stokes County Historical Society.)

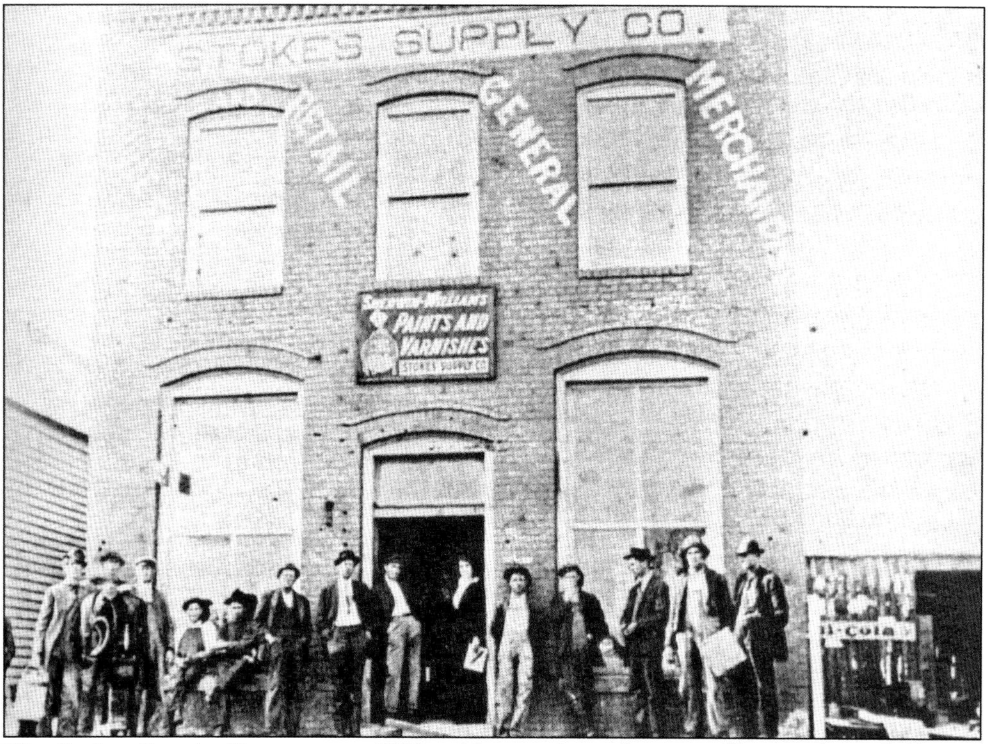

The Stokes Supply Company, c. 1920, sold everything from needles to wheat drills and housed the King Post Office for about two years. To the left of the doorway is James Bowen; in the doorway are William Hartman (left) and Trilby Love (right). On March 9, 1911, James Riley, William Hartman, and others bought the store from Charles White. When Hartman became postmaster in 1920, he moved the post office into the back of the building. In 1925, the store closed when the owners couldn't turn a profit after extending credit to farmers whose crops failed. (Courtesy of Stokes County Historical Society.)

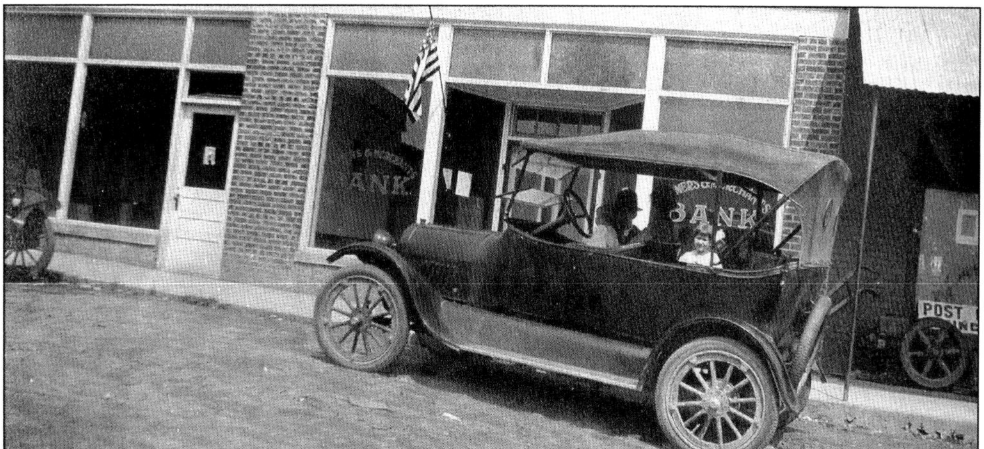

Farmers and Merchants Bank is captured in this photograph taken in King on July 4, 1920. In 1920, the Farmers and Merchants Bank became the second bank to open in King. It failed a few years later. Notice the sign in front of the building to the right of the bank, which reads "Post Office, King, NC." (Courtesy of Doris Rutledge and Hugh Kiser.)

From left to right, Jack Gunter, Tink Shore, Mack Hartman, Ruth Hartman, and Ruth Everette Boyles Kiser wait for the train at the King depot in the 1920s. (Courtesy of Doris Rutledge and Hugh Kiser.)

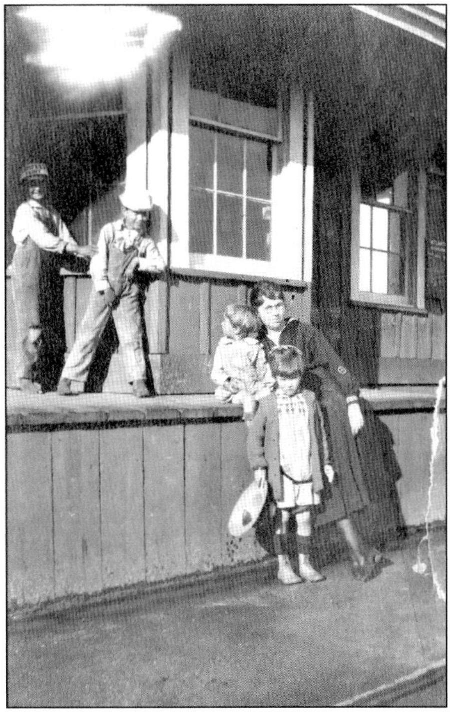

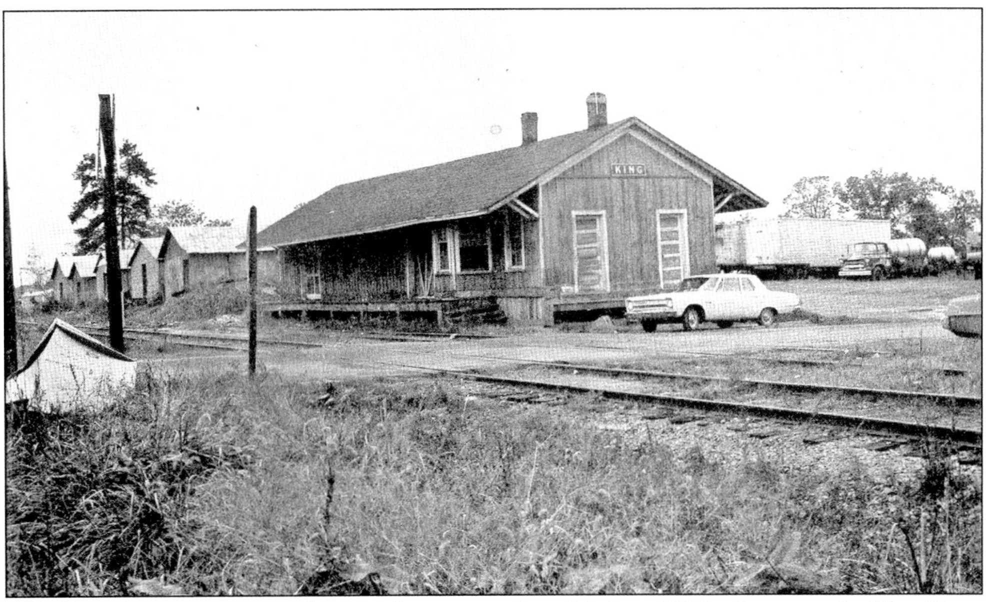

The King Depot was torn down a few years after this late-1960s photograph. The Cape Fear & Yadkin Valley Railroad only planned mail flag stops when it first laid tracks here in the 1880s. Nick Dalton, who founded the community of Dalton between King and Pinnacle, gave the railroad two miles of right-of-way through his prosperous community, with the condition that the railroad never build a depot between Rural Hall and Dalton, making his community a center of trade for local farmers. The people of King, wanting the train to stop, built a depot themselves and sold it to the railroad for $1. (Courtesy of Jim Moser.)

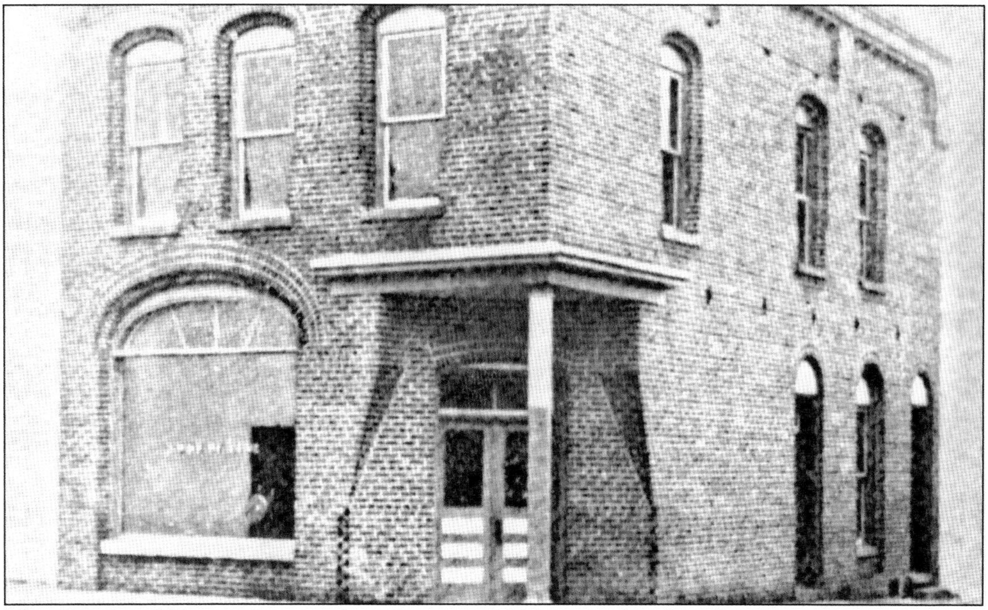

The Bank of King, chartered in January 1914, was the first bank to open in King. Community leader Virgil Grabs promoted the idea of a town bank, and the building, which still stands today at the corner of Main Street and Dalton Road, was built on Grabs's property. With several stockholders' support, Grabs was elected president. In the 1920s, the Bank of King became the King branch of the Bank of Stokes County. When the Great Depression hit, the bank failed. Soon after the bank closed, the building was used as a hardware store until chicken producer Holbin Johnson opened Johnson's Hatchery in the building in the early 1930s. Johnson produced chickens here until 1955, when the State Planter's Bank of Walnut Cove bought the building and opened a branch here. Below, from left to right, Arnold Moore, Ronnie White, William Marshall, and Walt McKinney are pictured in front of the newly opened State Planter's Bank. (Courtesy of Peggy Wall.)

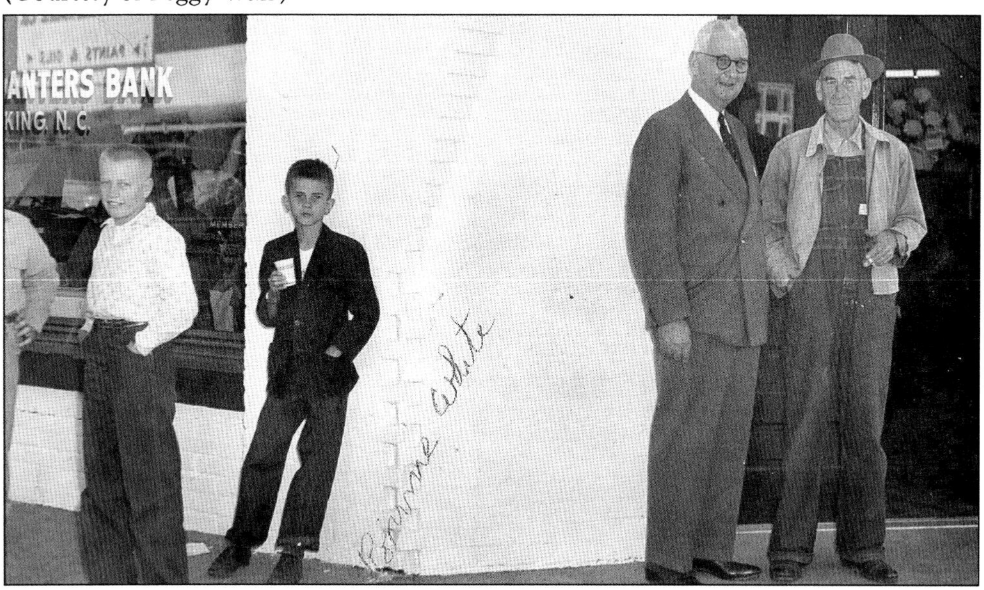

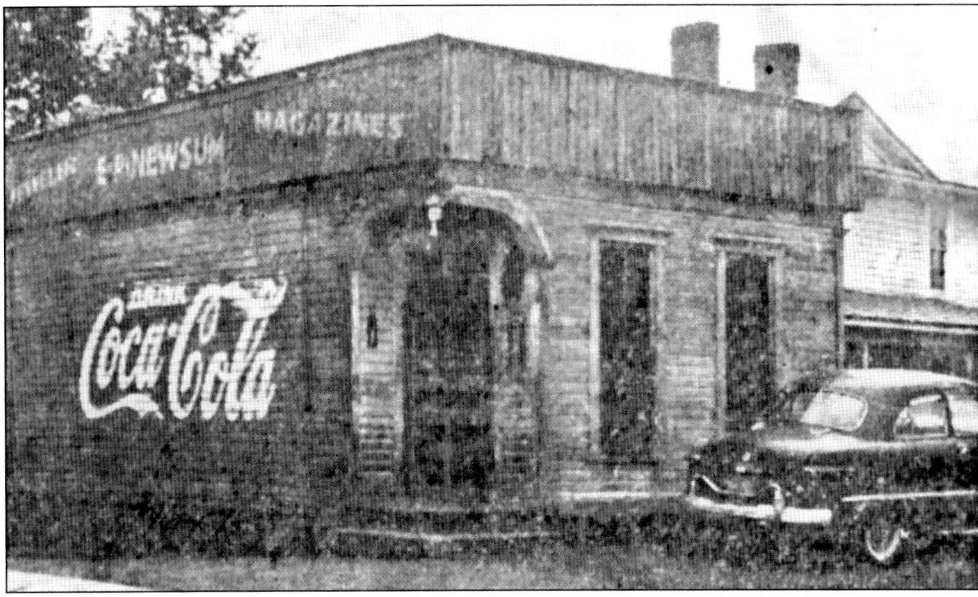

E. P. Newsum Store, seen here in the 1950s, became a King landmark at the corner of present-day Dalton Road and Main Street. E. P. Newsom spelled his last name "Newsum" after returning from the army. Newsom told friends that the army misspelled his last name; fearing he would not receive his pension if he corrected it, he kept the incorrect spelling. In 1907, he opened a back counter in Butner's Store selling jewelry. In 1908, he bought the corner lot across Hollow Road (today Dalton Road), where he sold everything from magazines to real estate. The store closed in the late 1950s to make room for a service station, seen below. Newsom never married and died in 1960. (Courtesy of Annie Sue Griffin.)

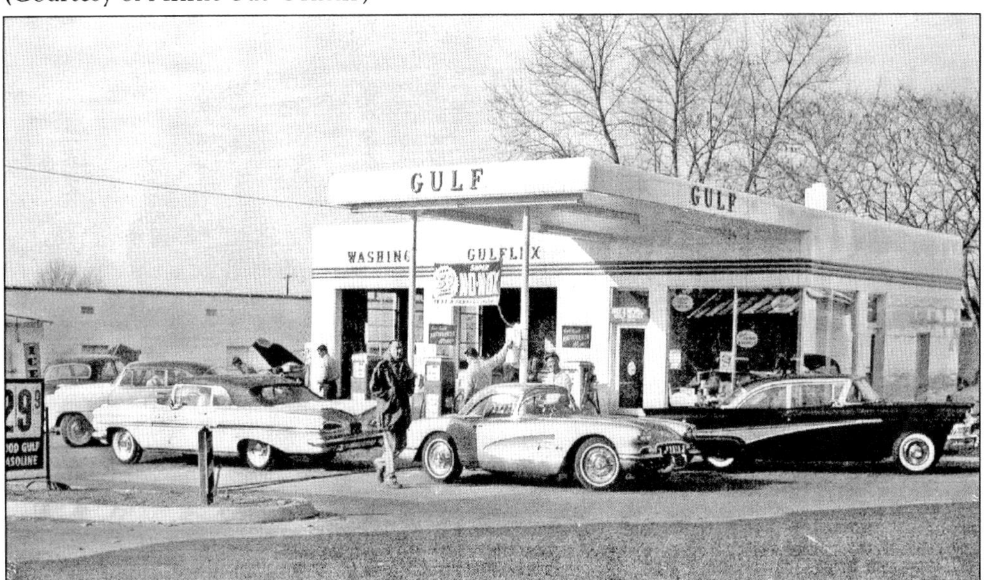

A Saturday morning at King Gulf Station in this 1959 photograph shows many filling up. From left to right are Newell Newsome's 1959 Chevrolet, Deb Holder's 1958 Corvette, and Keith Johnson's customized 1957 Ford. (Courtesy of Lewis Carroll.)

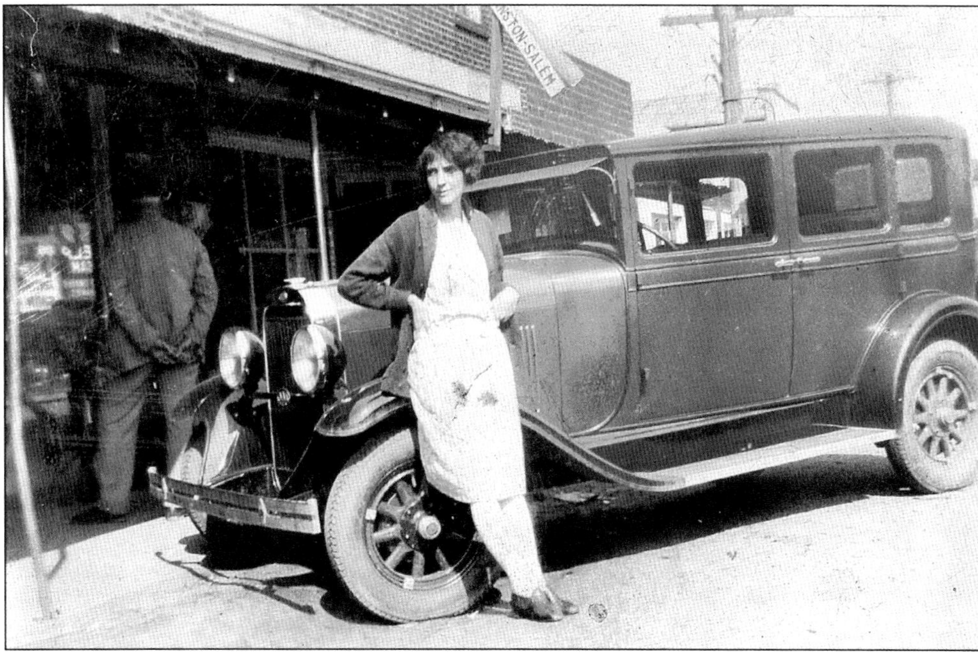

Trilby Love Tuttle Petree, seen *c.* 1930, served as King's postmaster from 1929 to 1941. (Courtesy of Bill Boles.)

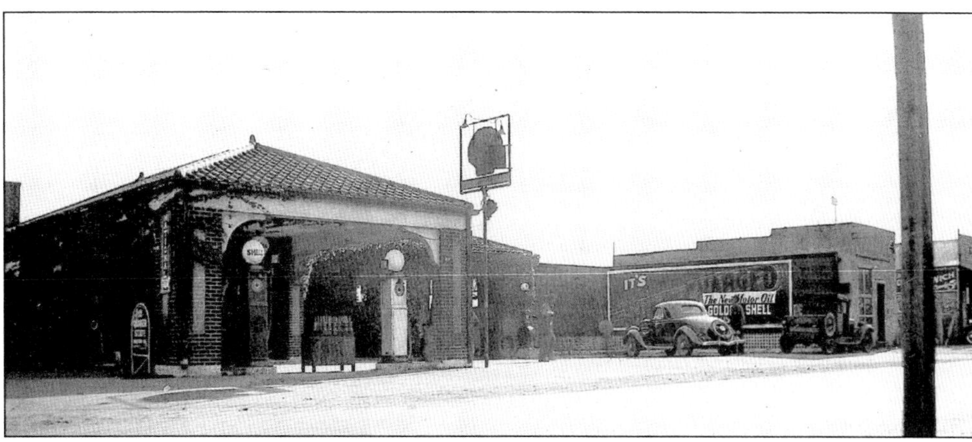

Stokes Motor Company, *c.* 1935, was located on present-day Dalton Road between Slate Funeral Home and downtown King. In 1929, O. O. Grabs Sr. built this garage and service station, leasing it to Chester "Chess" McGee, who operated it under the name Stokes Motor Company. In 1940, Chess McGee and C. S. Newsom bought the building and continued operating the Stokes Motor Company. (Courtesy of Eddie Marshall.)

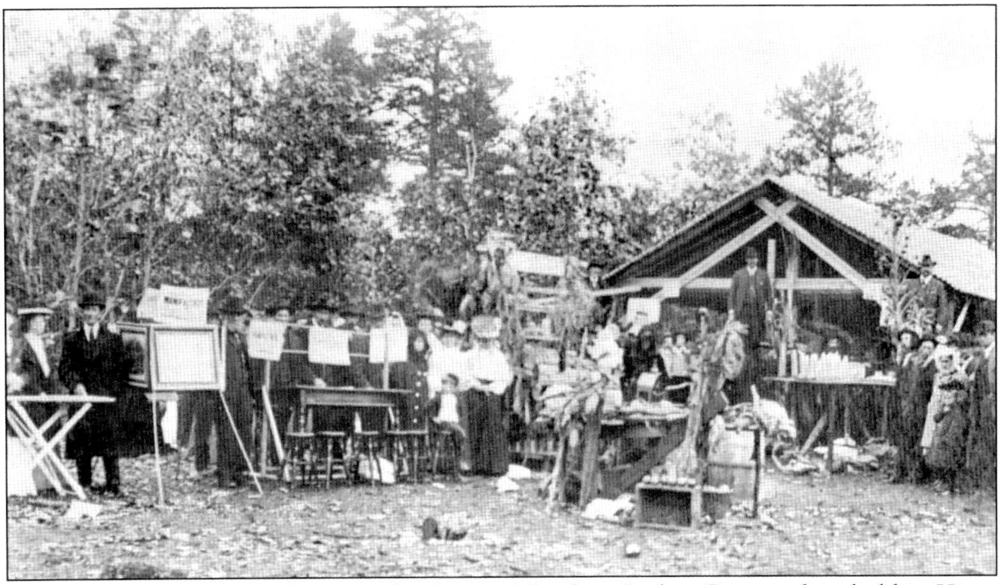

This is believed to be a photograph of one of the first Stokes County fairs held in King. The first fair was held at the King Tabernacle in 1906. After a successful first year, a Stokes County Fair Association was formed, and a new site was bought at the corner of present-day Mountain View Road and Helsabeck Road. On November 5 and 6, 1907, the first fair held at this site brought in between 1,500 and 2,000 people each day. (Courtesy of Stokes County Historical Society.)

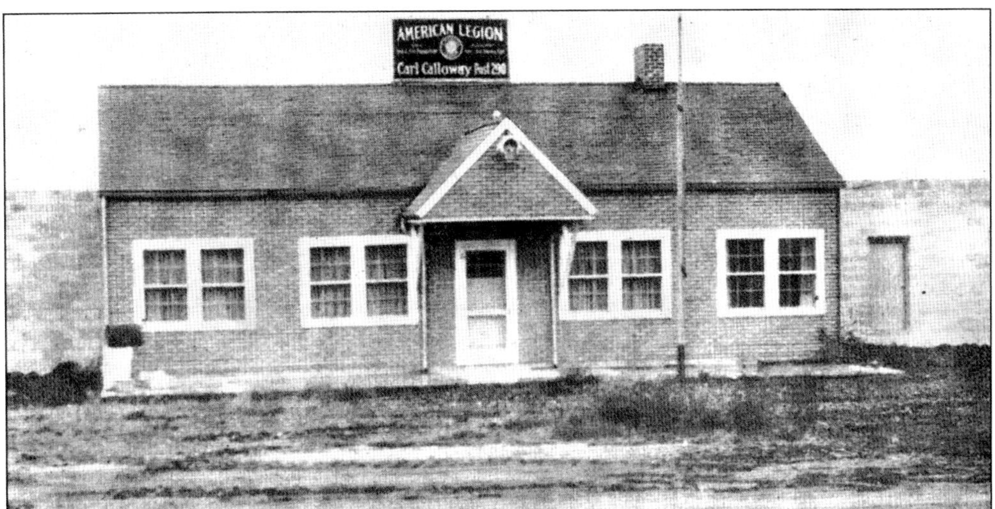

The American Legion Carl Calloway Post 290 was built in King c. 1946. The post was named after one of seven men from King killed during World War II. The grounds became the home of the Stokes County Fair in 1950. (Courtesy of Kathleen Mendenhall.)

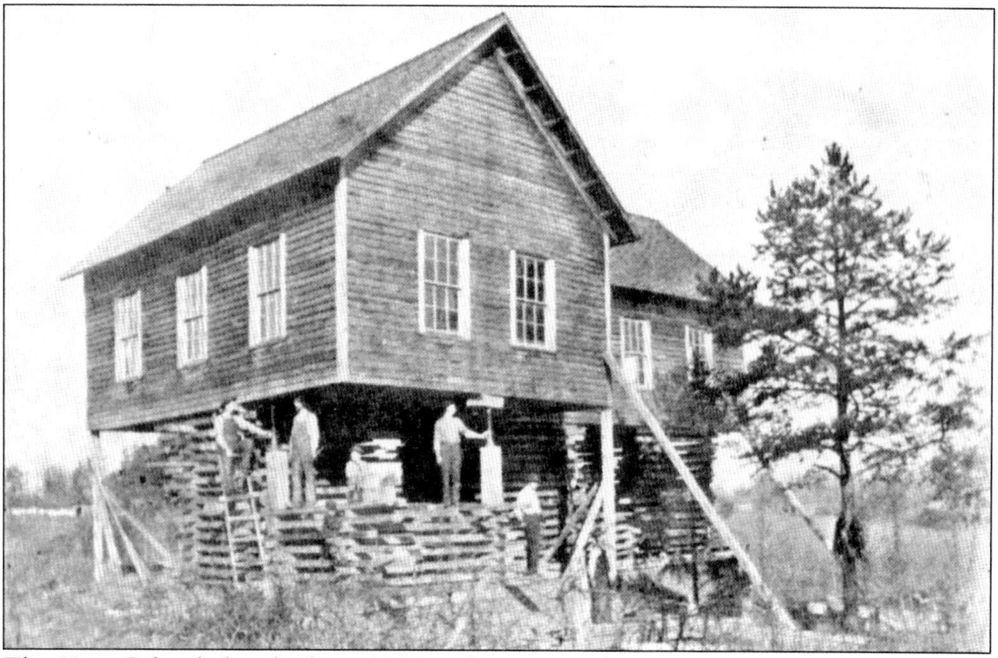

The King School, first built in 1904, is being raised in 1909 to add more classrooms underneath for Stokes County's first high school. The King High School began after the Stokes County School Board consolidated the Hustler and Hard Luck Schools in 1904. The school board ordered the new school to take the King name, but there was already a King School, named after Alexander King (Charles King's brother), in the Capella community. The Capella community school changed its name to Capella, and the King name went to the new consolidated school in King.

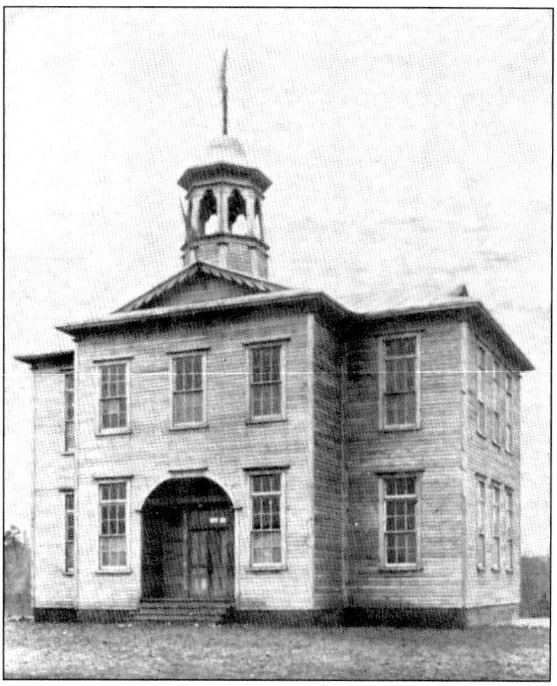

State High School (left) was built in 1910, after the first King High School (above) did not meet state structural guidelines. In July 1910, Virgil Grabs won the contract to build the new high school. He worked fast, building the new school in five months. The school was built specifically to state standards, the reason it was officially called the State High School, but it was always commonly known as King High School. Students came from across Stokes County, boarding in area homes to attend. (Courtesy of Marshall Boyles.)

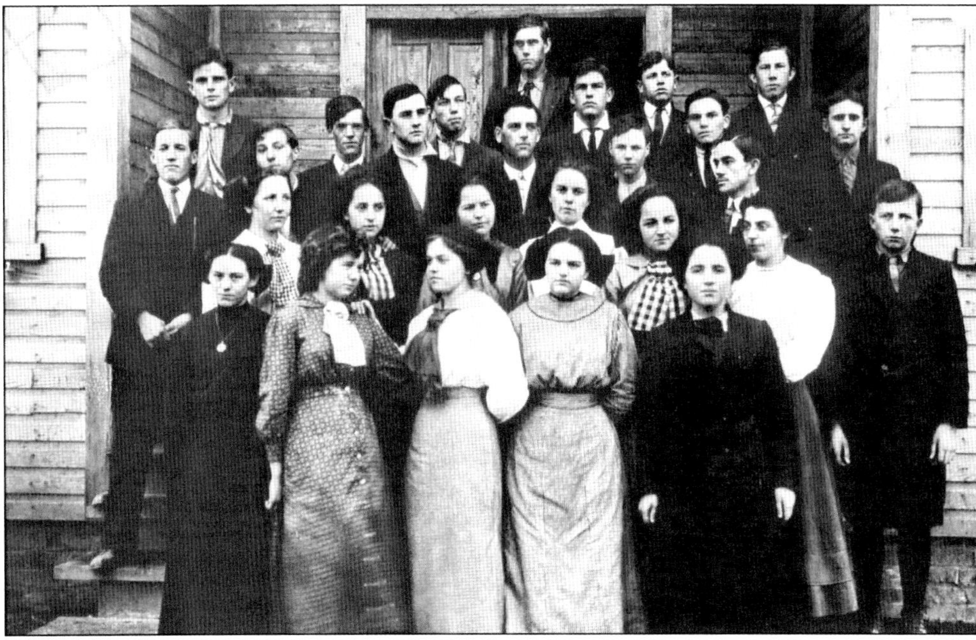

The entire King High School student body is photographed on the front steps of the school in 1912. (Courtesy of Becky Rains Moser.)

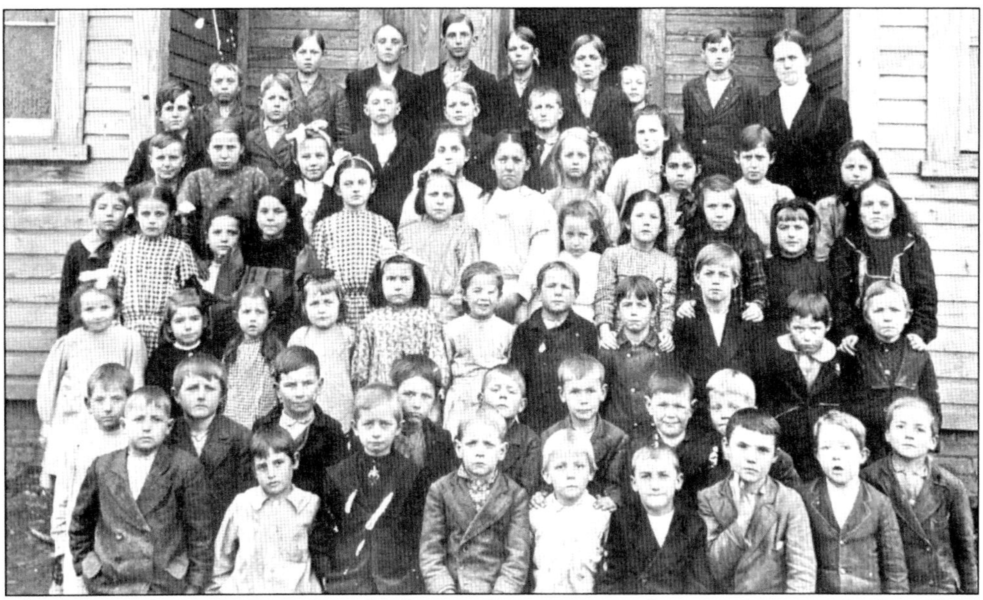

The entire elementary student body—grades one to eight—is photographed c. 1920 with its only teacher, Jennie Reid. (Courtesy of Becky Rains Moser.)

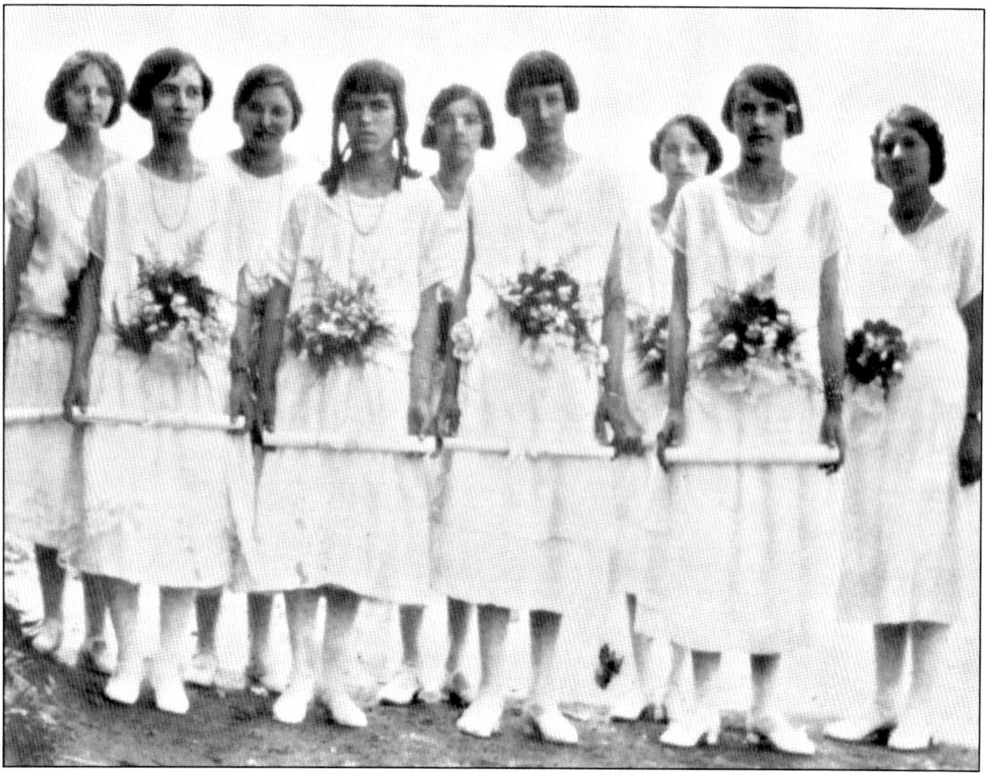

The King High School class of 1925 was all females. Included here are Irene Baker, Mildred Carroll, Oneida Caudle, Cleo Cromer, Gertrude Masencup, Lois Meadows, Sara Mitchell, Clara Pulliam, and Nellie Thomas posing for their graduation photograph. (Courtesy of Becky Rains Moser.)

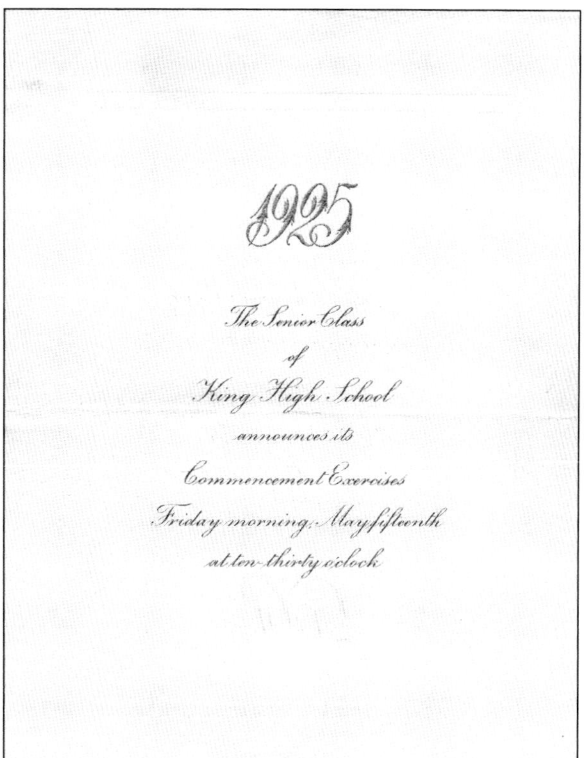

1925

The Senior Class
of
King High School
announces its
Commencement Exercises
Friday morning, May fifteenth
at ten thirty o'clock

The all-female class of 1925 graduated on Friday morning, May 15, 1925. Their graduation announcement notes the young women chose rose and silver as their class colors, sweet pea as their class flower, and "Not at the Top, but Climbing" as their class motto. (Courtesy of Eunice Lawson Collection.)

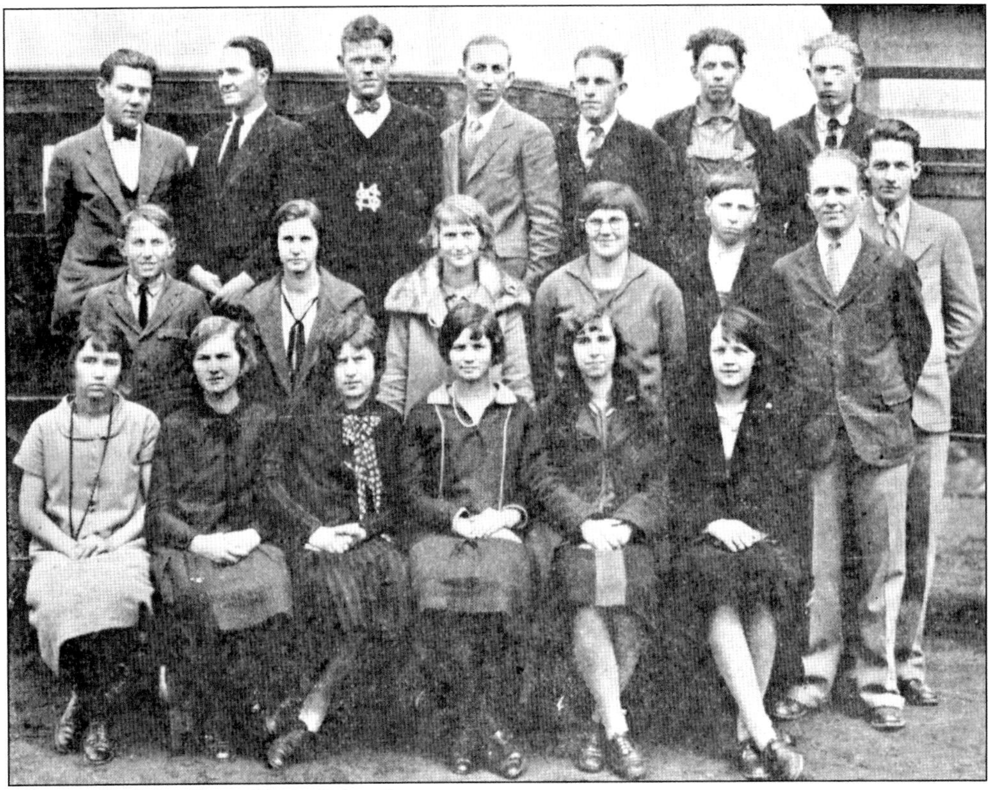

The staff of the King High School newspaper, the *King Breeze*, in 1926 was, from left to right, (first row) Mattie Ferguson, Inez Kiser, Odessa Boyles, Eunice Lawson, unidentified, and Irene Alley; (second row) Bernard Mitchell, unidentified, Opal Ingram, Tonza Smith, Sam Ray Smith, John Reynolds, and Edward Holder; (third row) Luther France, Norm Hooker, Austin Garner, Fount Smith, Ollie Ray Smith, Robert Carroll, and Glenn Hamm. (Courtesy of Eunice Lawson Collection.)

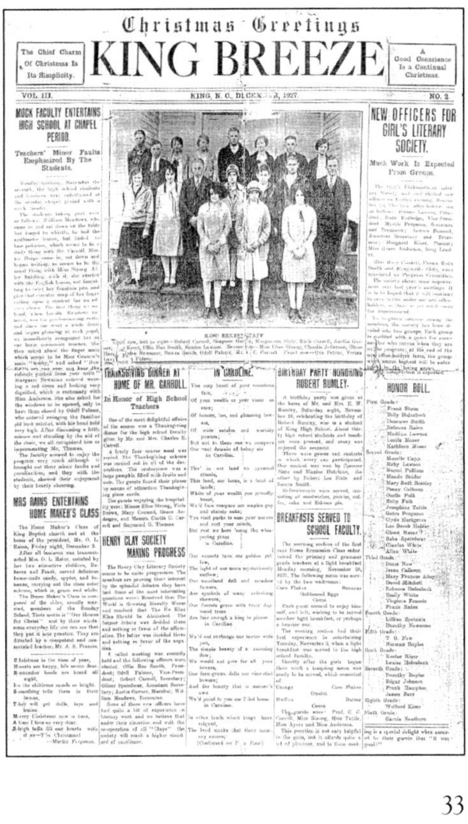

Christmas Greetings

The Chief Charm Of Christmas Is Its Simplicity.

KING BREEZE

A Good Conscience Is a Continual Christmas.

VOL. III. KING, N. C., DECEMBER, 1927. NO. 2

MOCK FACULTY ENTERTAINS HIGH SCHOOL AT CHAPEL PERIOD.

Teachers' Minor Faults Emphasized By The Students.

NEW OFFICERS FOR GIRL'S LITERARY SOCIETY.

Much Work Is Expected From Groups.

KING BREEZE STAFF

THANKSGIVING DINNER AT HOME OF MR. CARROLL.

In Honor of High School Teachers

IN CAROLINE.

BIRTHDAY PARTY HONORING ROBERT RUMLEY.

HONOR ROLL.

MRS RAINS ENTERTAINS HOME MAKER'S CLASS

HENRY CLAY SOCIETY MAKING PROGRESS

BREAKFASTS SERVED TO SCHOOL FACULTY.

Shown here is the front page of the December 1927 edition of the *King Breeze*. (Courtesy of Lewis Carroll.)

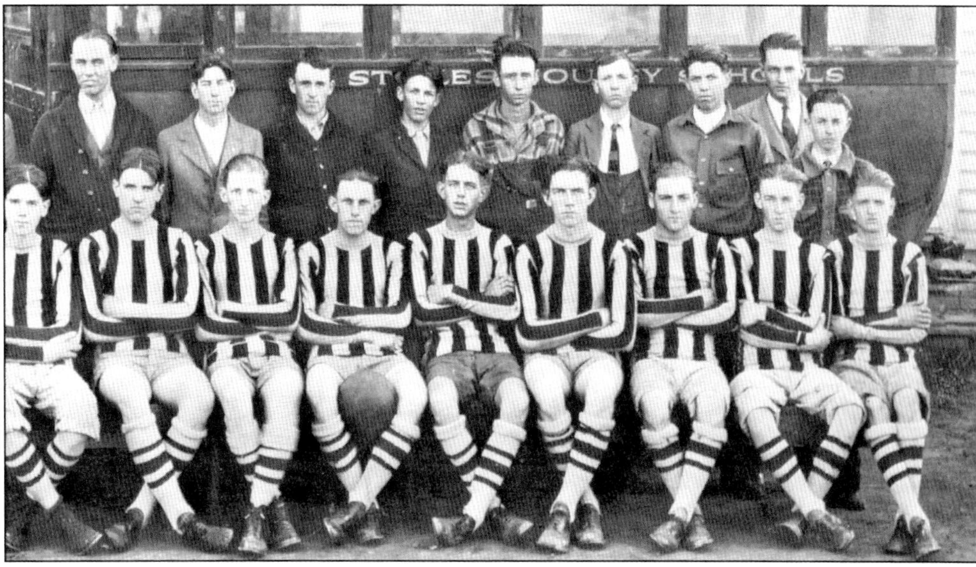

The King High School soccer team is pictured in 1927. From left to right are (first row) Homer Ferguson, Bill Meadow, Worth Gentry, Ollie Ray Smith, Spencer "Snip" Hutchens, Bahnson Hall, Carl Webster, Carlos Jones, and Odell Palmer; (second row) Herman Smith, Max Hutchens, Troy Spainhour, Homer Edwards, Guy Newsom, Simpson Garner, Robert Carroll, Coach Edward Holder, and Charles Hunter. (Courtesy of Becky Rains Moser.)

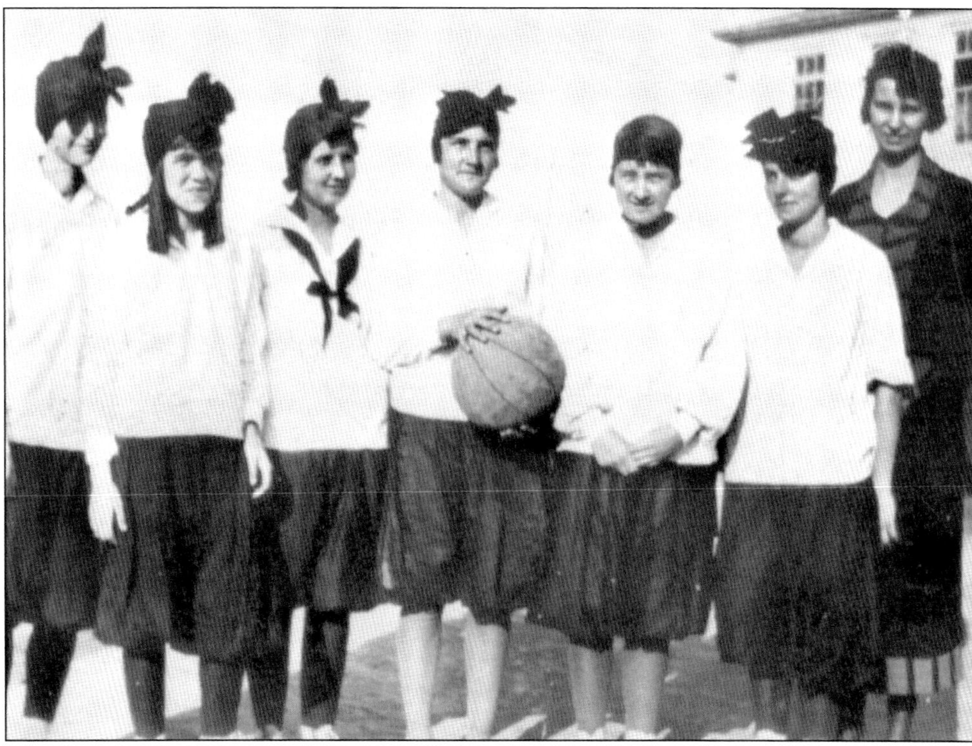

The King High School girls basketball team won the Stokes County Championship in 1925. (Courtesy of Becky Rains Moser.)

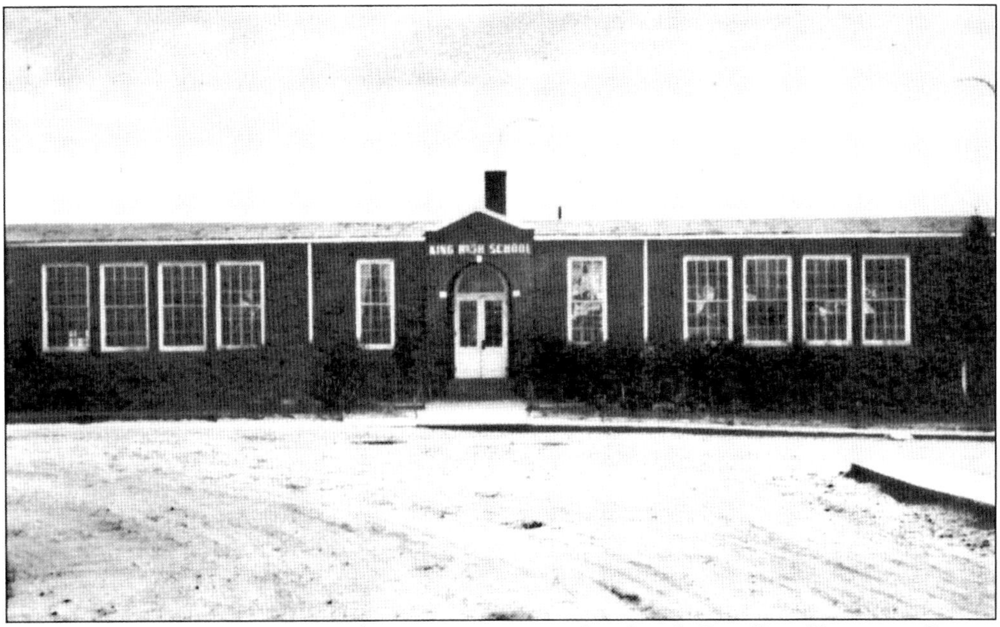

In August 1925, the surrounding community schools of Capella, Chestnut Grove, Creason, Dry Springs, Flat Shoals, Friendship, Haw Pond, Mount Olive, Mountain View, Oak Grove, and Pine Log voted 461-307 to consolidate with the King High School System and increase their taxes to build a new, modern high school. In 1928, students moved into King High School (above), which introduced many students to indoor bathrooms, drinking fountains, electricity, and central heating. (Courtesy of Becky Rains Moser.)

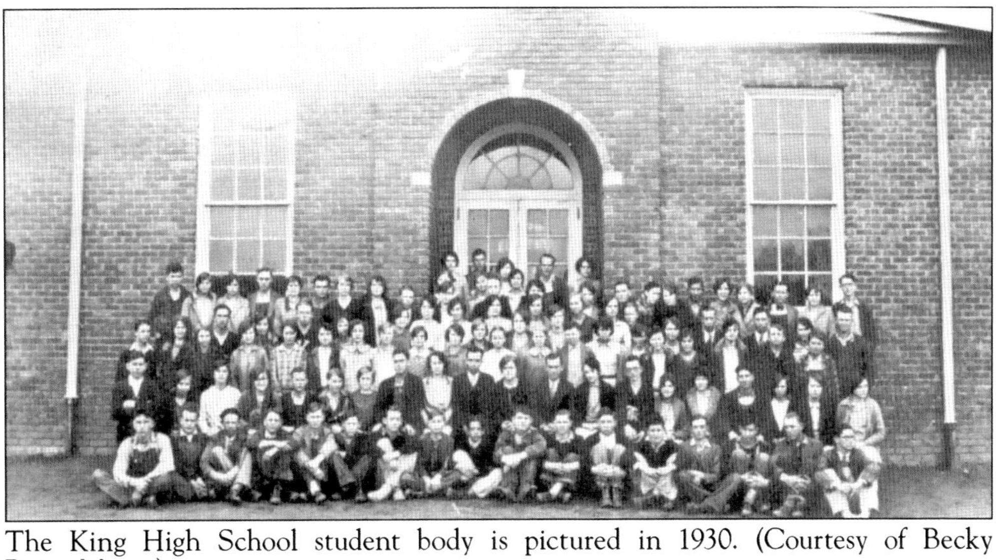

The King High School student body is pictured in 1930. (Courtesy of Becky Rains Moser.)

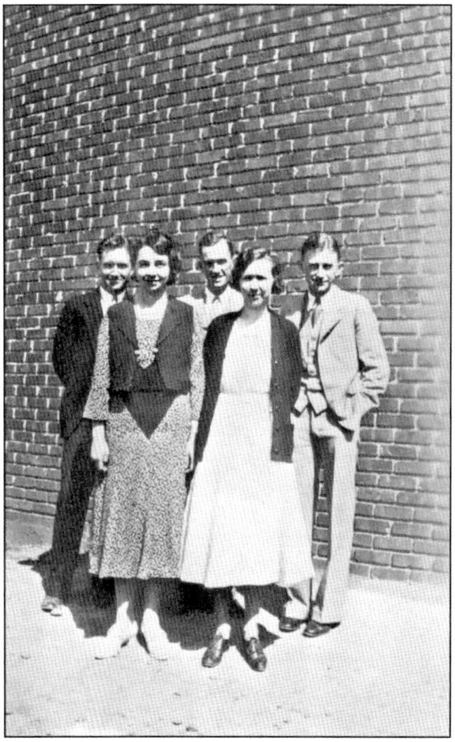

The King High School faculty was photographed in 1931. (Courtesy of Becky Rains Moser.)

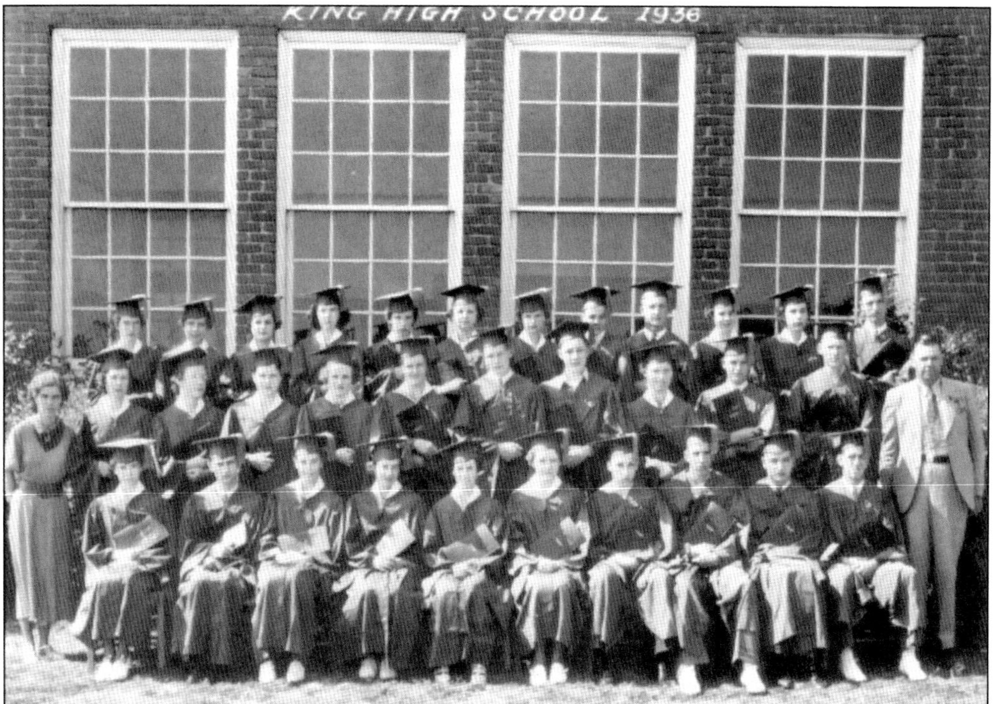

The King High School class of 1936 poses for their class picture. (Courtesy of Becky Rains Moser.)

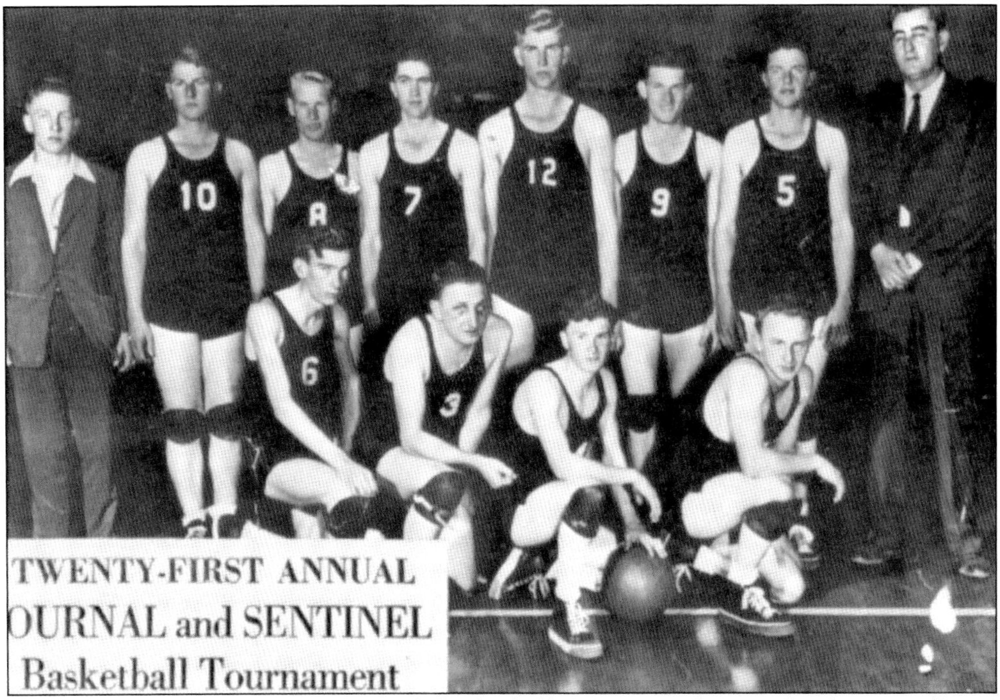

The King High School boys and girls basketball teams were known for their excellence in the sport. In 1947, both the boys team (seen above), coached by O. T. Neal, and the girls team (seen below), coached by Nell Voss, won the *Winston-Salem Journal and Sentinel* Basketball Tournament. Both teams drew enormous crowds when they took to the court. The girls basketball team's winning streak started when the team was formed in the early 1920s. In their first four years, they did not lose one game. In the 54 years the King High School was open, the girls basketball team had 35 years of winning seasons. (Courtesy of Becky Rains Moser.)

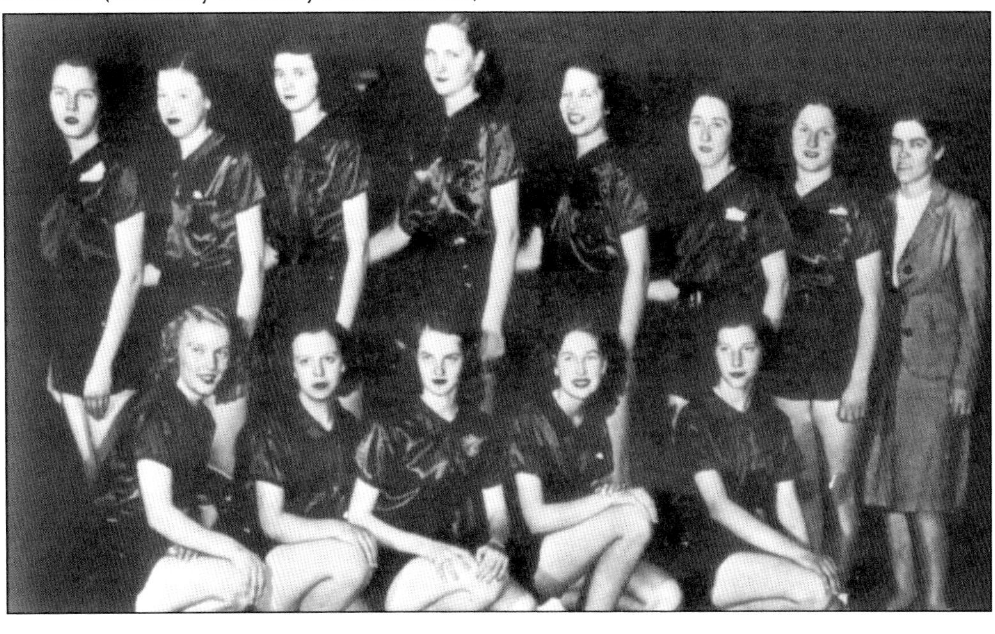

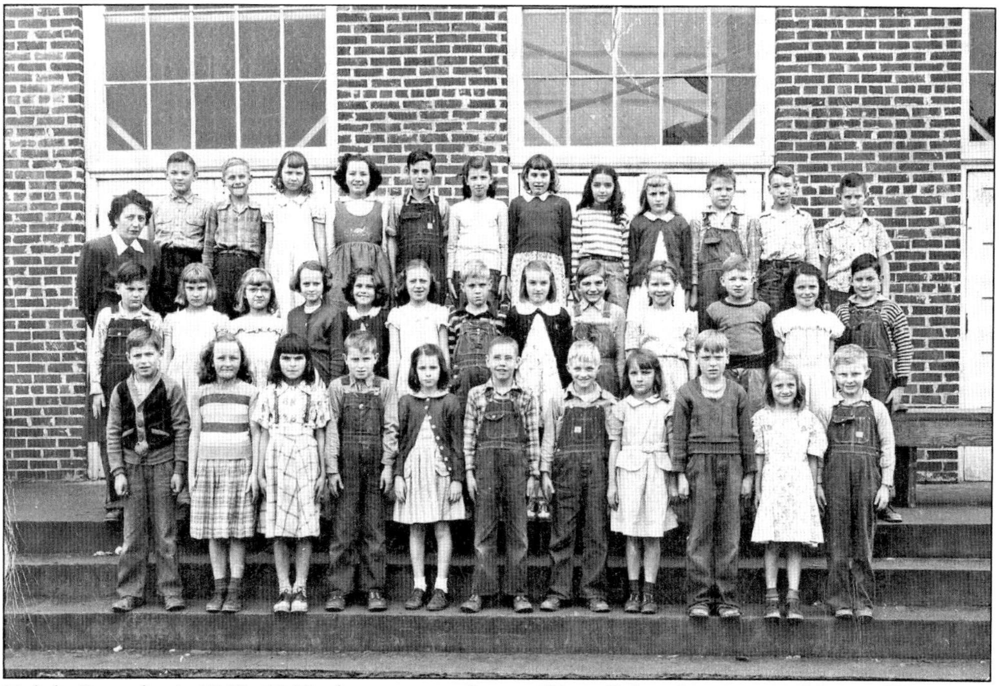

Eulala Brandon's 1948–1949 elementary class at King School is pictured here. (Courtesy of Virginia Moorefield Ortiz.)

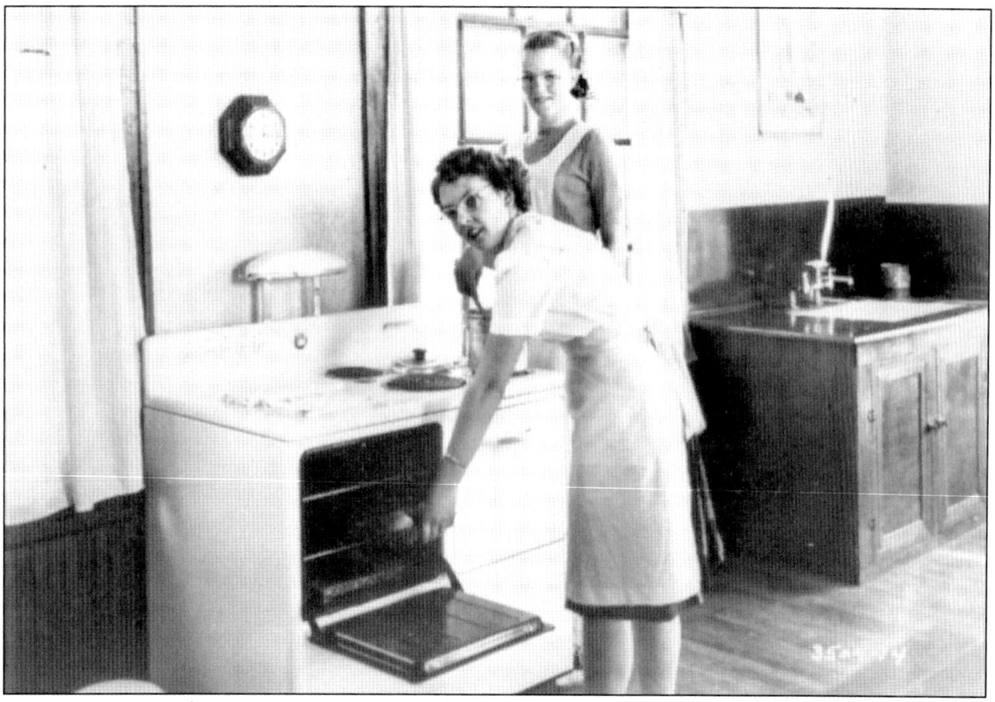

Future Homemakers Association members Mary Frances Long Watts (bending over) and Sally Meadows Hartgrove (standing) practice cooking in a home economics class at King High School, *c.* 1950. (Courtesy of Becky Rains Moser.)

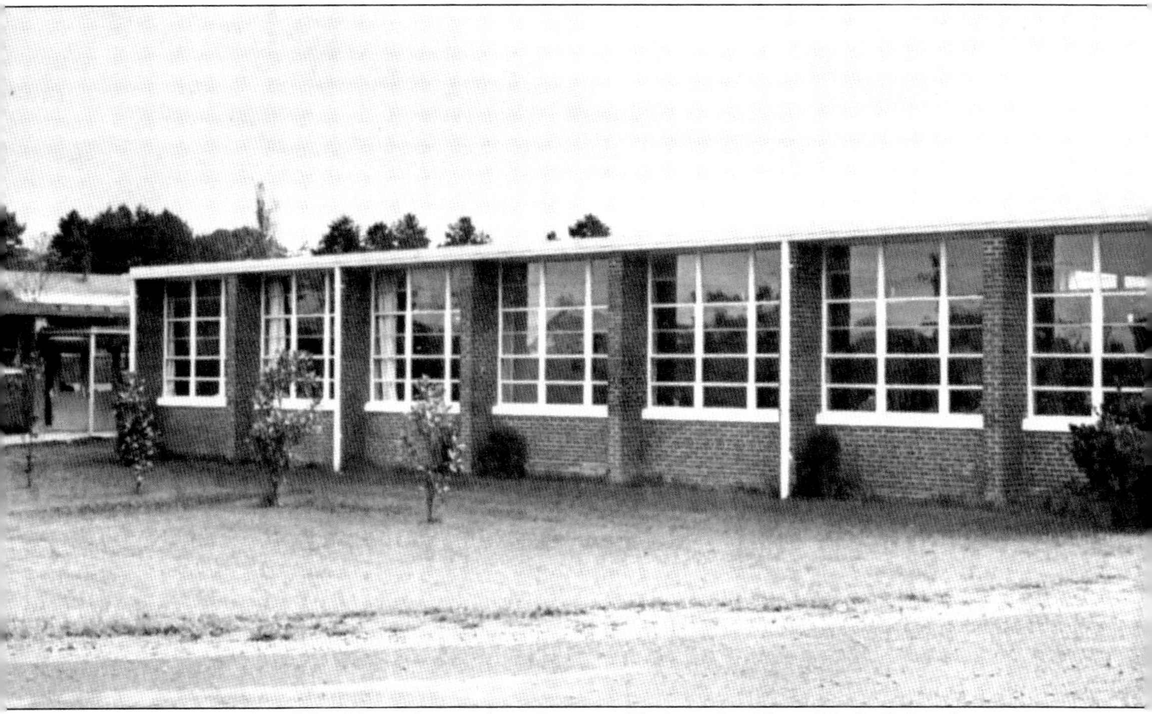

In 1952, a new school building (seen above) was added to the King High School campus at a cost of $90,000. Graduates of King High School had grown from one student in 1915 to 55 students in 1964. In 1965, King High School consolidated with Pine Hall, Pinnacle, Germanton, and Walnut Cove High Schools to form South Stokes High School. After the consolidation, the King High School building became King Elementary School, serving first through eighth grades. After four neighborhoods were constructed in King in the early 1970s, growth spilled into the elementary school. After parents protested the school was still using parts of the 1928 King High School building, it was closed. A new school building named King Primary opened in 1974. In the fall of 1975, to alleviate overcrowding at the primary school, Chestnut Grove Junior High School opened its doors on Chestnut Grove Road. The following year, construction began next door to the junior high for King Intermediate School to reduce the number of grades at the crowded King Primary School. With many young families moving to King, King Primary continued to grow. In 1997, to reduce overcrowding, King Intermediate became Mount Olive Elementary School, while King Primary changed its name back to King Elementary, giving King two elementary schools. With overcrowding issues at South Stokes High School, a new high school was planned for King. West Stokes High School opened in the fall of 1999. (Courtesy of Becky Rains Moser.)

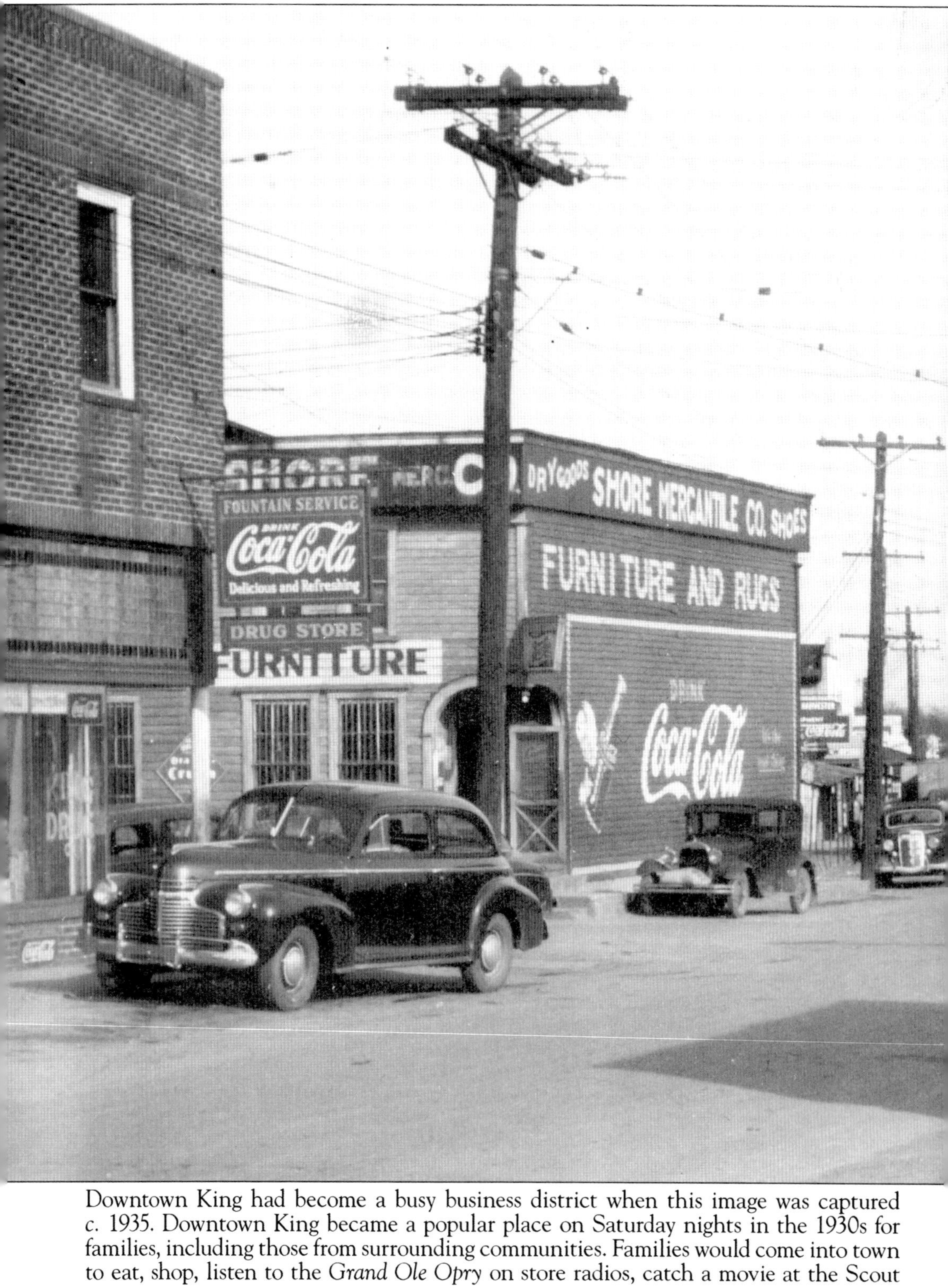

Downtown King had become a busy business district when this image was captured c. 1935. Downtown King became a popular place on Saturday nights in the 1930s for families, including those from surrounding communities. Families would come into town to eat, shop, listen to the *Grand Ole Opry* on store radios, catch a movie at the Scout

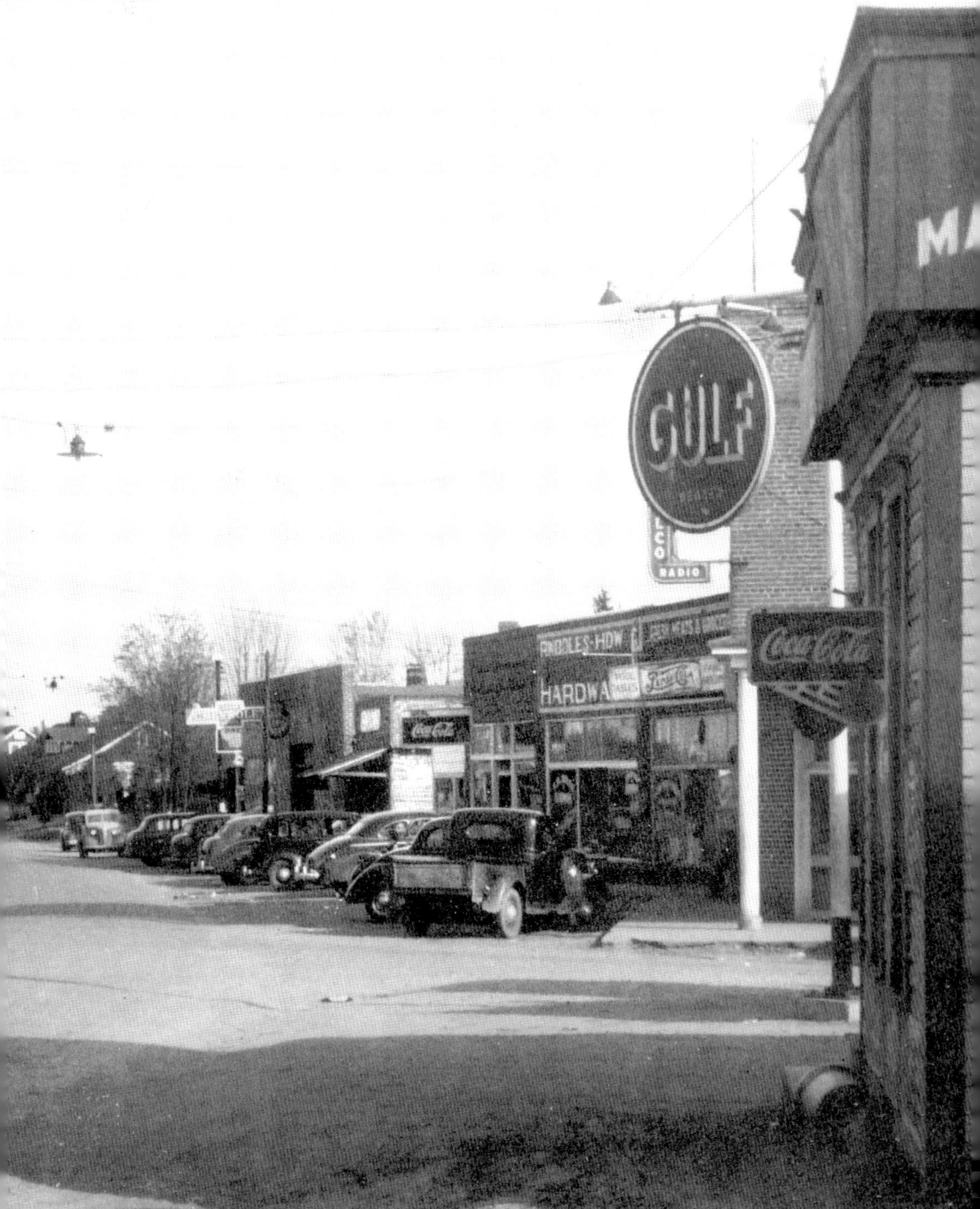

Theater, and visit with other families they had not seen all week. After World War II, families cut back on Saturday night trips into town, and with the birth of television, more people stayed home and stores started closing at sunset. (Courtesy of © *Winston-Salem Journal.*)

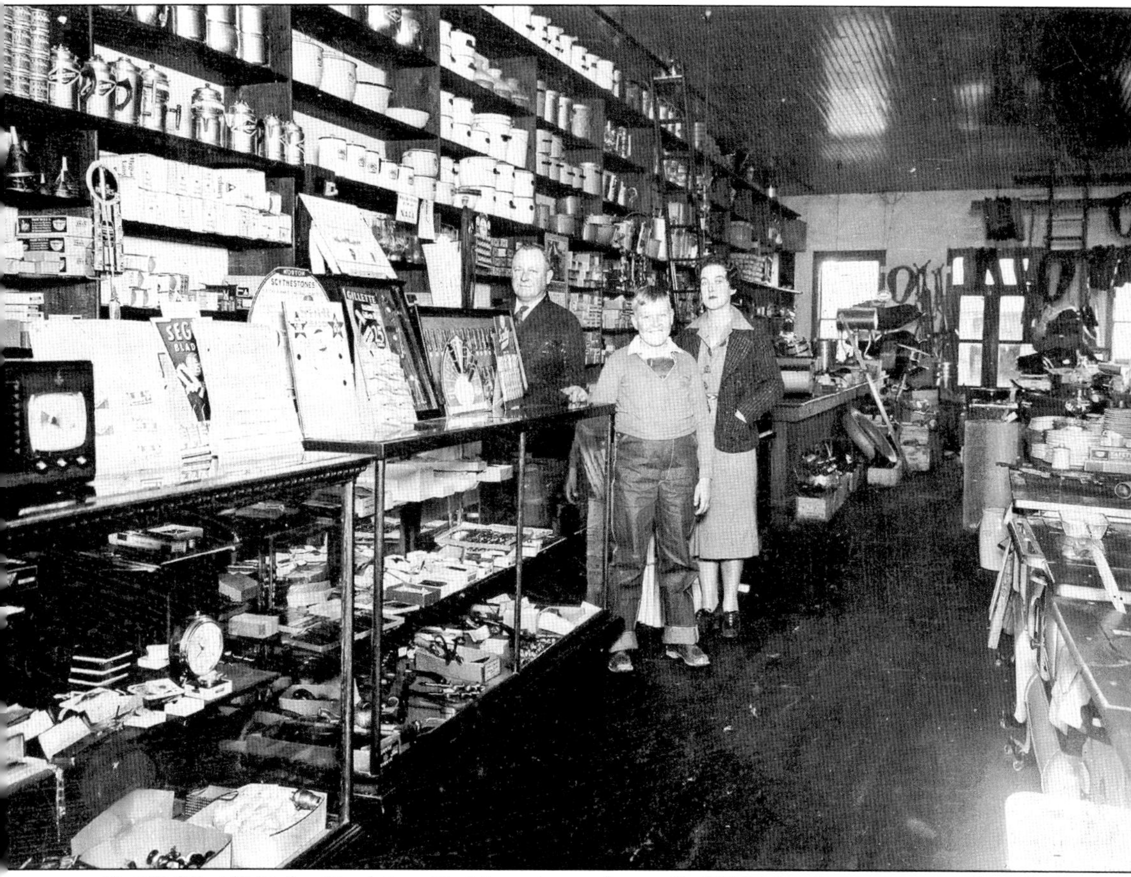

R. W. "Reid" Boles Sr., his wife, Nannie, and son, R. W. Boles Jr., are pictured in Boles Hardware in downtown King, *c.* 1938. (Courtesy of Trish Shouse.)

From left to right, W. Lawson, C. Dillon, and ? Lawson are in front of the King Radio Shop and King Barber Shop in downtown King, c. 1935. (Courtesy of Annie Sue Griffin.)

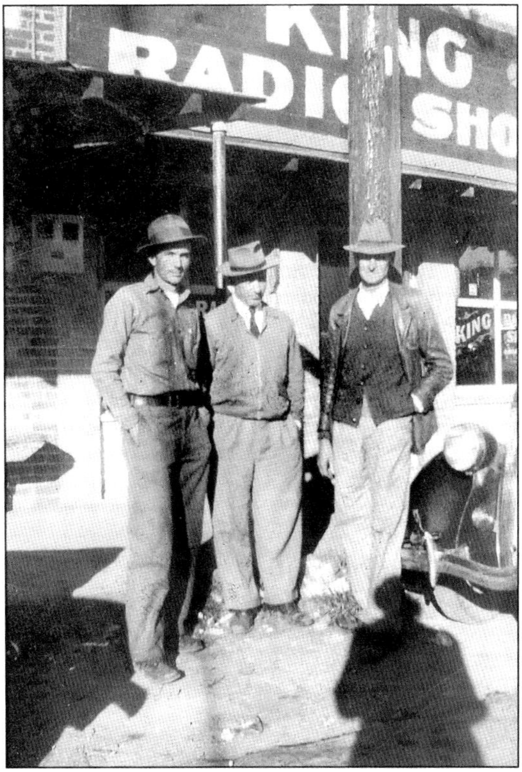

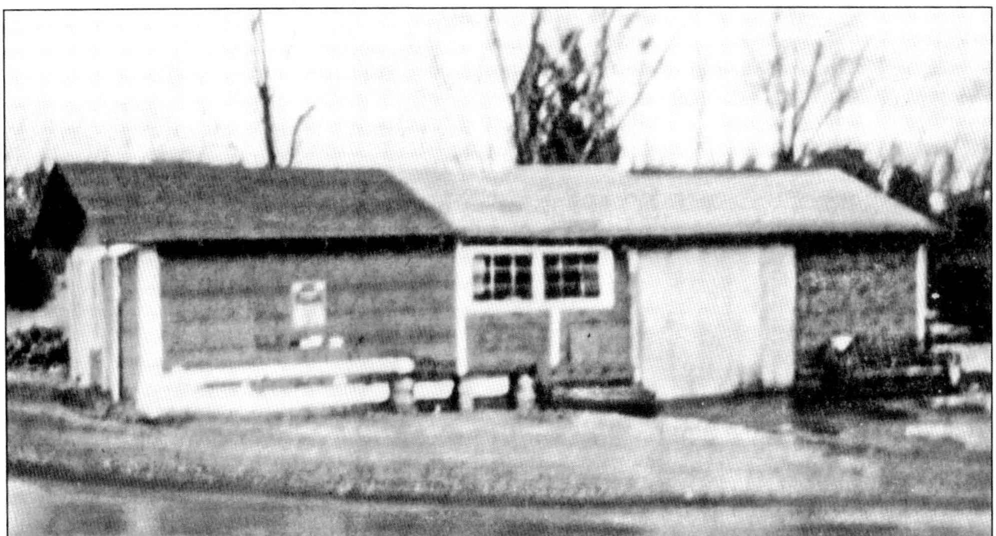

The Glory Hole, a country store owned by Roy McGee, was a common place where neighbors shared topics of politics and humor. Originally a blacksmith shop built by Joe Jones, the building stood on South Main near Meadowbrook Drive. When a new post office was planned for its location, men sawed the store in half and moved it up Pulliam Street. Politicians including former governors Jim Hunt and James Holshouser stopped in to gain votes. The store closed shortly after the death of Roy McGee in 1993 and was torn down the following year. (Courtesy of Bobby "Crow" McGee.)

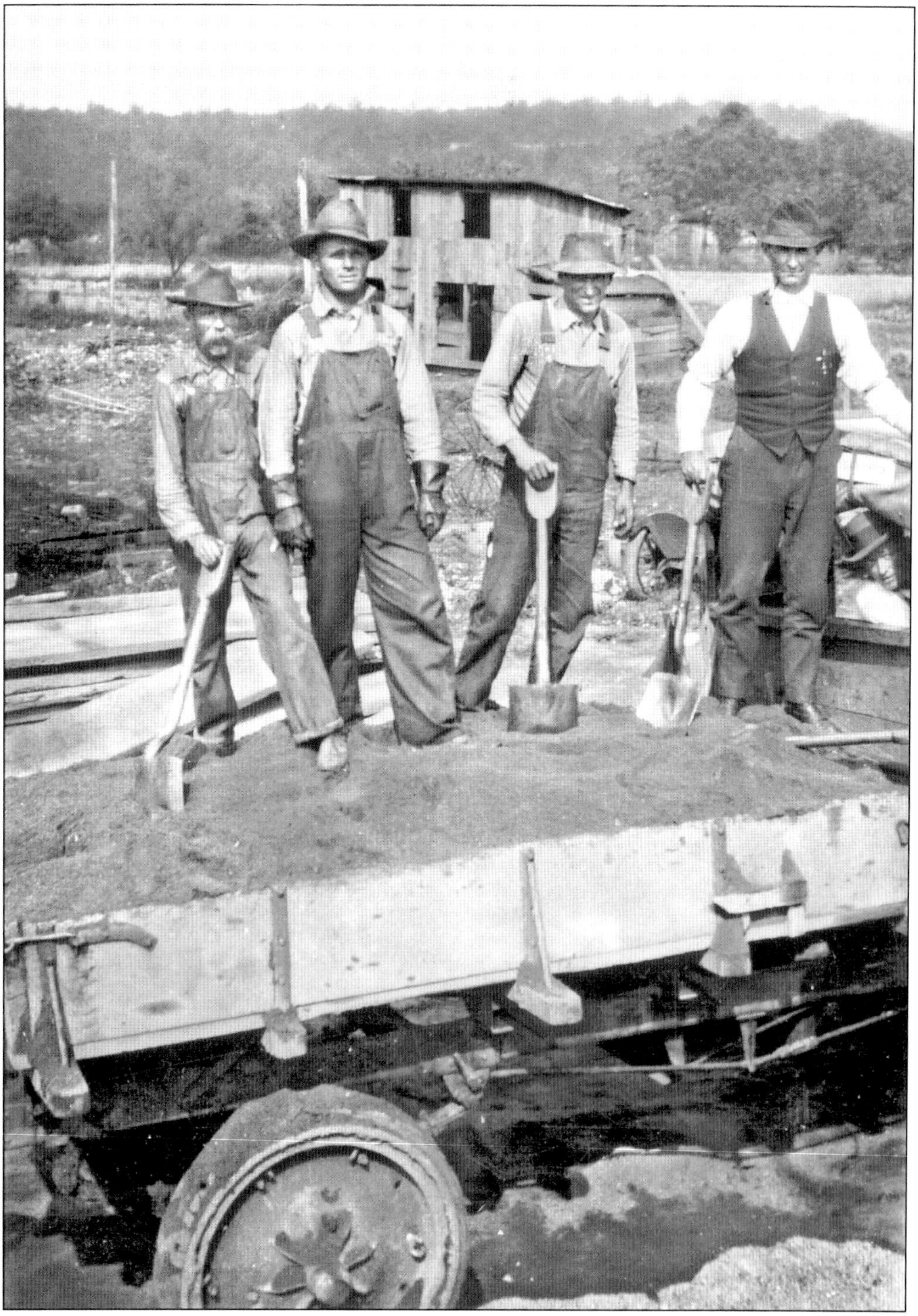

Unidentified men are photographed building the National Highway (today Old Highway 52/King Street), *c.* 1936. In 1935, state engineers surveyed the route that stretched from the Great Lakes to Florida. The highway opened in July 1937. (Courtesy of Becky Rains Moser.)

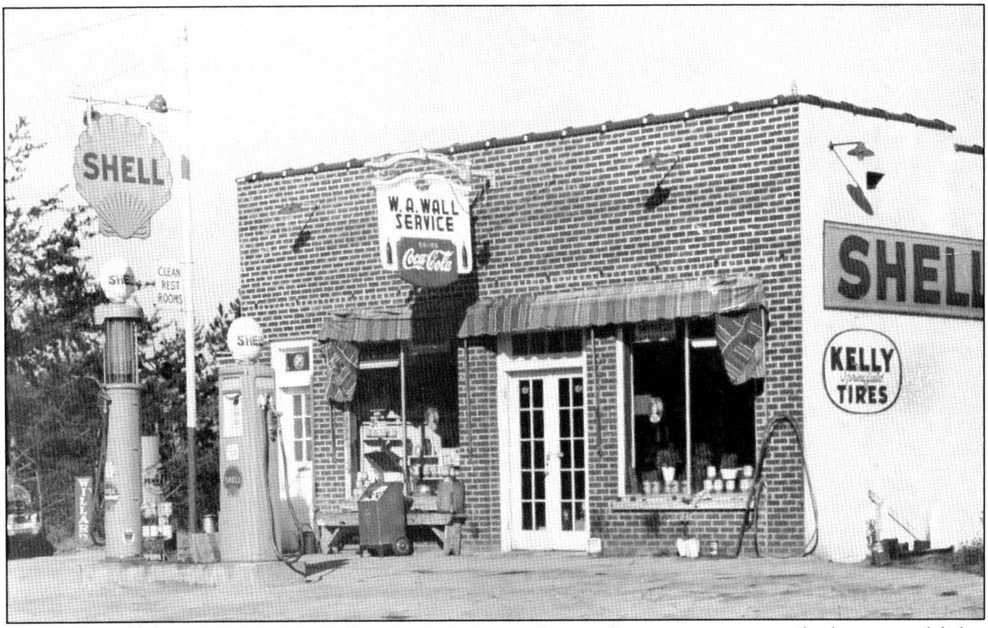

Many small businesses started sprouting up along the concrete road that would be named (Old) Highway 52 (today King Street). William Austin Wall built a Shell service station (seen above) in 1947 on the highway. He died two years later, and his children, Jake Wall and Roberta Wall Merritt, took over the store. Jake; his wife, Peggy; and their children, Rick, Craig, Brent, and Randy, continued to run the company, which became Wall Tire Company. They added onto the building and started new businesses there, including King's first newspaper, the *King Times-News*. (Courtesy of Peggy Wall.)

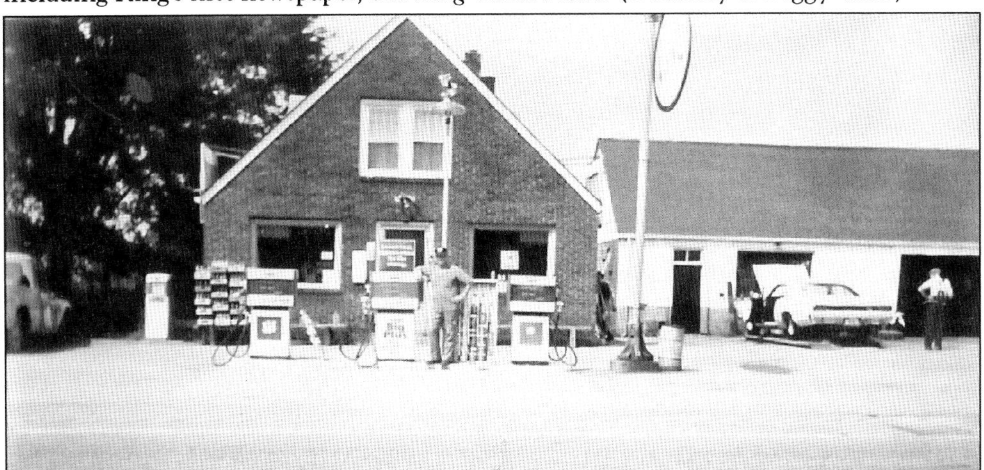

A passerby from Los Angeles traveling on (Old) Highway 52 (today King Street) took this photograph of J. Clyde Moorefield in front of his Esso service station in 1960. J. Clyde Moorefield opened the store in 1945. His family, who lived upstairs, worked in the store, including his wife, Myrtle, who pumped gas and checked the oil and the air in customers' tires. Moorefield built a garage next door in 1948 and built a new garage in 1961. His son Clyde took over the business in 1982. In 1990, the store was torn down to make way for King's Cabin Salon, while the garage remained open as Moorefield's Automotive. (Courtesy of Moorefield family.)

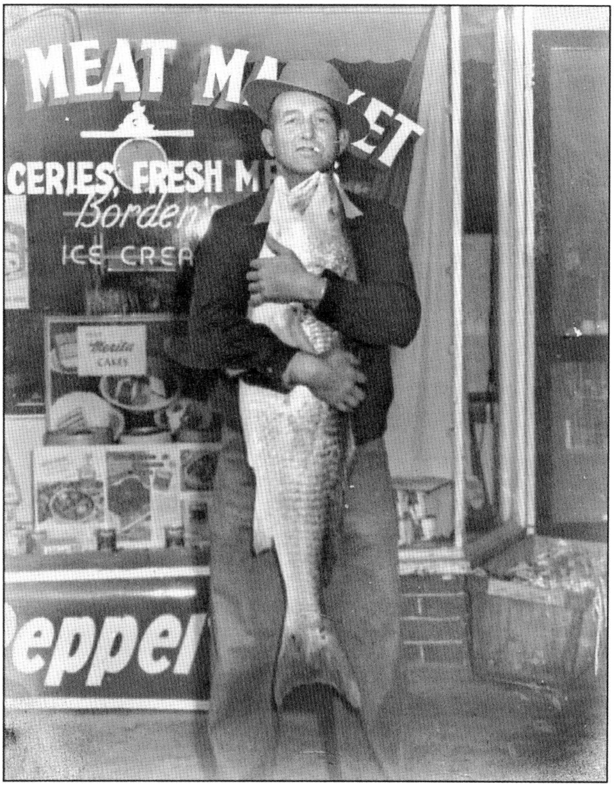

H. L. "Lynn" Southern stands in front of the King Meat Market with a 46-pound puppy drum he caught off Ocracoke Island in 1954. Southern loved fishing and working with the Boy Scouts, always making sure the less fortunate boys had adequate supplies, equipment, and transportation. (Courtesy of Lewis Carroll.)

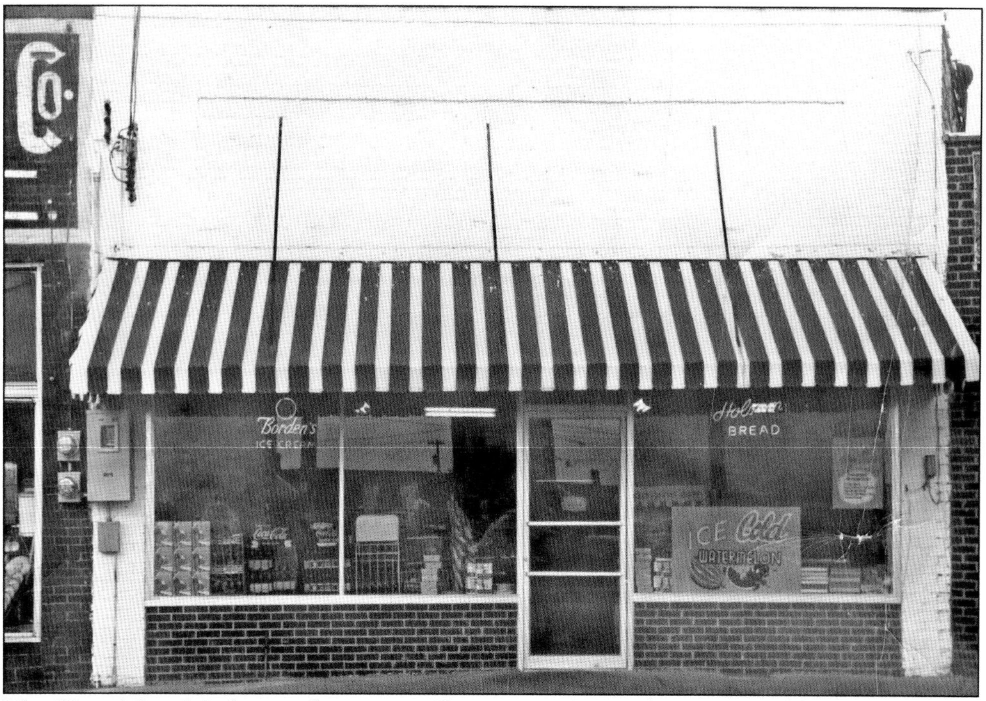

The King Meat Market in downtown King, c. 1942, was first operated by Mr. and Mrs. Dewey Long, who later sold it to Bill and "Kooler" Law. (Courtesy of Brent Wall.)

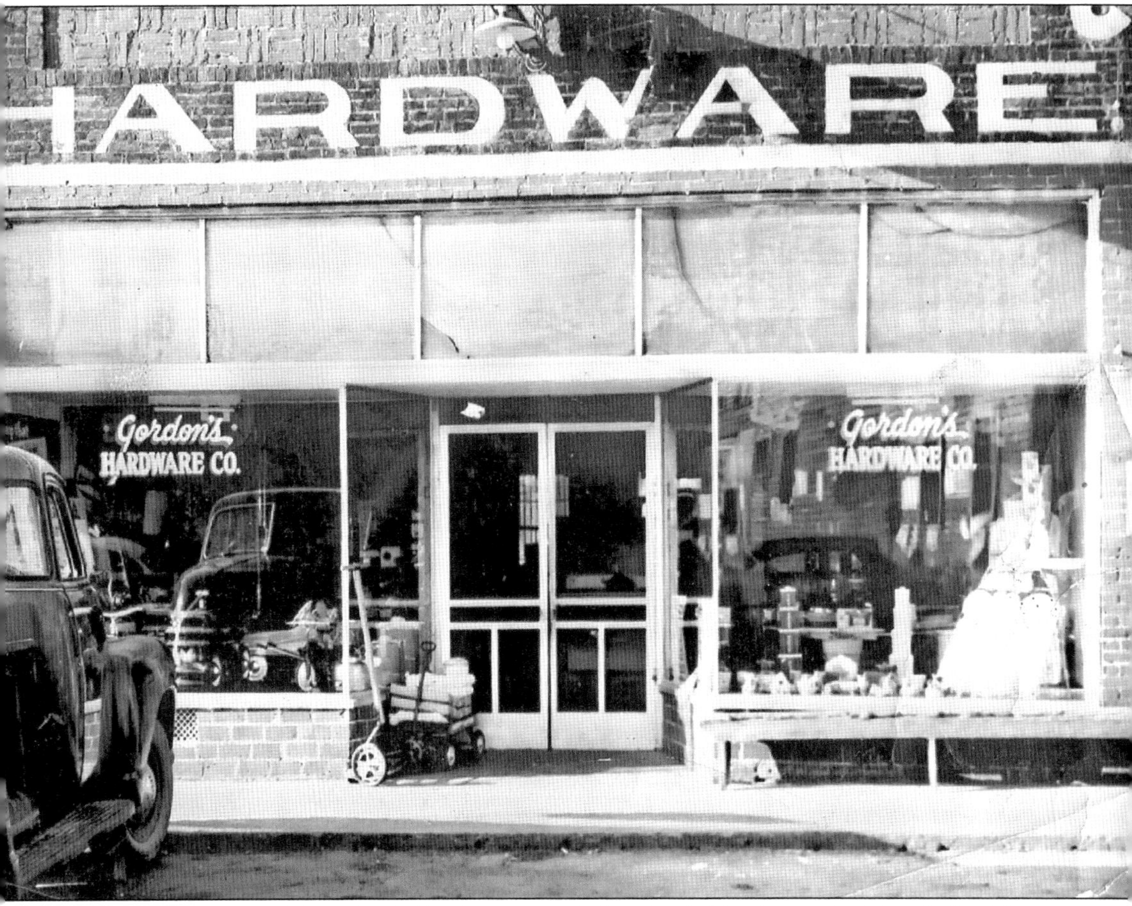

Brothers Loman and Mitchell Gordon opened Gordon's Hardware in May 1952. The brothers sold everything from stovepipes to Radio Flyer wagons and offered store credit to farmers from the early spring until they cashed in their crop in the fall. They also served as an early-day ATM because you could cash a check here on Saturday. With the brothers' retirement in 1989, the store closed. (Courtesy of Lewis Carroll.)

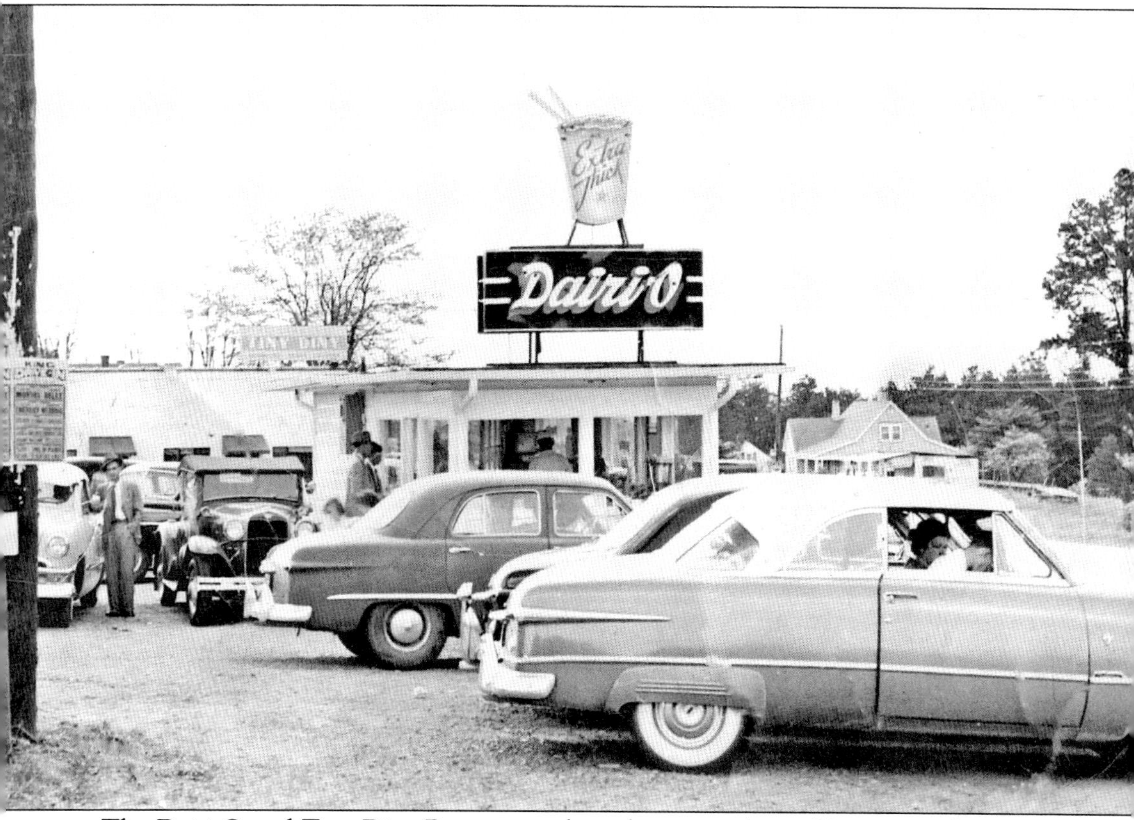

The Dairi-O and Tiny Diny Restaurants have been popular in King since they opened in the early 1950s. The Tiny Diny Restaurant, seen behind the Dairi-O in the above 1952 photograph, was first opened in June 1950 by the Barber family. The Dairi-O opened two years later, first serving only ice cream and milk shakes and later adding food. (Courtesy of Coster Collins.)

King and Stokes County's first stoplight was raised by the King Lions Club on July 17, 1952, at the intersection of present-day Main and Dalton Road in downtown King. (Courtesy of the Forsyth County Public Library Photograph Collection.)

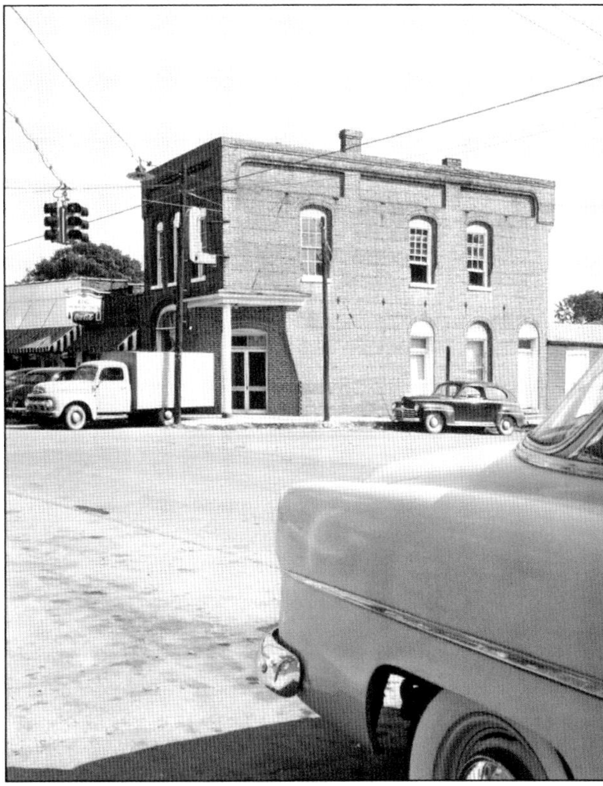

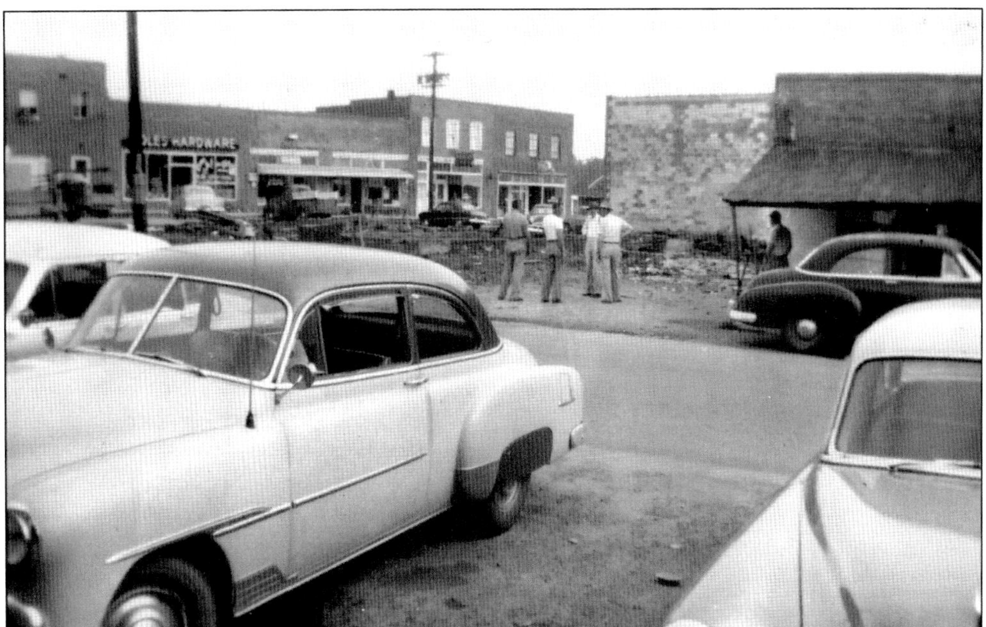

In 1956, the wooden frame building of Shore Mercantile Company, a landmark on the corner of present-day Main Street and Dalton Road in King since before 1900, was torn down for a modern brick building. The building to the right of the site in this photograph was once the King Post Office. (Courtesy of Peggy Wall.)

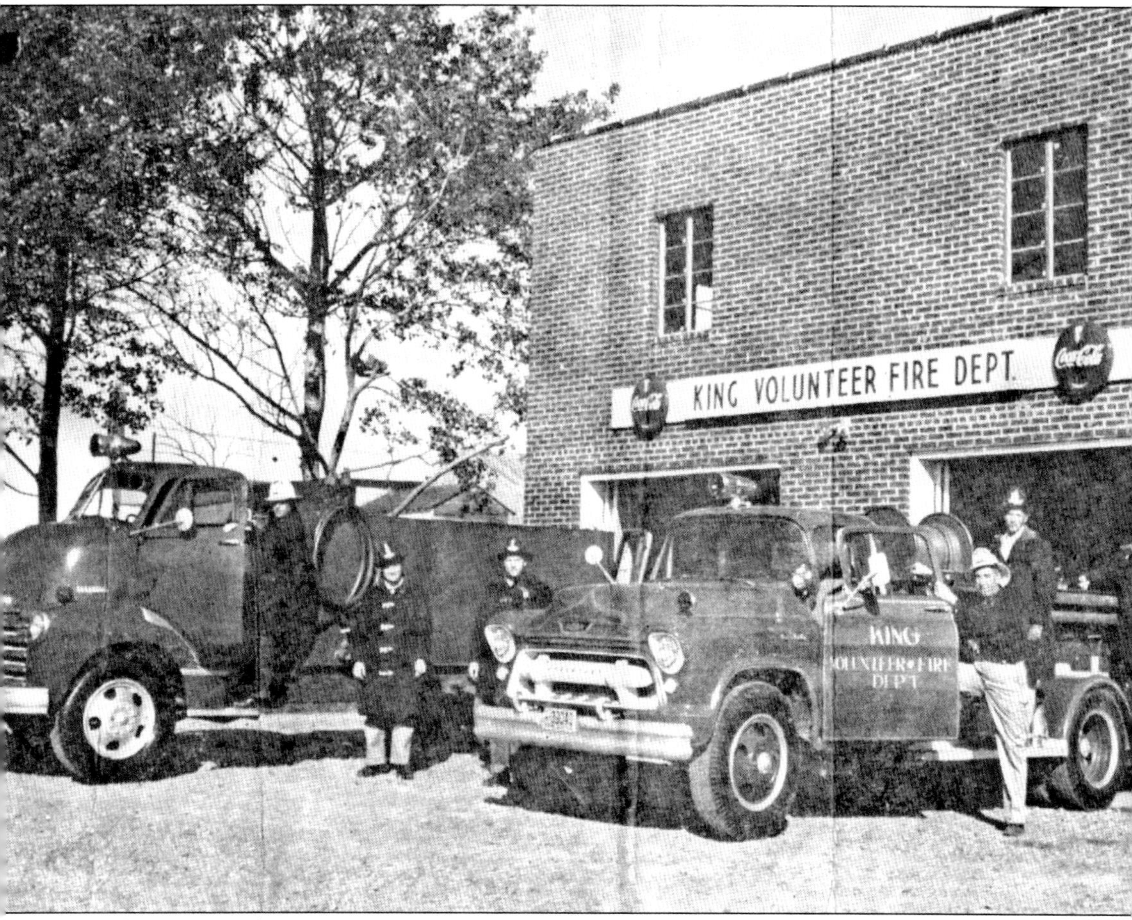

The King Volunteer Fire Department is pictured *c.* 1956. Before 1955, the only fire protection in King was a 50-pound dry chemical extinguisher on wheels that was rolled out on the sidewalk during the day. Before the extinguisher, people in town would gather and start a bucket brigade. The King Lions Club looked into starting a town fire department in 1955. Shortly after, construction began on a two-story, two-bay fire station. Almost all the material to build the fire department was donated. A 1955 Chevrolet pumper was ordered (above), and firefighters built a 1,400-gallon tank for a 1952 Chevrolet chassis (also seen above) to be used for a tanker. The fire department joined the Forsyth County Fire Association to receive help and training. In 1958, additional bays were added to the right of the station to make room for the rescue squad. In 1961 and 1973, additional pumpers were purchased. In 1984, another bay was added. In 1988, construction began on a new fire department on West King Street. The old station became King City Hall. A full-time paid fire chief was hired in 1995, and the following year, the first paid full-time firefighter started. In 2000, the city took full ownership of the City of King Fire Department. In 1955, the volunteer department served about 1,000 people; today it serves more than 20,000 in the King Fire District. (Courtesy of City of King Fire Department.)

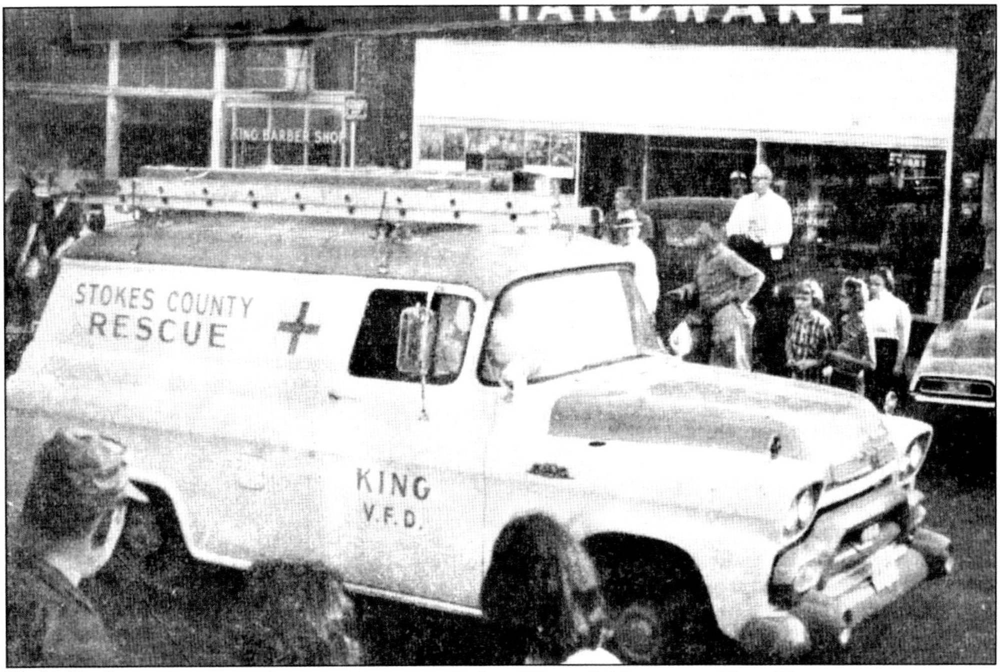

The Stokes County Rescue Squad of the King Volunteer Fire Department moves through downtown in a King parade, *c.* 1958. Firefighters converted a Krispy Kreme delivery truck into Stokes County's first rescue squad in 1958. (Courtesy of City of King Fire Department.)

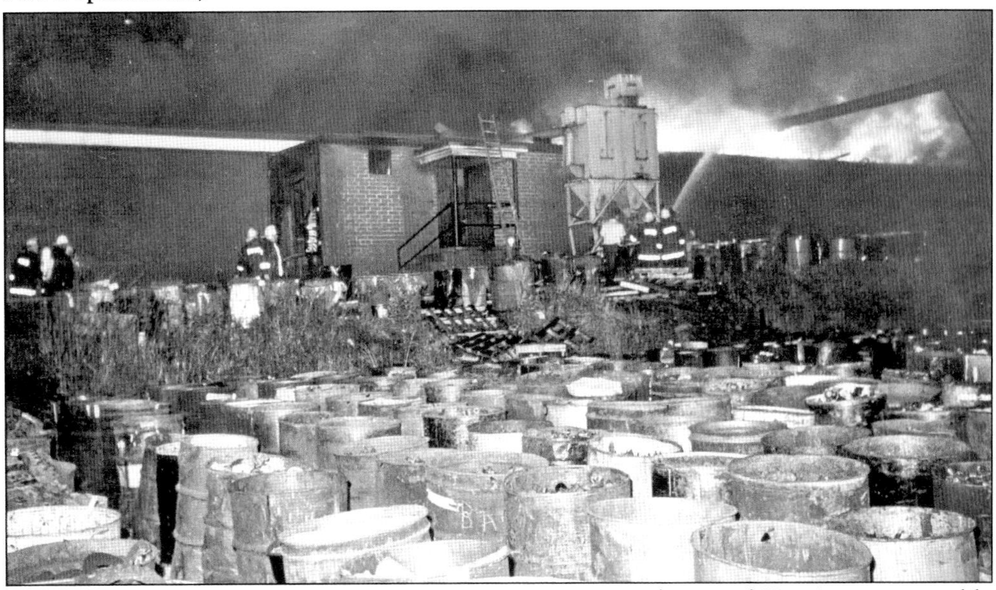

In 1975, the King Volunteer Fire Department answered one of King's most notable events. A fire destroyed two thirds of the Hastings Company, the town's largest employer at the time. Neighboring Sauratown Volunteer Fire Department and a ladder truck from Lewisville Fire Department responded to assist the King Volunteer Fire Department. No one got hurt during the fire, and the Hastings Company rebuilt. (Courtesy of City of King Fire Department.)

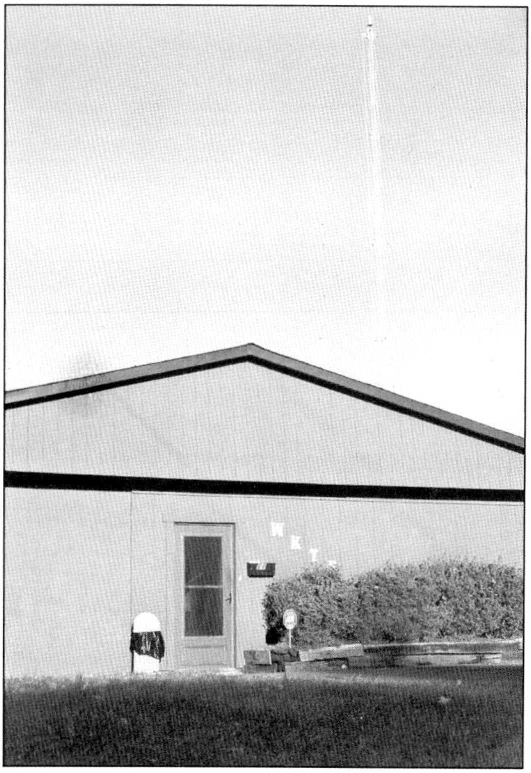

King's first and only radio station, WKTE AM, signed on in 1963 playing rock-and-roll music, switching to country rock by 1974 and all country a year later. The station brought well-known entertainers like Conway Twitty, Alabama, George Straight, Loretta Lynn, Crystal Gale, Hank Williams Jr., Marty Stuart, and Lester Flatt to King for interviews. In 2002, the station switched to a gospel and bluegrass format.

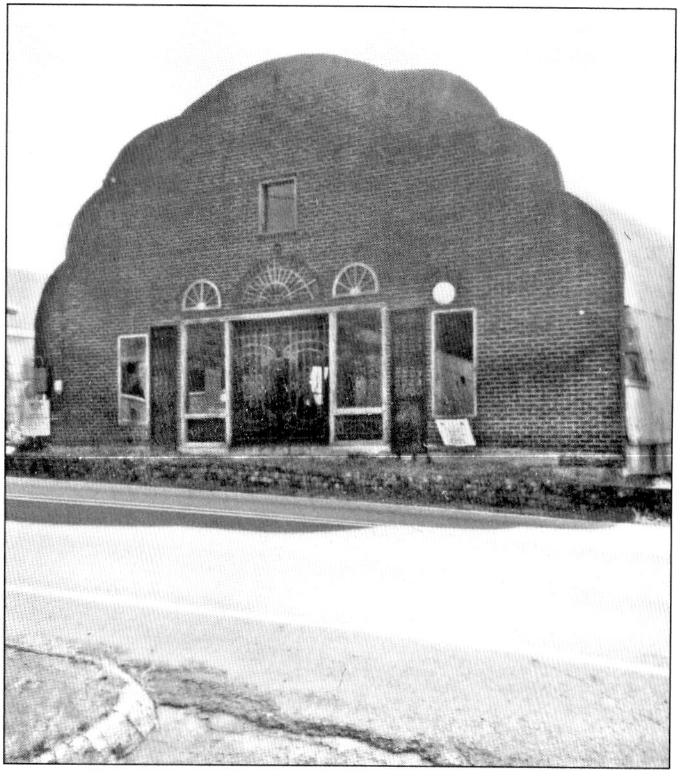

The King Theater began in 1928 as the Scout Theater. Boy Scouts showed movies in a small building next to the former King Furniture Company; then the theater, managed by Debs and Meyer Holder, moved into this building on South Main Street. When *Uncle Tom's Cabin* played, a miniature log cabin was built outside the theater. The replica caught the eye of *Box Office Magazine*, which wrote a feature about it. By the 1940s, Jessie Booth and his son, Jim, ran the theater until it closed and the drive-in opened at the corner of East King Street and Mountain View Road. (Courtesy of Juanita Gordy.)

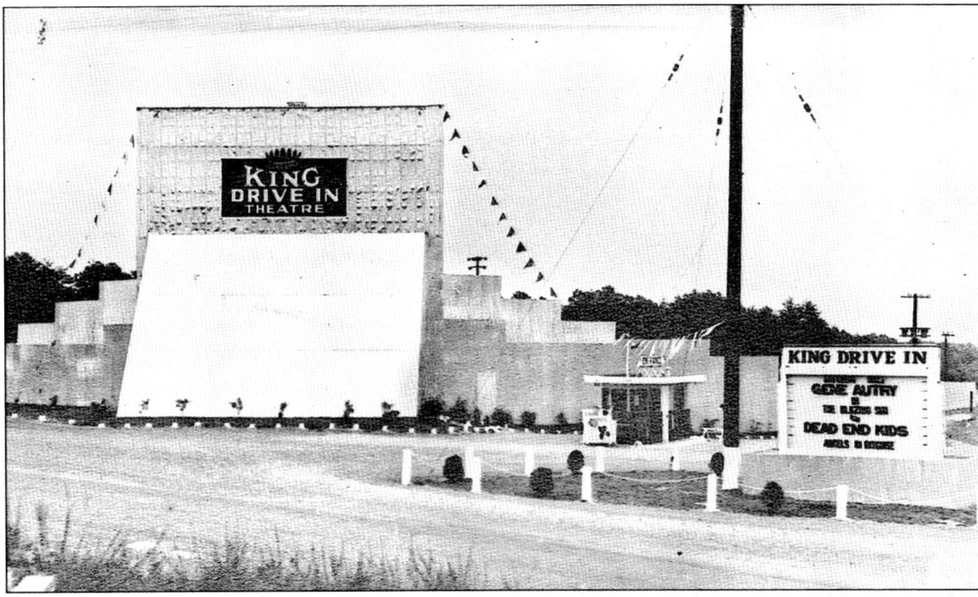

The King Drive-In sat at the corner of East King Street and Mountain View Road in 1950. (Courtesy of Eddie Marshall.)

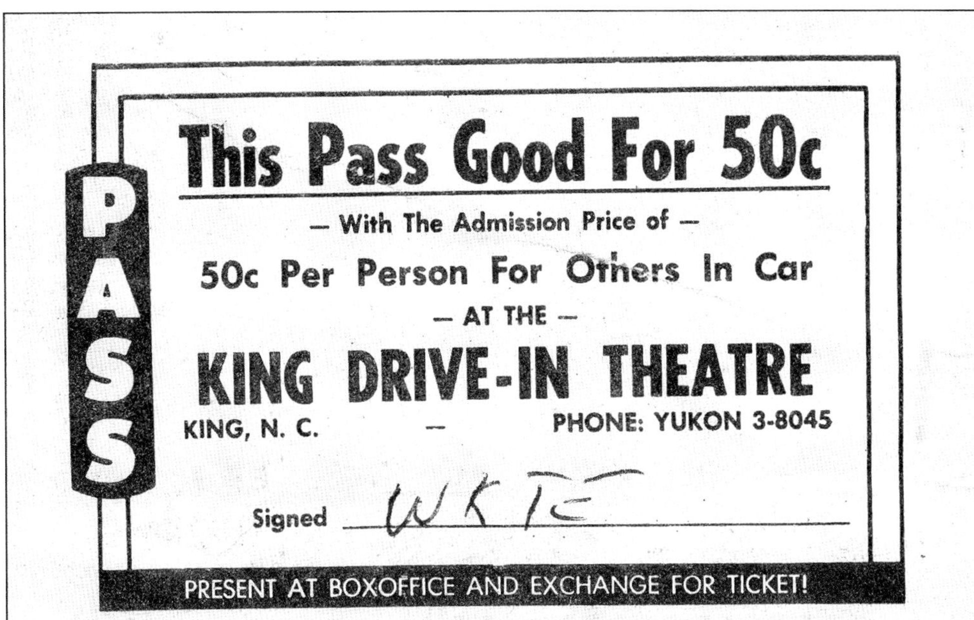

This 50¢ pass to the King Drive-In was won from a contest on WKTE AM radio. (Courtesy of Adeline Kiser.)

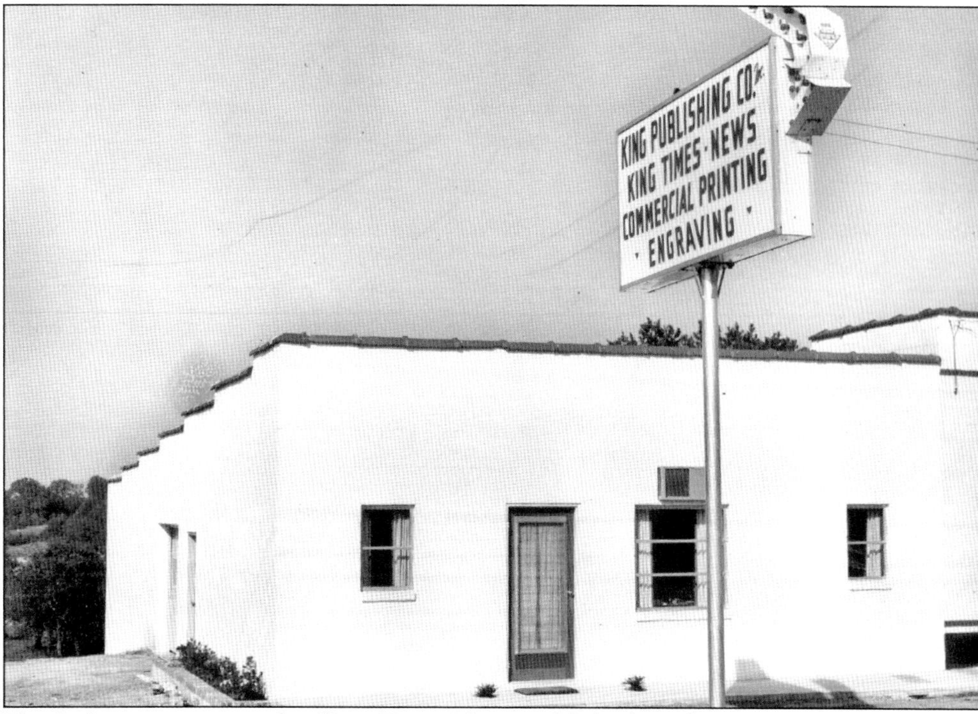

King's first newspaper, the *King Times-News*, published its first issue on December 7, 1961. Jake and Peggy Wall founded the newspaper. In 1968, they sold the newspaper to Steve Neal, who moved the offices and presses to the vacant former First Baptist Church building. The paper changed owners several times before being consolidated with the *Danbury Reporter* to become *The Stokes News* in 2002. (Courtesy of Peggy Wall.)

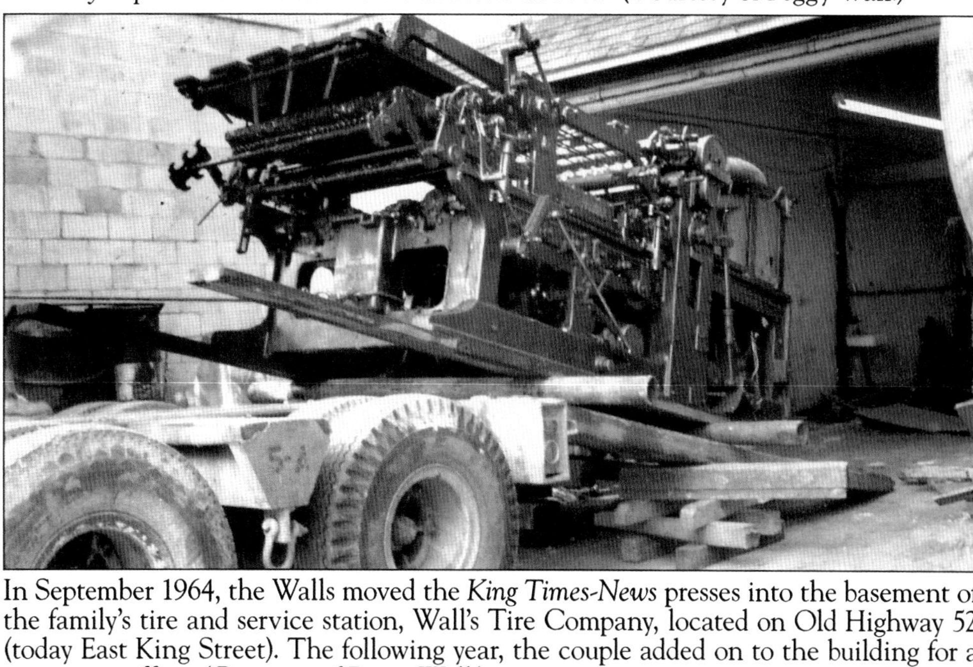

In September 1964, the Walls moved the *King Times-News* presses into the basement of the family's tire and service station, Wall's Tire Company, located on Old Highway 52 (today East King Street). The following year, the couple added on to the building for a newspaper office. (Courtesy of Peggy Wall.)

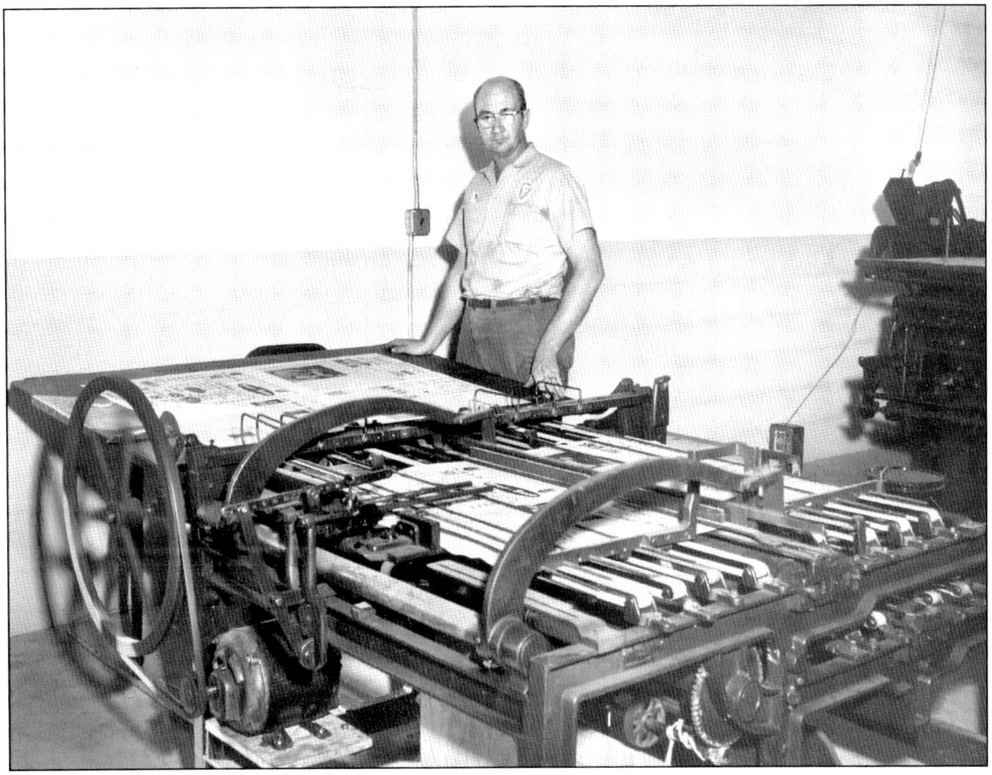

Newspaper founder Jake Wall stands at the original newspaper folder in October 1964. (Courtesy of Peggy Wall.)

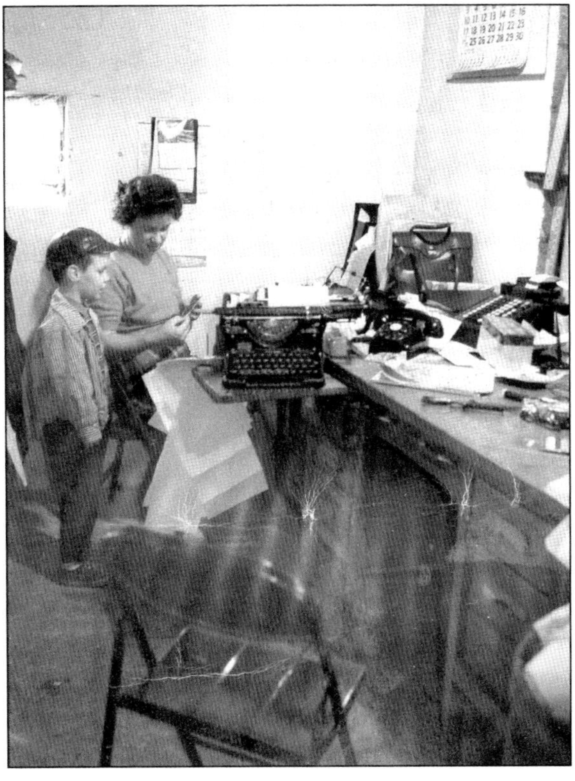

Newspaper founder and reporter Peggy Wall and her son, Brent, are seen in the *King Times-News* office in 1963. (Courtesy of Peggy Wall.)

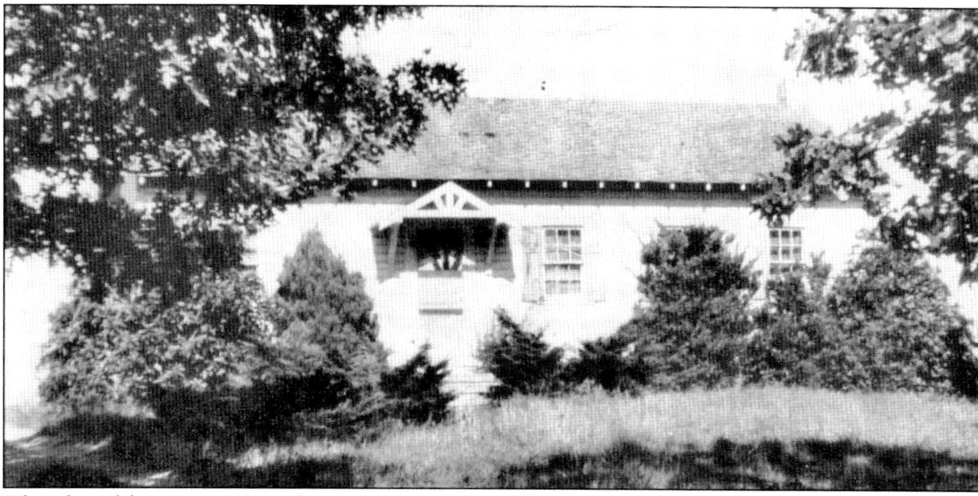

The first library in King began in the King Woman's Club building (seen above) on Dalton Road *c.* 1943. The women's club stocked the building with books from the North Carolina Library Commission and operated a library one afternoon a week. When the service stopped, the community relied on a bookmobile service that delivered books to Wall Service Station and later the FCX building. In 1967, community volunteers brought a library back to the former woman's club building, naming it the Lula Pulliam Memorial Library because Pulliam originally donated the land for King Woman's Club. In 1980, the library moved downtown until 1996, when a new King Public Library opened on the corner of Dalton Road and Pilot View Drive. (Courtesy of Roberta Wall Merritt.)

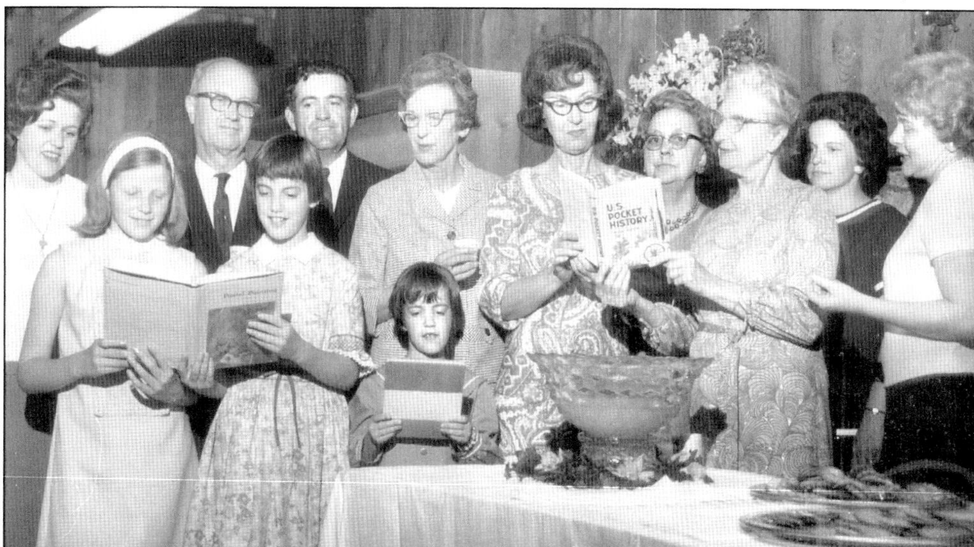

The Lula Pulliam Memorial Library is dedicated by some of its founding volunteers on April 2, 1967, in the former King Woman's Club building. The adults, from left to right, are Dottie Shelton, Dr. I. A. Booe, Moir Sizemore, Mary Ella Booe, Jane Boles, Jessie Garner, Clara Helsabeck, Lola Stanley, and Patsy Ginns. The children are, from left to right, Lou Ellen Rierson, Karen Sizemore, and Gwen Sizemore. The library opened with no restrooms and used a stove for heat. In 1969, Edith Smith was hired as the first permanent librarian. (Courtesy of Peggy Wall.)

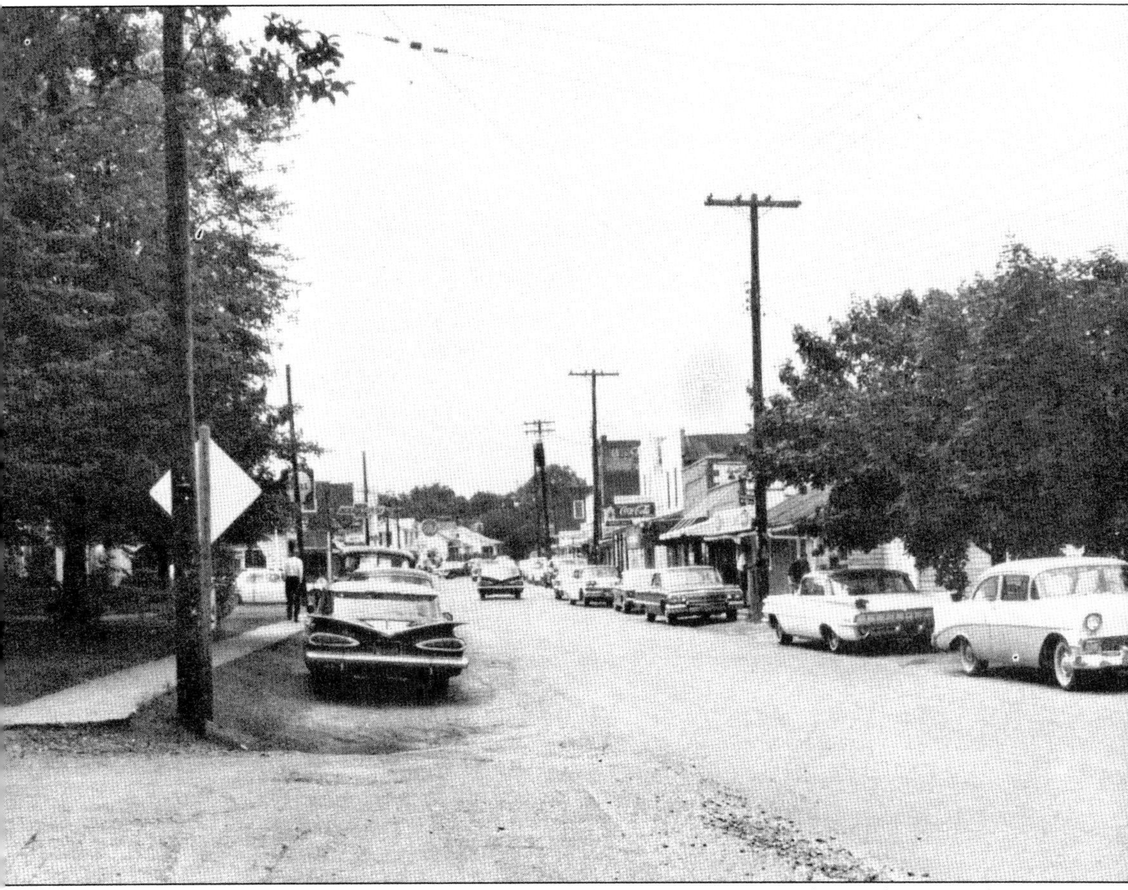

This *c.* 1964 photograph of downtown King looks west on present-day Dalton Road.

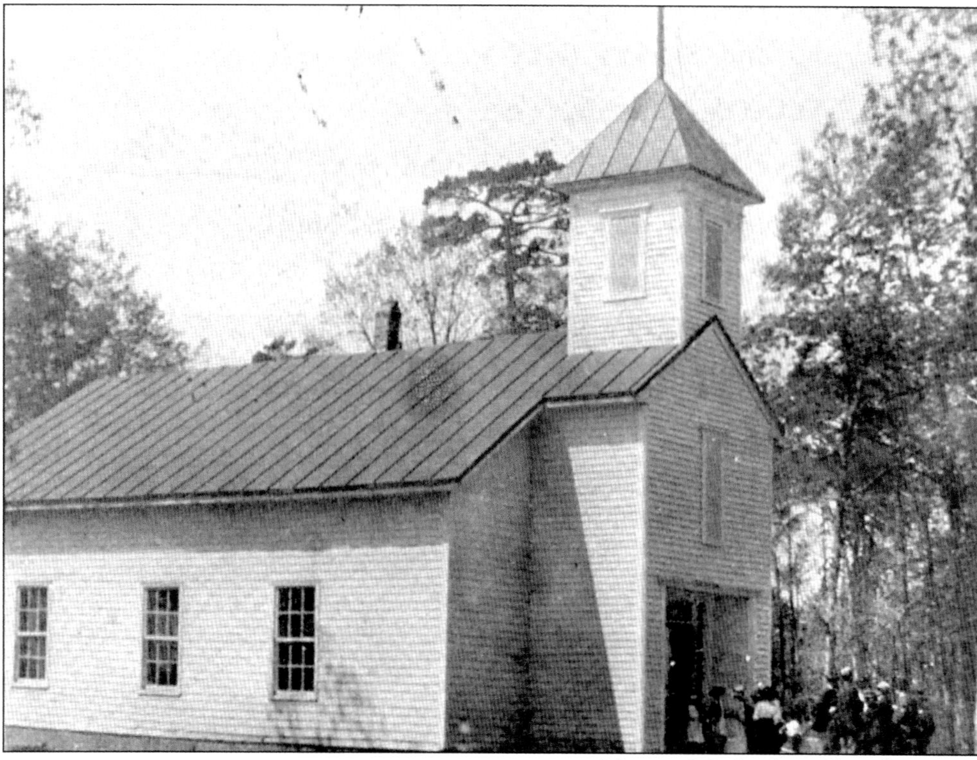

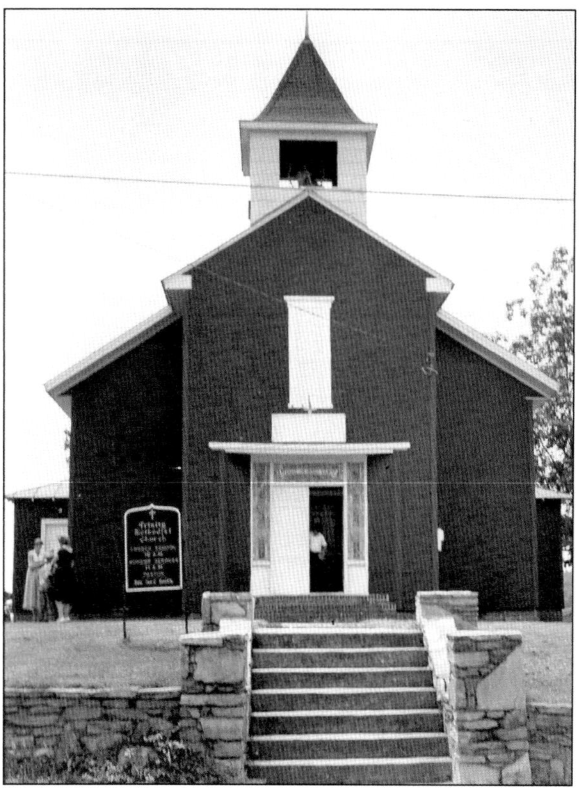

Trinity Methodist Church, *c.* 1918, began in the Spainhour Schoolhouse just across the road from the church's present location in 1873, before the railroad and King (King's Cabin) began. The first church building was built and dedicated *c.* 1880. (Courtesy of Trinity United Methodist Church.)

In the early 1940s, members grassed the church lawn for the first time, built a rock wall, and poured a sidewalk, as seen in this *c.* 1950 photograph. The last sermon preached in this building was in 1974, when the congregation moved into a new building built behind it. (Courtesy of Trinity United Methodist Church.)

The First Baptist Church of King, formed in January 1898 as Missionary Baptist Church, held its first sermon the following month. The same year, members discussed building a church and purchased land on Old Hollow Road (today East King Street). In April 1899, members congregated under an arbor on the property until the first building, seen at right, was completed in March 1900. Sometime after 1905, the church became known as King Baptist Church. (Courtesy of First Baptist Church of King.)

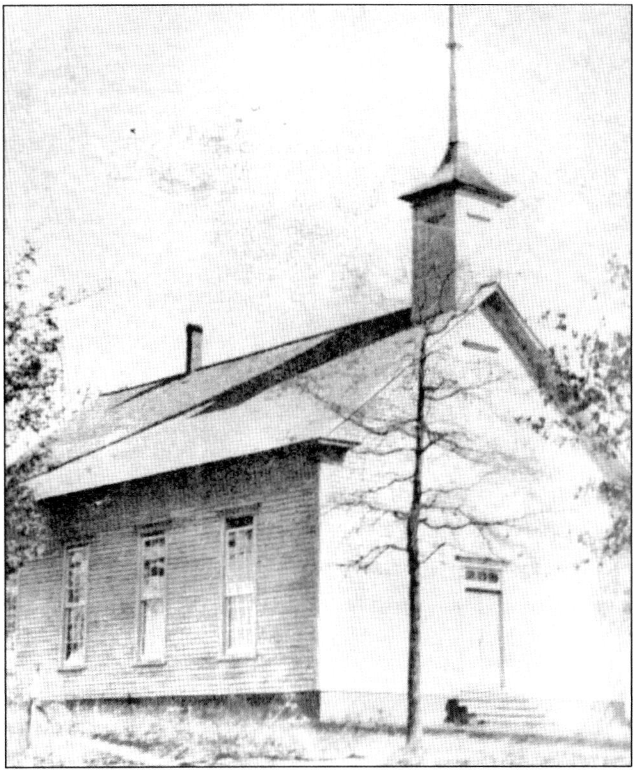

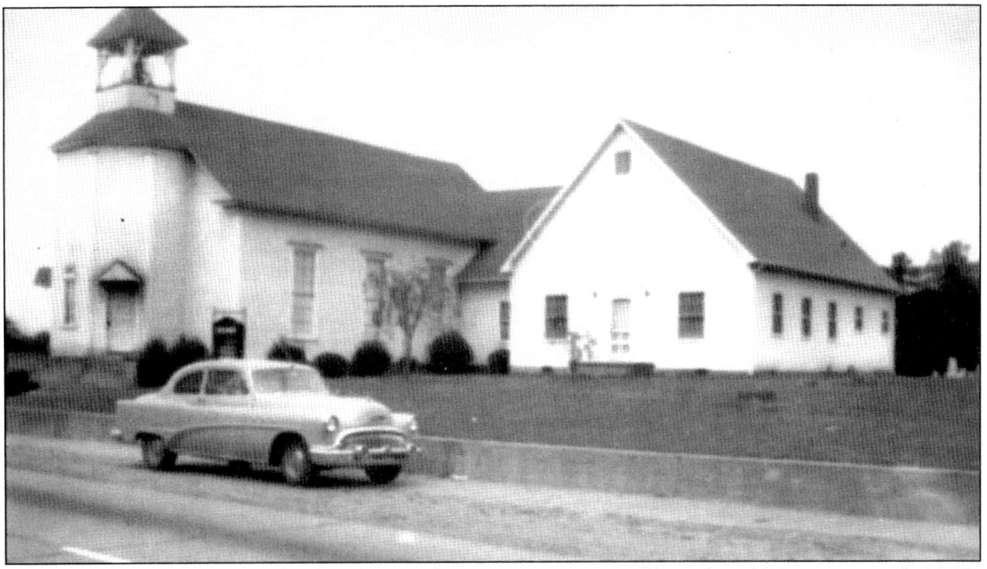

King Baptist Church, which changed to First Baptist Church of King around 1960, held its last service here on present-day East King Street in January 1967. The church bought four acres of land across the railroad tracks on Kirby Road in 1956 to build a larger sanctuary. In 1966, the church broke ground on the new sanctuary and moved in the following year. In 1968, the congregation sold the old sanctuary, seen above, to publisher Steve Neal, who used it to house the offices and presses of the *King Times-News*. (Courtesy of Peggy Wall.)

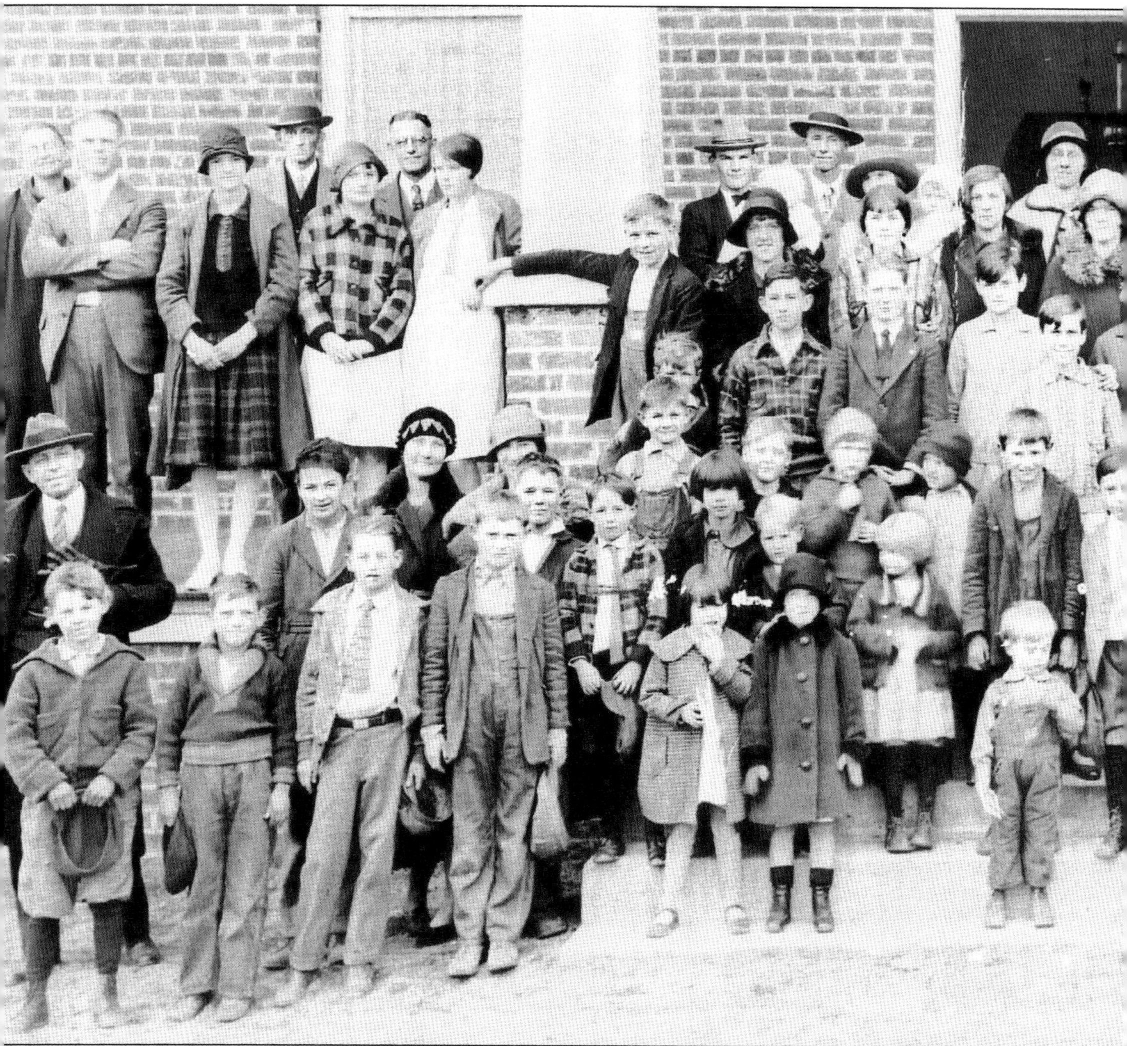

In 1902, First Christian Church of King began as the Galatia Church at the corner of present-day Meadowbrook Drive and Ingram Road. The area was considered part of the Five Forks community at the time. In 1923, the Galatia congregation decided to sell the church property and move to King. In July 1924, the Galatia congregation, along with members of other area Churches of Christ, formed King Church of Christ and built the church seen above on the corner of present-day Pilot View Drive and Dalton Road. In 1979, the church moved back to the property where the Galatia Church first met. The former King Church of Christ building was later sold to St. Elizabeth Episcopal Church. King Church of Christ later became known as First Christian Church of King. The King Church of Christ congregation, seen above *c.* 1927, is as follows, from left to right: (first row) unidentified, Bud Burge, Dare White, Muertis Caudle, Edith Beasley Blakely, Opal Southern Dobbins, Robert Columbus White, Merle Newsom Pratt, Junior Wolff, Lucille Southern Throckmorton, Emily Spainhour Vogler, two unidentified, Dorothy Spainhour Holland, Mozelle Kapp Kirby, unidentified, and Robert Spainhour; (second row) Dr. E. M. Griffin, Jim "Sweeten" Boyles, Moir Baker, Alan White, Mary Ruth Beasley, Ovaline Caudle Loggins, Lucille White, Ruby Spainhour, Alice Briggs Spainhour, unidentified, Brent Moore, Coster Collins, Ralton Griffin, and Anna

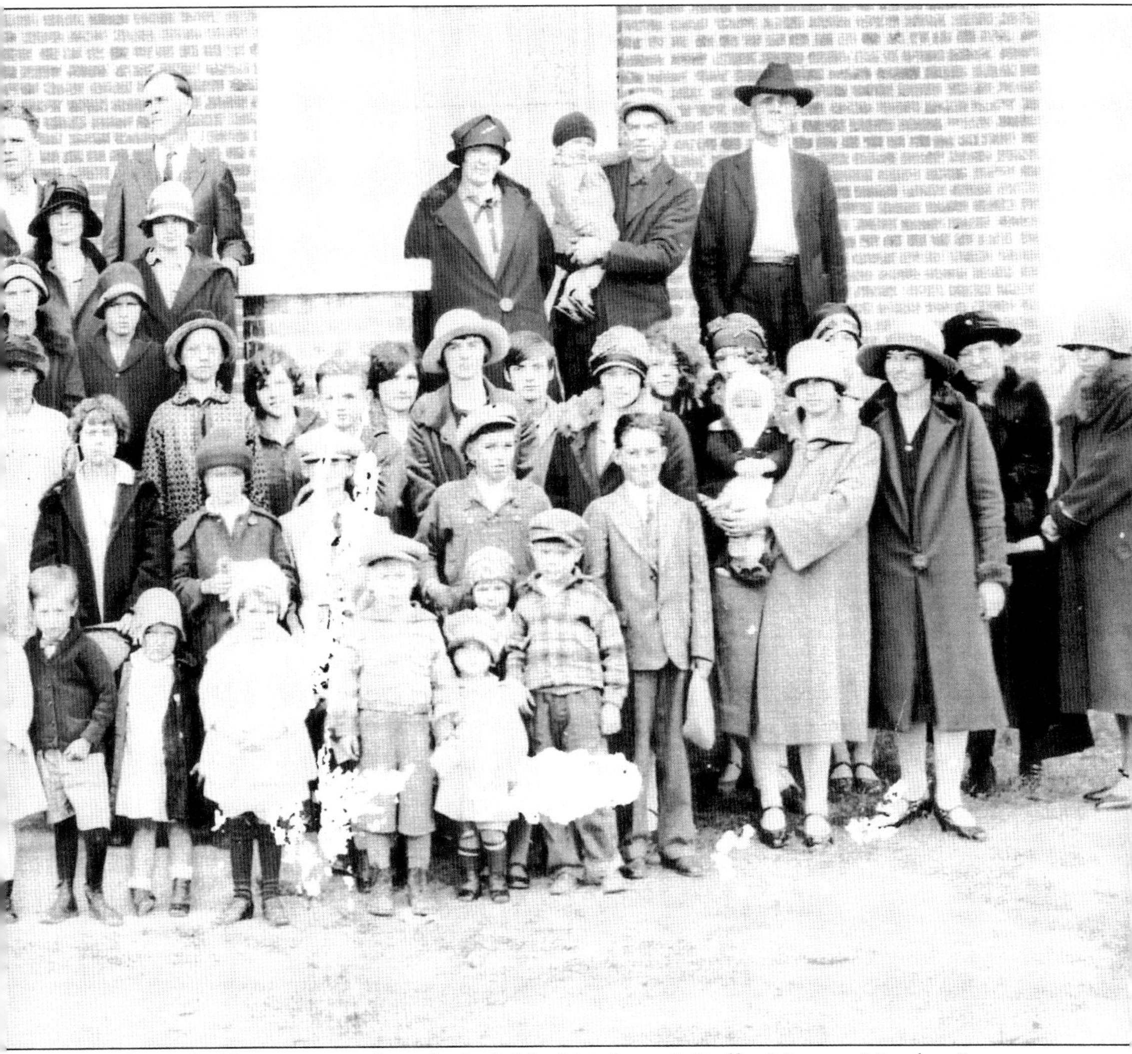

Spainhour holding an unidentified child; (third row) Della Moore, Martha Ingram Harding Grabs, Fred White, Baxter Moore, Virgie White, Laura Boyles, Ed White, Renard Griffin, Melissa Newsom, Ola Newsom Spainhour (or possibly her sister Minnie Newsom), Vivian Newsom Rumley, Norman Alexander White, Oneida Caudle, Marie Goff Rierson, Avis Newsom Doub, Madonna Burge, Mina Burge Hauser, Albright Caudle Holder, Lucille Kirby Wall, Lalah Newsom Smith, Leiza Helsabeck, Ola Slate Grabs, and unidentified; (fourth row) Pryan Joseph White, Tink Shore, Raymond Moore, Nedra Newsom Whitman, Ruthie Burge Hayworth, Lia Southern Bowen, Myrtle Wolff, and Della Newsom Baker; (fifth row) Wyatt Caudle, Viola Southern Cromer, Luna Burge Tuttle, Vivian Burge Hunt, Betsy Burge White, Anne Spainhour Murray, Ersie Garner Barber, and Sula Boyles Hauser; (sixth row) Martha Jane Newsom Shore, Norman Newsom, Gladys Spainhour Newsom, Fred Shore, Mae "Sis" Newsom McGee, Phil Spainhour, Edith Moore Hauser, Austin Wall holding Roberta Wall, Gid Newsom, Anne Spainhour holding Allen Spainhour, Mae Goff Wall, Judson Spainhour, Felix Spainhour, Hessie Bennett, Wyatt "Pete" Southern holding Olene Southern Booth, and Martin Spainhour. (Courtesy of Norma Newsom Cox.)

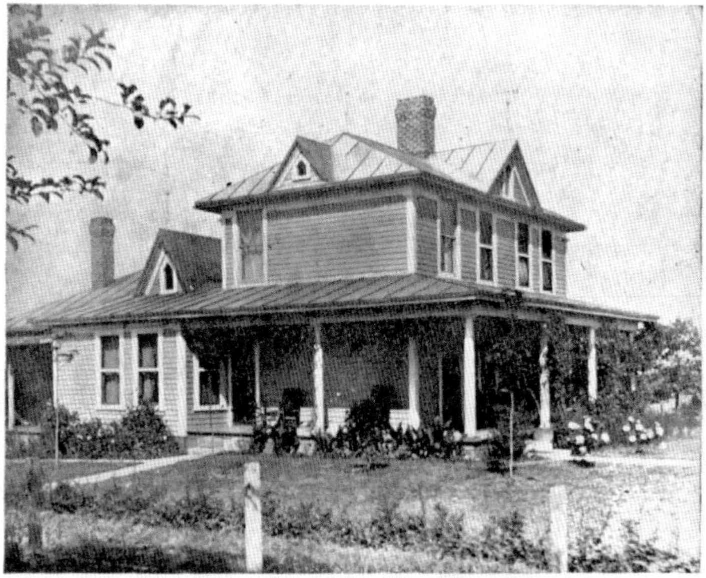

The S. W. Pulliam Residence, West Main Street, King, N. C.

PUB. BY E. P. NEWSUM, KING, N. C.

The King Moravian Church congregation held its first service in the King School auditorium in July 1924. In October 1924, the church's 15 charter members met for services in the home of Simeon and Lula Grabs Pulliam, seen above. Simeon and Lula donated the land across from their home for the first church building. The first brick was laid on April 27, 1925. At their deaths, the Pulliams donated their home, built in 1909 and captured in this postcard, to the church as a parsonage and today used as a church office.

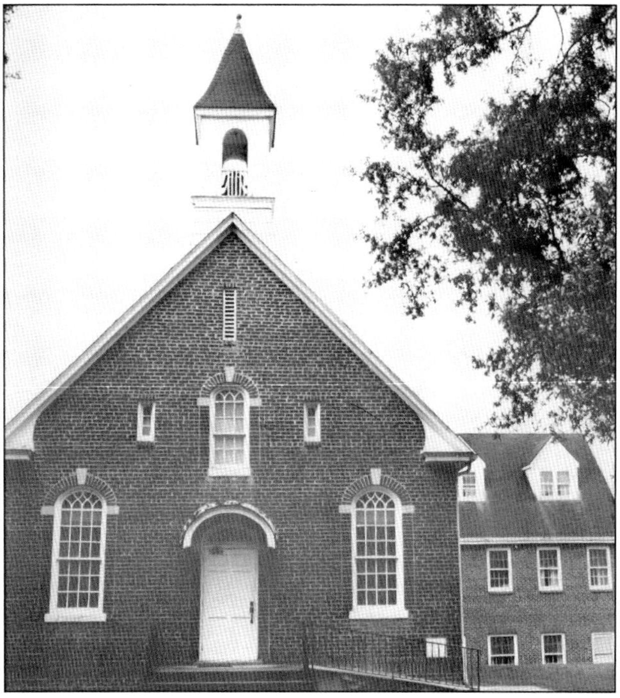

In 1951, King Moravian Church expanded with the construction of the Christian Education Building. A new sanctuary was added and dedicated in 1993. The old sanctuary, seen here, continues to be used for church functions. (Courtesy of King Moravian Church.)

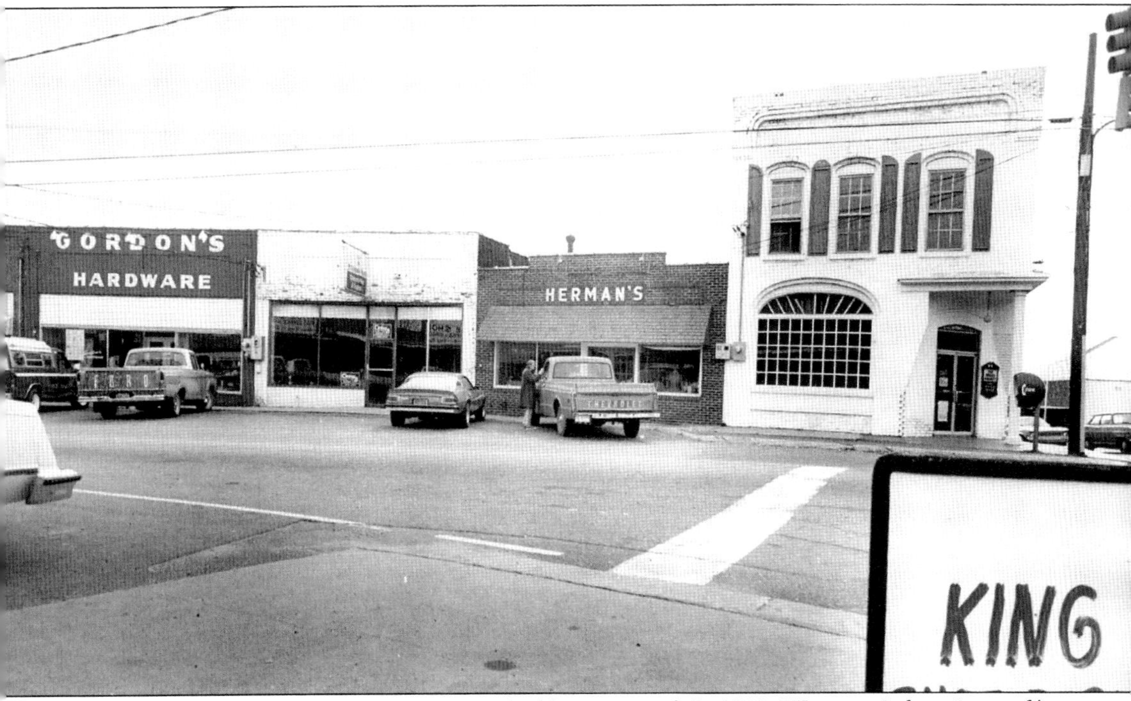

Shown here is downtown King in 1982. (Courtesy of © 1982 *Winston-Salem Journal*/ David Rolfe.)

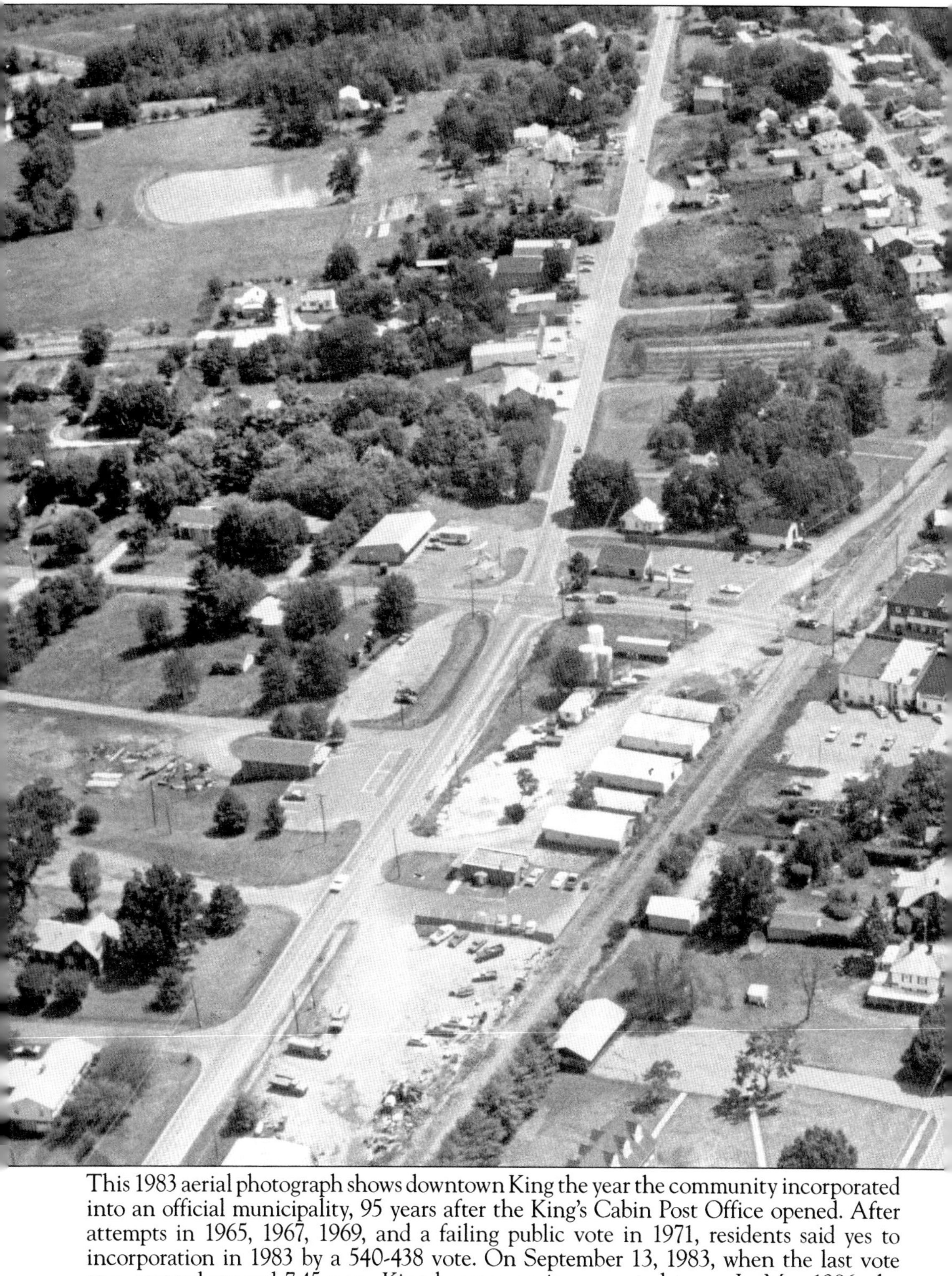

This 1983 aerial photograph shows downtown King the year the community incorporated into an official municipality, 95 years after the King's Cabin Post Office opened. After attempts in 1965, 1967, 1969, and a failing public vote in 1971, residents said yes to incorporation in 1983 by a 540-438 vote. On September 13, 1983, when the last vote was counted around 7:45 p.m., King became an incorporated town. In May 1986, the

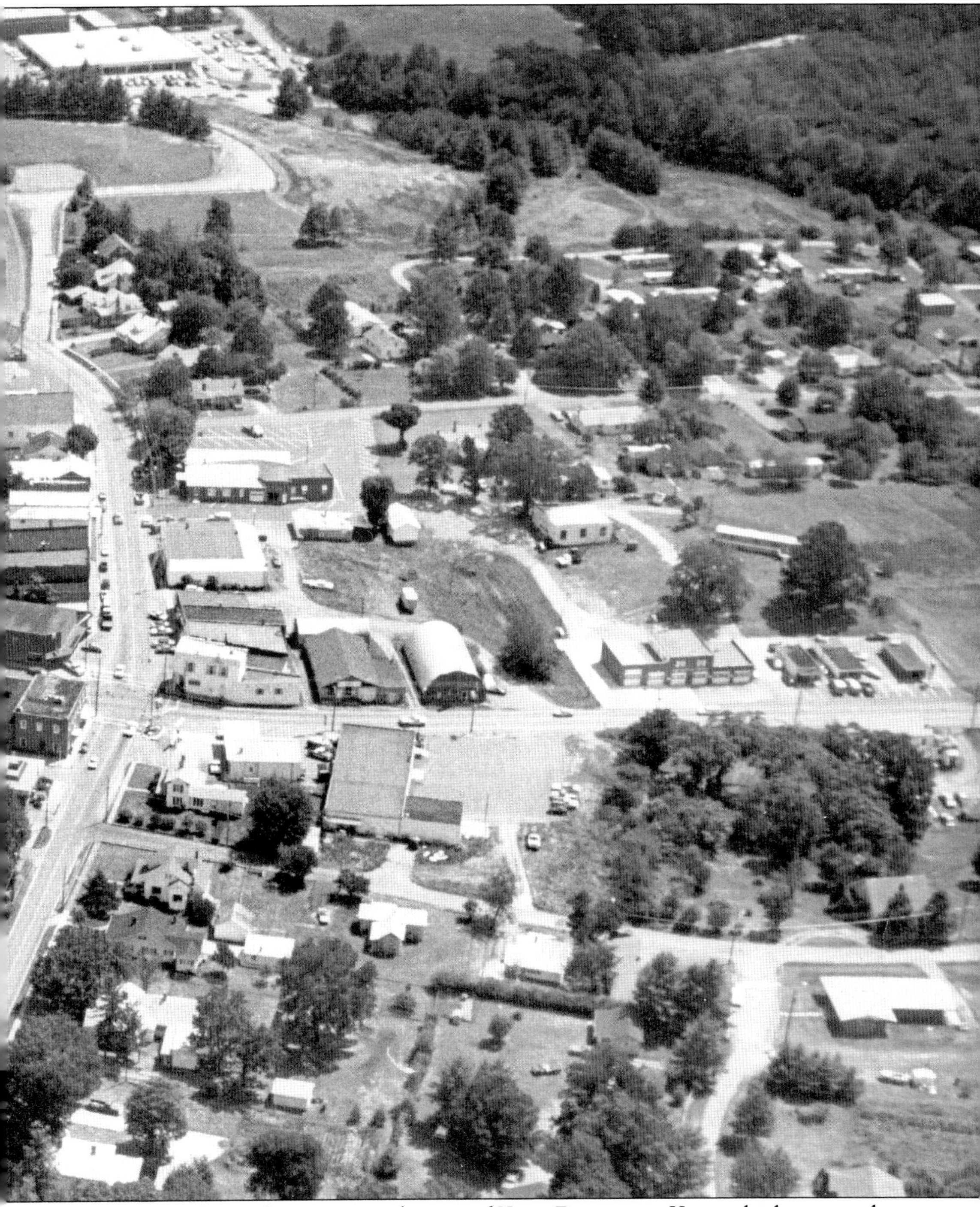

town of King changed its name to the city of King. Downtown King, which was used as a backdrop in the 1998 made-for-television movie *The Patron Saint of Liars*, became the King Historic District after being placed on the National Register of Historic Places in 2002. (Courtesy of © 1983 *Winston-Salem Journal*/David Rolfe.)

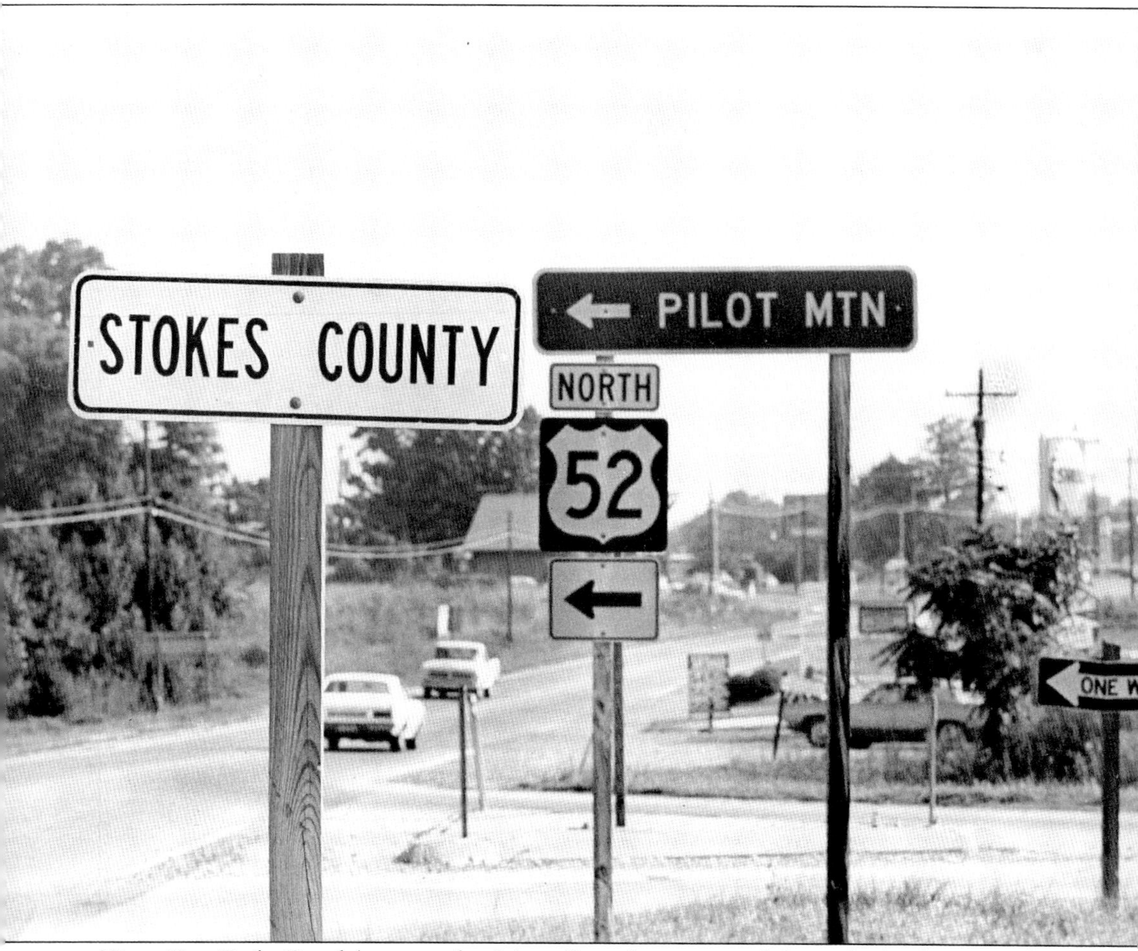

King–Five Forks Road (present-day Main Street) is captured from the bridge at Highway 52 (future Interstate 74) looking north toward King in 1974. After the 1960s construction of the four-lane Highway 52, with an interchange built at Five Forks, the town of King started moving in this direction. The rich farmland of Five Forks slowly began to vanish as King and its commerce shifted away from downtown and toward the four-lane highway. The shift was later fueled by R. J. Reynolds Tobacco Company, who in 1980 started building the world's largest cigarette manufacturing plant in Tobaccoville. Soon fast-food chains and shopping centers flourished near the interchange. Many of the new businesses had a Tobaccoville address until King incorporated in 1983 and turned its Main Street toward the four-lane highway (King's original Main Street was present-day Dalton Road). The King Post Office moved away from downtown and closer to the highway in 1987. (Courtesy of © 1974 *Winston-Salem Journal*.)

Two

Quiet Places

We knew everybody up and down the road here. Few know what its like to grow up in a country store with a potbelly stove and water cooled drink box.

—Norma Newsom Cox, recalling growing up in her father's store at Five Forks

King's prosperity was blessed by the railroad, while her neighbors became places of stillness filled with quiet beauty. These surrounding communities began much like King did, with people coming together at crossroads, schools, and churches. Some took on an identity thanks to a post office, which officially gave them a name. Capella, Chestnut Grove, Dalton, Mount Olive (whose post office was named Ale), Dry Springs, Five Forks, Mizpah (today known as Mountain View), Poplar Springs (whose post office was first named Helsabeck and later shortened to Helsa), Quaker Gap, Oak Grove (whose post office was named Slate), and Timmon's Crossroads each became places in their own right, with businesses, churches, and schools.

In 1879, the general assembly authorized the consolidation of the Western Railroad and the Mount Airy Railroad, and five years later, surveys were conducted to connect Mount Airy with the rest of the world. The connection would require tracks to be laid through southwest Stokes County. Three surveys were conducted, one bringing the tracks through Mount Olive, another laying tracks through Five Forks, and the third, which was chosen, placed tracks through the open fields of King's Cabin. The fate of each surrounding community was sealed, as people moved from the quiet countryside to be closer to the sounds of a locomotive.

With the introduction of Rural Free Delivery (RFD), surrounding post offices slowly consolidated with King, where the mail was delivered by train. Many of these small community post offices became rural mail routes of King, and by 1951, all were gone. In 1928, community schools started to consolidate with King School. These quiet places are now fading from maps, and some are completely silenced thanks to King's growth. Their past identity is only preserved in the names of churches, schools, road signs, reflections from aged minds, and photographs. The following collection of images reflects these places of the past now resting in the stillness of history.

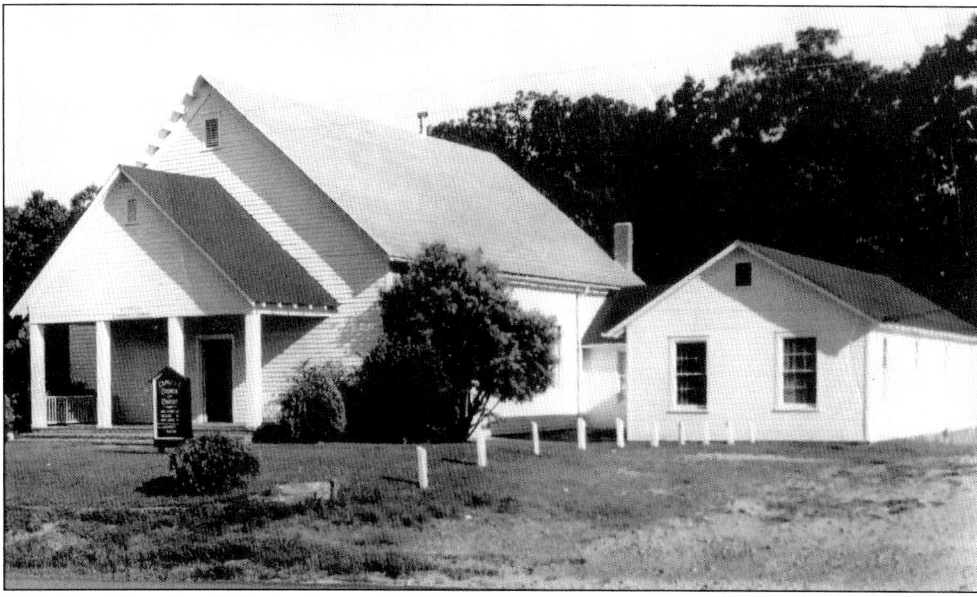

Capella Church of Christ began in 1900 in the homes of its first members. In 1901, the congregation built its first church on Flat Shoals Road. In 1921, a new church was built. Sunday School rooms were added in 1945, and a front porch was added in 1951. During the 1960s, the church was clad in brick, and more classrooms, a restroom, and a baptistry were added, along with the sanctuary being remolded. (Courtesy of Jack and Annie Lou Patterson.)

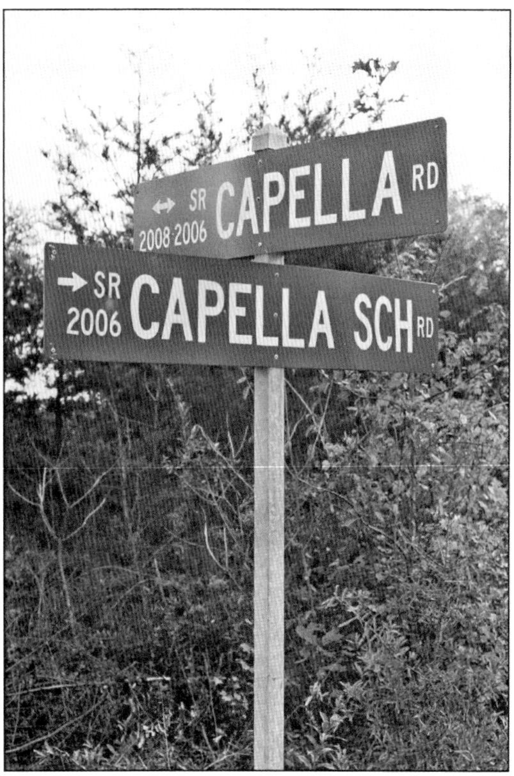

Capella began after the Quaker Gap Post Office moved farther away from the community, forcing residents to travel for their mail. Capella postmaster Sid Reynolds opened a new post office in 1901 in a corner of his home on Robertson Ridge Road. Some believe the post office was named after the star Capella, which at the time may have been seen bright in the night sky. Others believe the name came after postmaster Reynolds sent two names to the postal service for consideration: "Ella" after his wife and "Morella Carolle" after a neighbor. The postal service combined the two to form Capella. The post office closed in 1903, when it became a rural route of King.

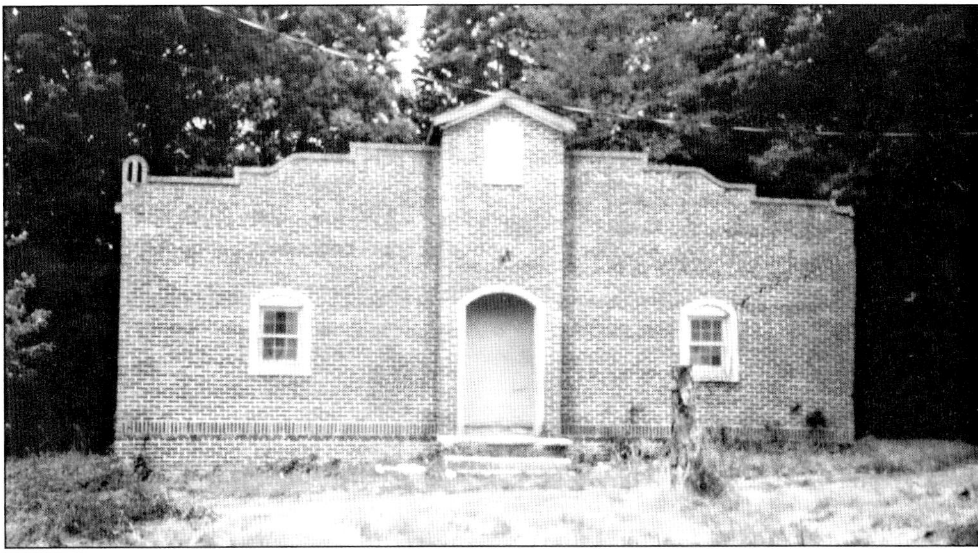

Capella School was first known simply as School District #70 and later named King School after Alexander King, a community leader, a landowner, and a brother of Charles King, whose home, King's Cabin, became the namesake of King. Alexander King, Henry Tuttle, and Drury Boyles served as the school committeemen in 1839, the first year of free public schools in North Carolina. In 1904, the school board ordered that the name be changed to Capella School so that a new school in King could take the King name. Capella School consolidated with King School in 1946. (Courtesy of Doug East.)

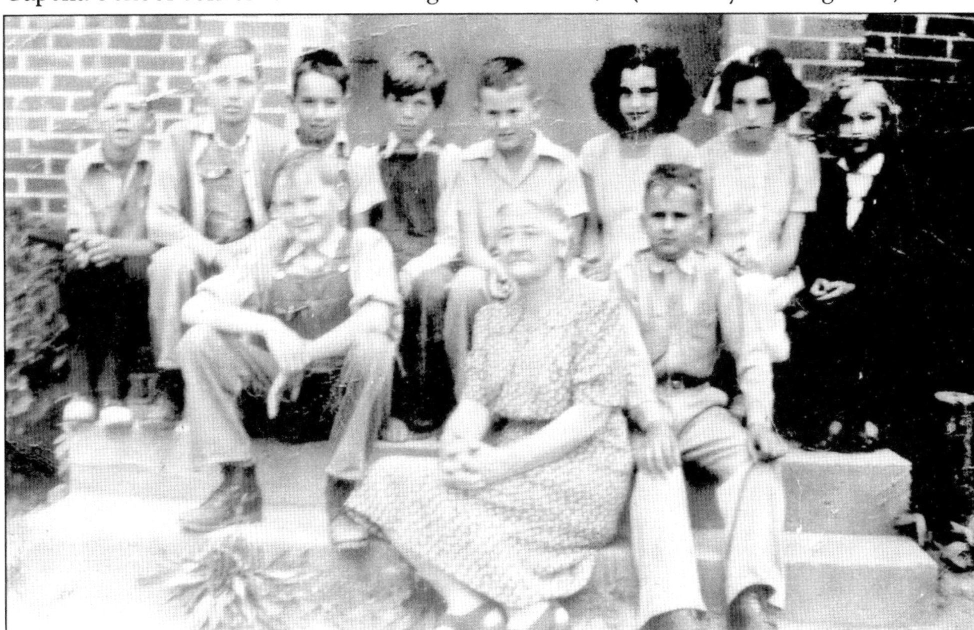

Shown are the fourth- and fifth-grade classes of Capella School during the last year it was open in 1946. From left to right are (first row) Carl Smith, Hessie Barr (fourth- through seventh-grade teacher), and Clarence Hall; (second row) David Bennett, William Covington, Marvin Tuttle, Carroll East, Billy Wade Hall, Betty Hunter Tucker, Doris Hall Covington, and Wilma Covington Smith. (Courtesy of Betty Hunter Tucker.)

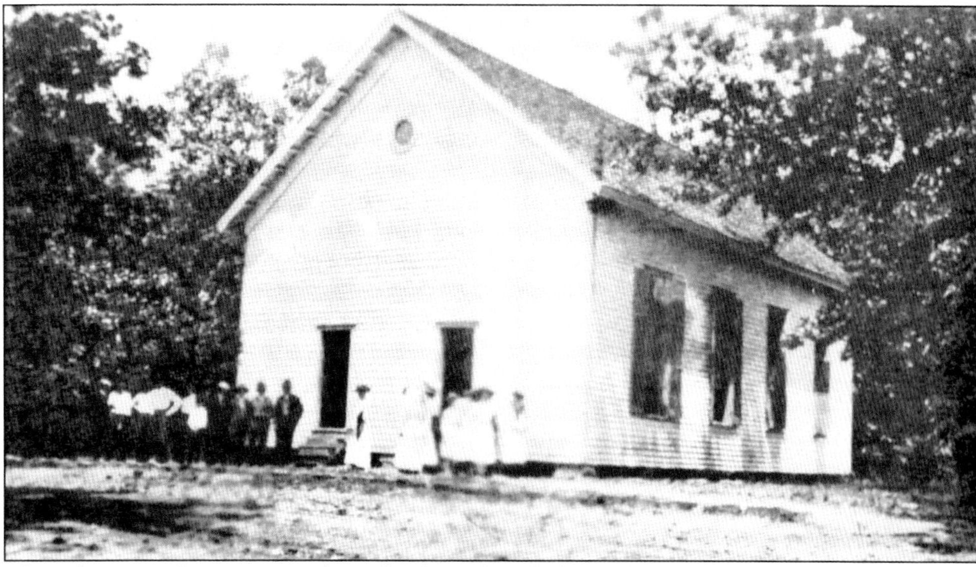

The Chestnut Grove United Methodist Church formed in 1857 as Sauratown Mission. In 1859, the congregation paid David Nicholas Dalton $4 for one acre on which to build a log church. The church was almost abandoned during the Civil War, but the congregation came back, building a small frame church. A small school named Chestnut Grove was built near the church before 1877. In 1890, the congregation built a larger church, seen above in 1916, and changed its name to Chestnut Grove. (Courtesy of Chestnut Grove United Methodist Church.)

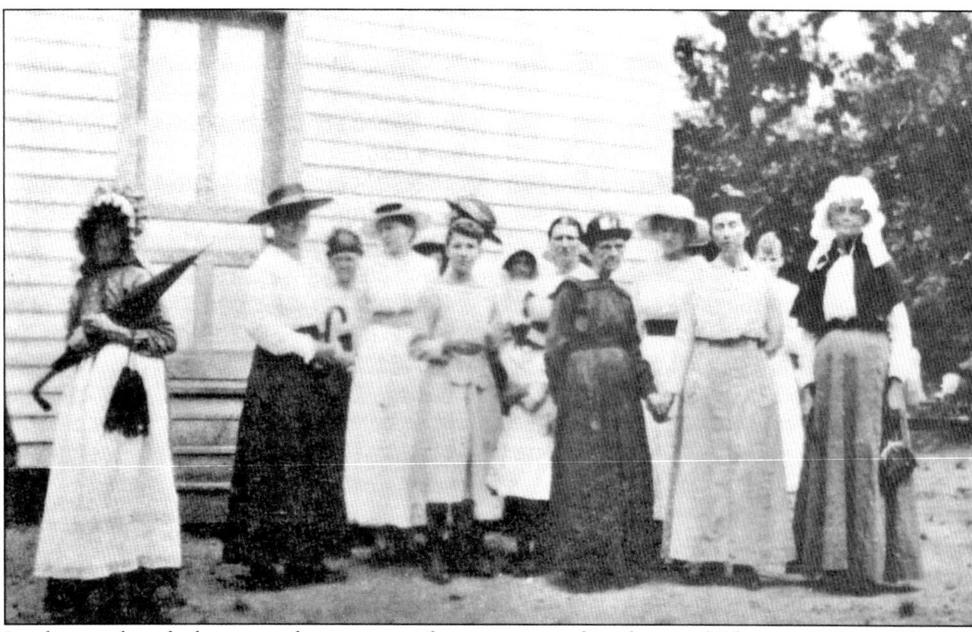

In this undated photograph, a group of women stand in front of Chestnut Grove United Methodist Church. In 1949, classrooms were added, and in 1957, the sanctuary was remodeled. In 1971, more classrooms, a fellowship hall, and a kitchen were added. The vestibule was added and the church was clad in brick in 1980. (Courtesy of Chestnut Grove United Methodist Church.)

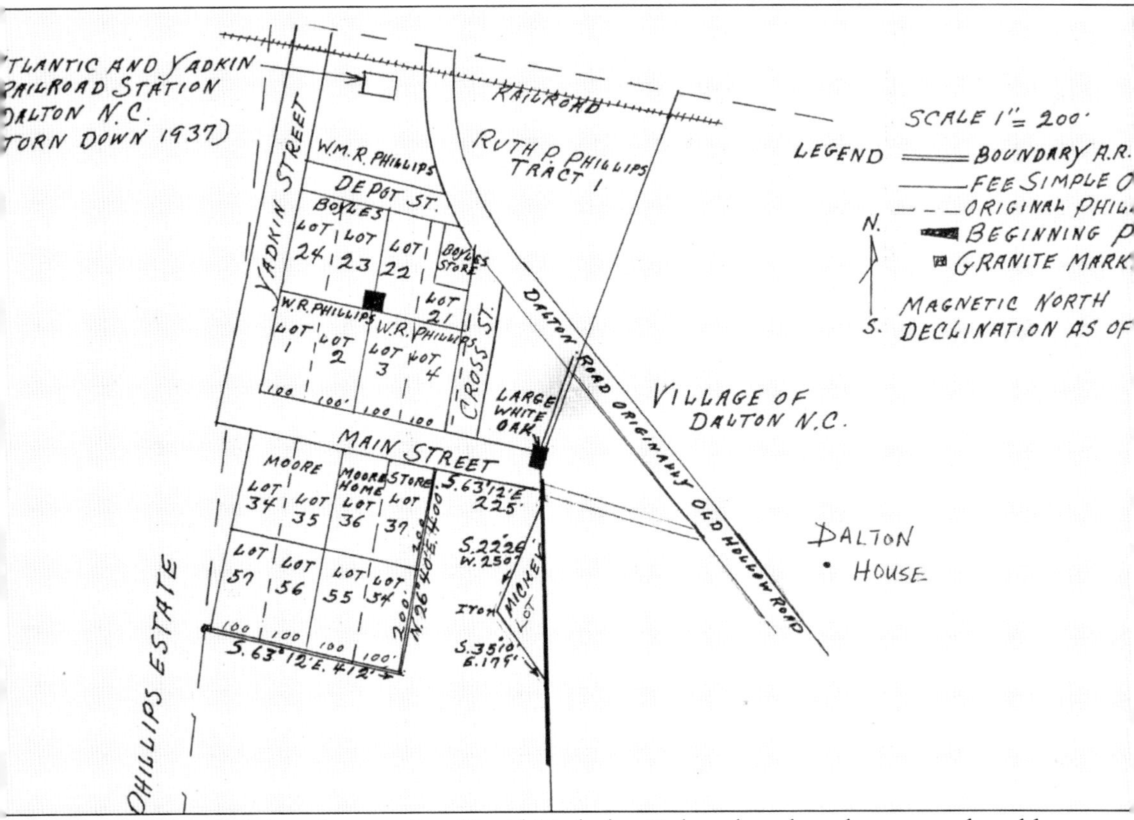

The village of Dalton began after David Nicholas Dalton bought a home on the old Hollow Road (today Dalton Road) near the Little Yadkin River in 1854. The community had become a trading post and was originally called Little Yadkin. Dalton expanded his home into a hotel, accommodating travelers going between Winston-Salem and Mount Airy. He created a thriving community around his home, laying it out in lots as seen in the map above. In 1856, Dalton bought eight acres, a flour and corn mill, a blacksmith shop, and the Little Yadkin Post Office, which changed its name to Dalton in 1876. The Dalton Institute, one of the best private schools in the area, opened in 1872, and the railroad started laying tracks in 1886. The railroad built a station, stationmaster's house, and a water tank. Little Yadkin Methodist Episcopal, Dalton Chapel Methodist Primitive, Trinity Methodist, Chestnut Grove Methodist, and the original Mount Olive Baptist Churches were all considered a part of the Dalton community and sometimes served by its post office. In 1890, the population of Dalton was 87. David "Nick" Dalton married twice and had 18 children. The community started to fade after his death in 1895 and lost its identity when the post office closed and consolidated with Pinnacle in 1951. (Courtesy of Margaret Phillips McClanahan.)

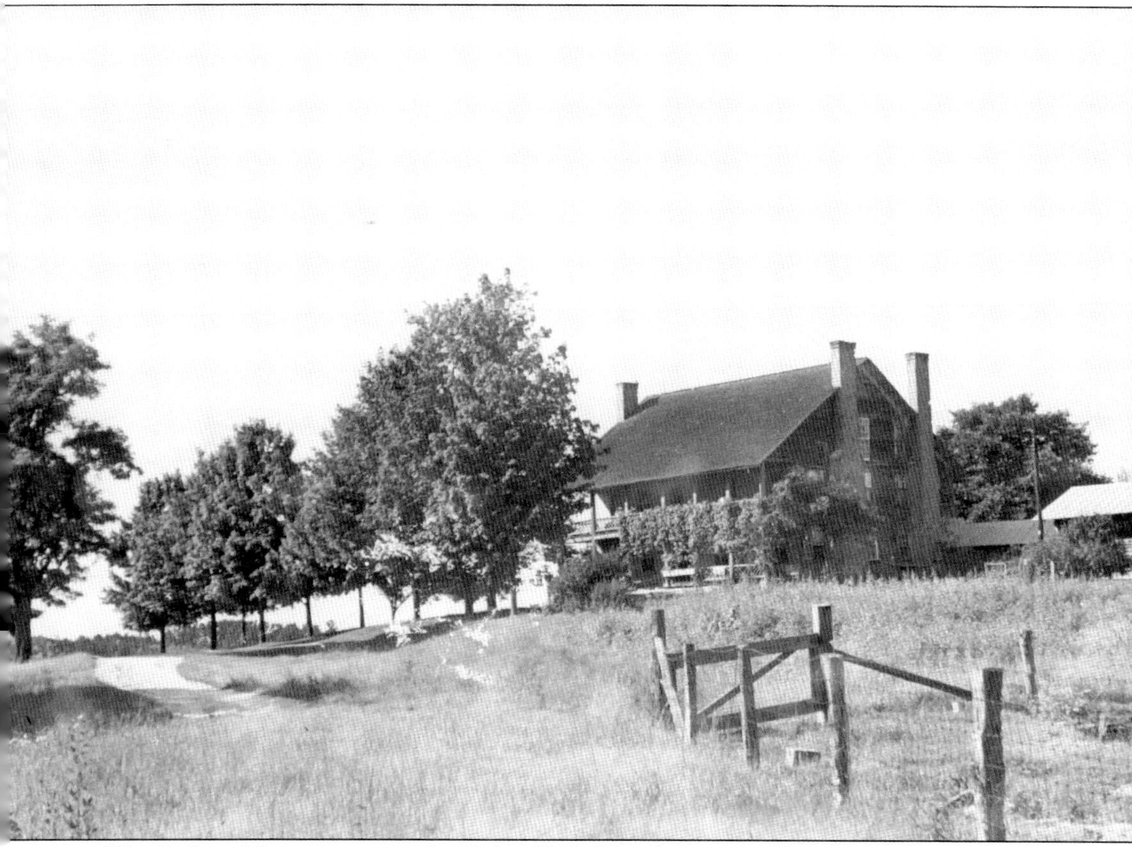

The Dalton Home is pictured in May 1942. The four-story, 22-room home was used as a hotel with a ballroom on the third floor and an underground passageway leading to the kitchen and smokehouse, which stood to the right of the home. The home was demolished in the 1990s. (Courtesy of the Forsyth County Public Library Photograph Collection.)

Scales Dalton, one of the owners of the Dalton Home in 1942, points out the rock walls that protect the underground passageway between the home and the kitchen. Servants used the passageway to protect themselves and the food from the weather elements. (Courtesy of the Forsyth County Public Library Photograph Collection.)

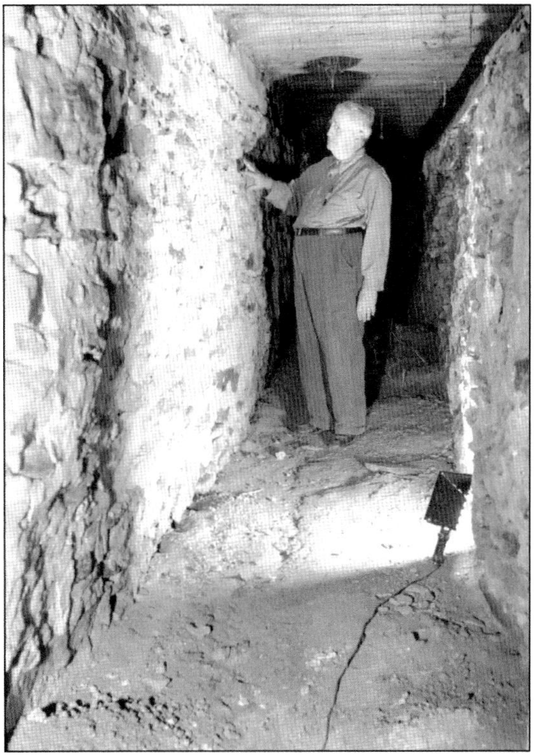

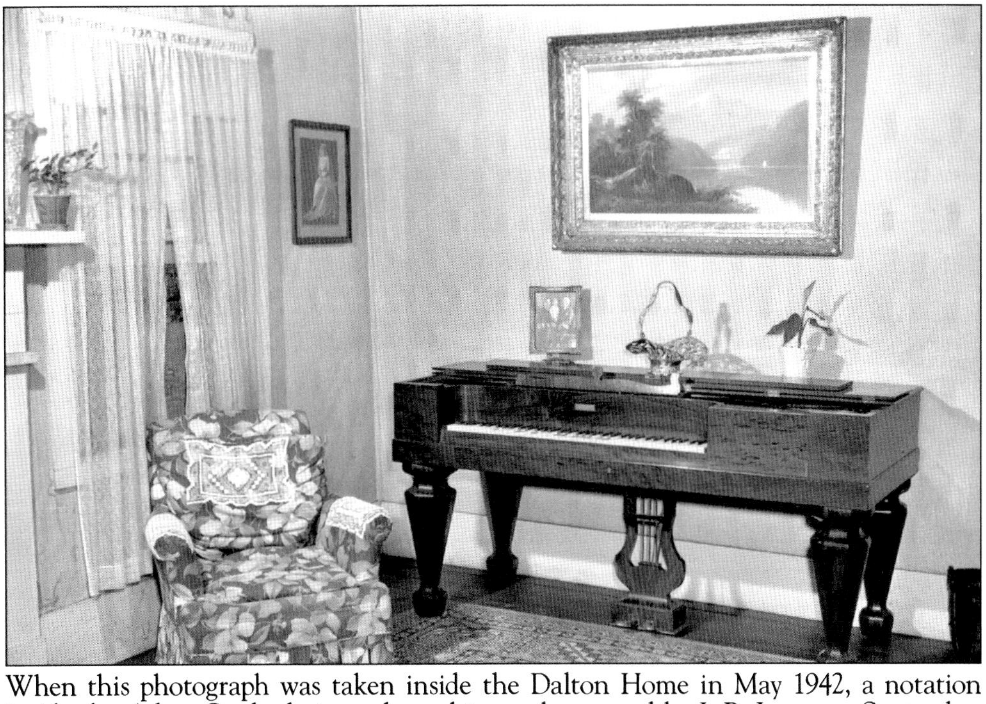

When this photograph was taken inside the Dalton Home in May 1942, a notation inside the Adam Stodard piano showed it was last tuned by I. B. Jones on September 5, 1851. The piano was originally purchased by David "Nick" Dalton. (Courtesy of the Forsyth County Public Library Photograph Collection.)

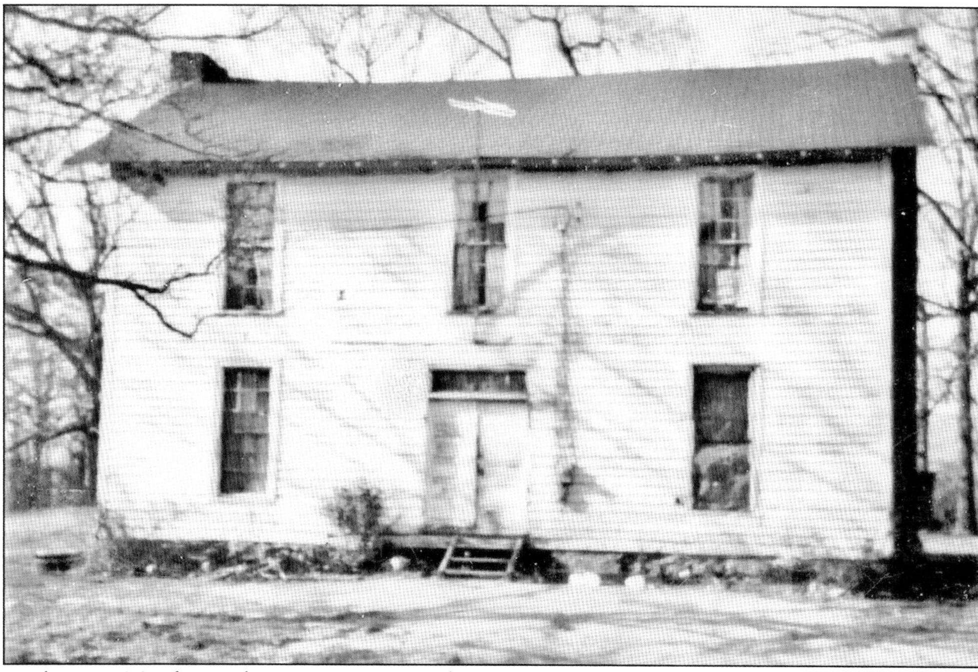

Built in 1872, the Dalton Institute was known as one of the best private schools in the area. As many as 25 male and female students attended each year from as far away as Mount Airy and High Point. Dalton Institute turned out many students who went into medicine and law. Tuition per session included $10 for primary English; $15 for higher English; and $18 for languages, with $7 to $8 per month for board, including fuel and washing. The institute closed in 1908. (Courtesy of Jean Stone Hall.)

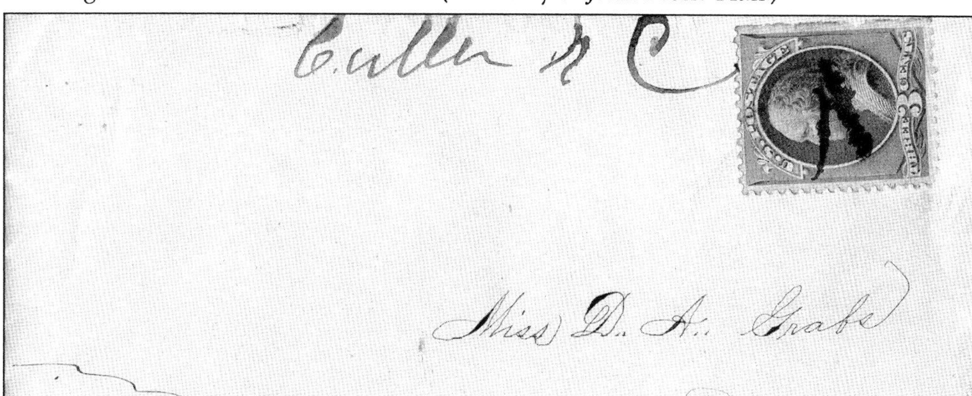

A letter addressed to Miss D. A. Grabs, Dalton, North Carolina, Stokes County, was sent from Culler, North Carolina, today known as Pinnacle. The Dalton Post Office opened in 1875 after changing names from the Little Yadkin Post Office, which opened in 1841. The Dalton Post Office continued to serve the community until July 1951, when it closed and consolidated with Pinnacle. (Courtesy of Susan Petree.)

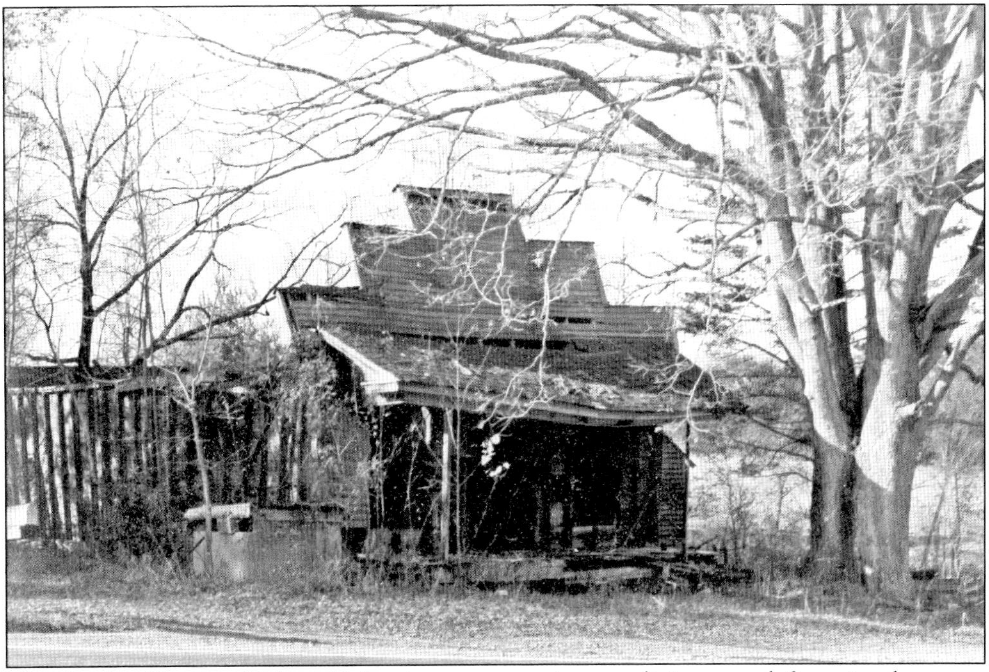

The Boyles Store, which sold hardware, groceries, medicines, and farm implements, opened in Dalton around 1912. John Sidney Boyles ran the store and the Dalton Post Office from May 1913 until his death in 1951. His wife, Dora, ran the post office for a few months before it closed in July 1951. (Courtesy of Jim Moser.)

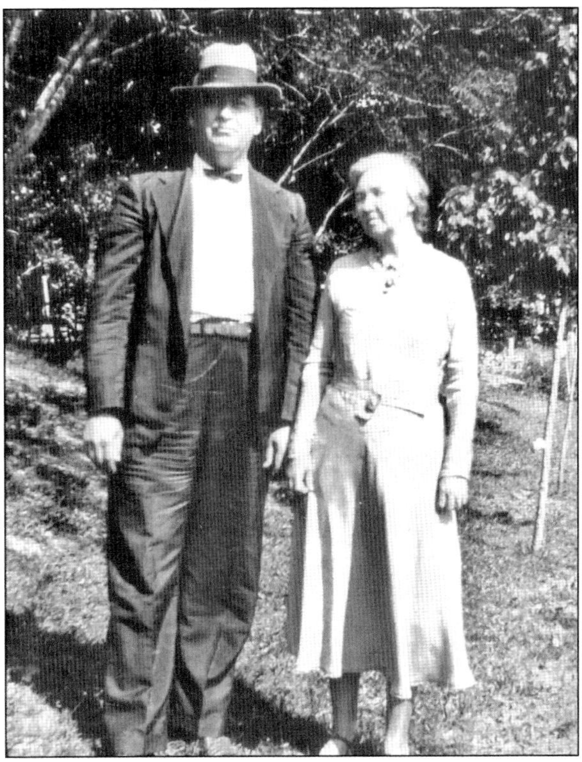

Dalton postmaster and merchant John Boyles is seen here with his wife, Dora, *c.* 1940 in Dalton. (Courtesy of Jim Boyles.)

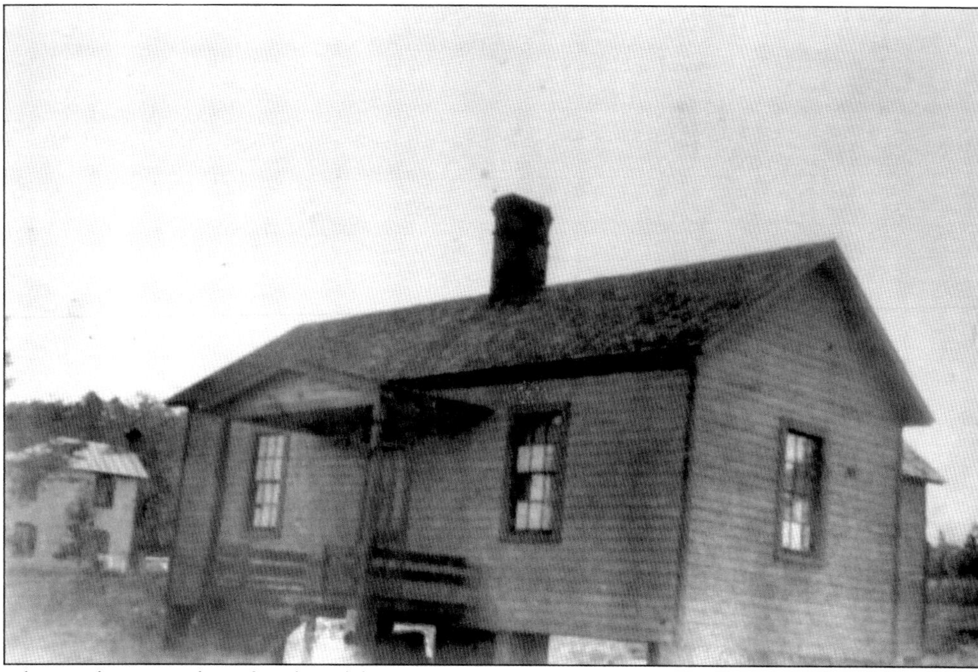

These photographs of railroad homes were taken near the railroad stop at Dalton, c. 1925. The photographs came from the engineer's notebooks and were recorded in the Interstate Commerce Commission (ICC) Valuation project of 1916–1936. (Courtesy of U.S. National Archives.)

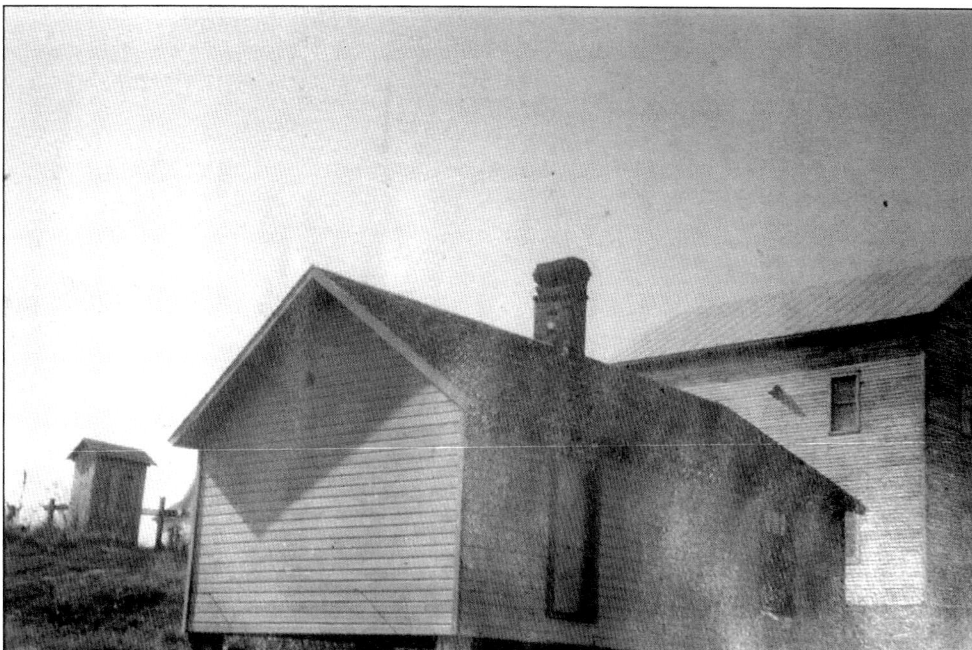

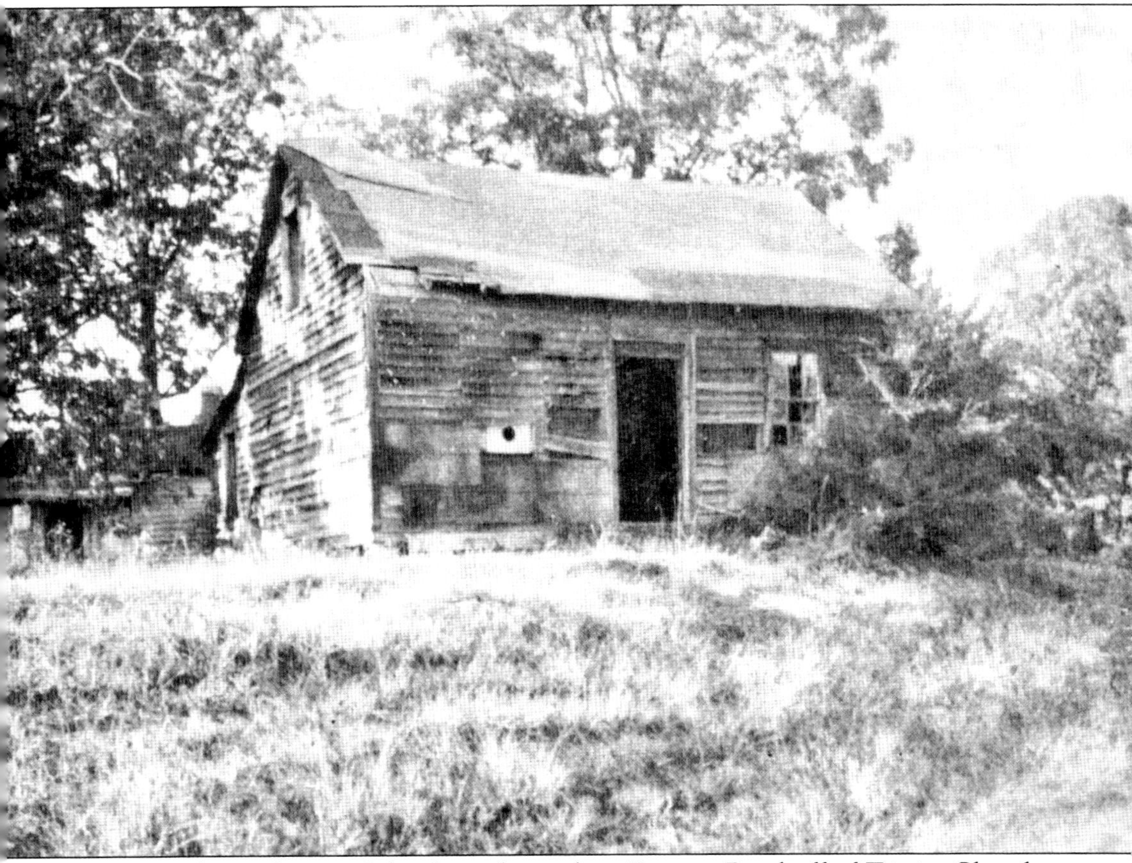

The original Dry Springs School was located on Rierson Road off of Trinity Church Road. The school was built in 1880 and served the Dry Springs community until it consolidated with King School in 1928. (Courtesy of Bobbie "Crow" McGee.)

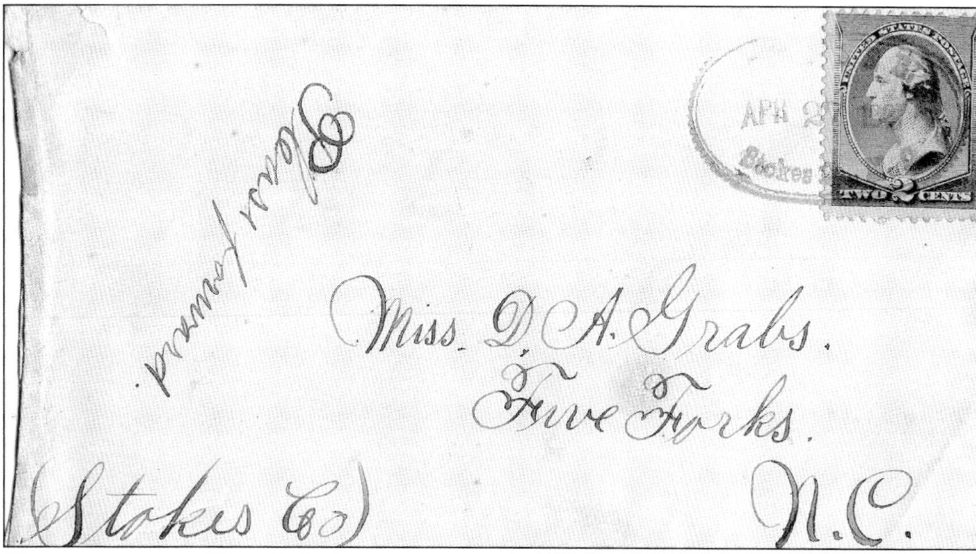

The community of Five Forks began as a stagecoach stop located today at the intersection of Main Street, Jefferson Church Road, and Ingram Road. When the stagecoach met the intersection, it split, creating a five-road juncture. In 1871, the Five Forks Post Office opened, as seen in the above letter addressed to Miss D. A. Grabs. Five Forks had several stores, a tavern, a blacksmith shop, and a private school. The village faded when business started moving toward the railroad at King's Cabin. The post office consolidated with King in 1895. Postmaster G. G. Boles loaded everything from the Five Forks Post Office into a wheelbarrow and pushed it to King. (Courtesy of Susan Petree.)

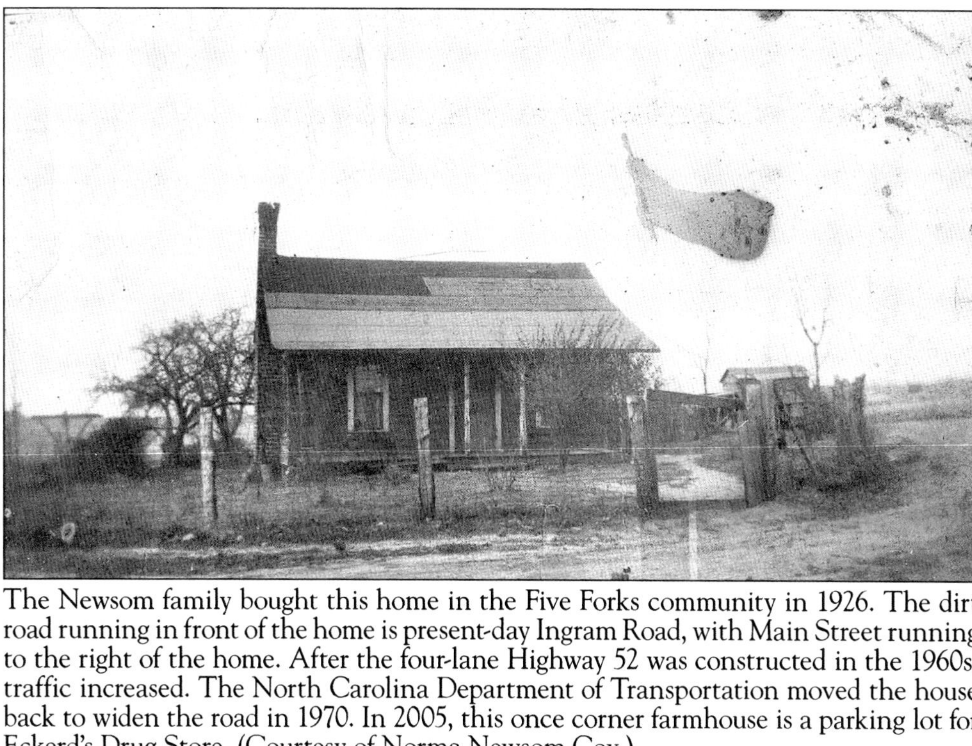

The Newsom family bought this home in the Five Forks community in 1926. The dirt road running in front of the home is present-day Ingram Road, with Main Street running to the right of the home. After the four-lane Highway 52 was constructed in the 1960s, traffic increased. The North Carolina Department of Transportation moved the house back to widen the road in 1970. In 2005, this once corner farmhouse is a parking lot for Eckerd's Drug Store. (Courtesy of Norma Newsom Cox.)

Gilmer Newsom Store, *c.* 1930, was located in Five Forks on the corner of present-day Ingram Road and Main Street in King. In this photograph, Ingram Road is between the cars and the shrubs under the snow, while Main Street is in the foreground. (Courtesy of Norma Newsom Cox.)

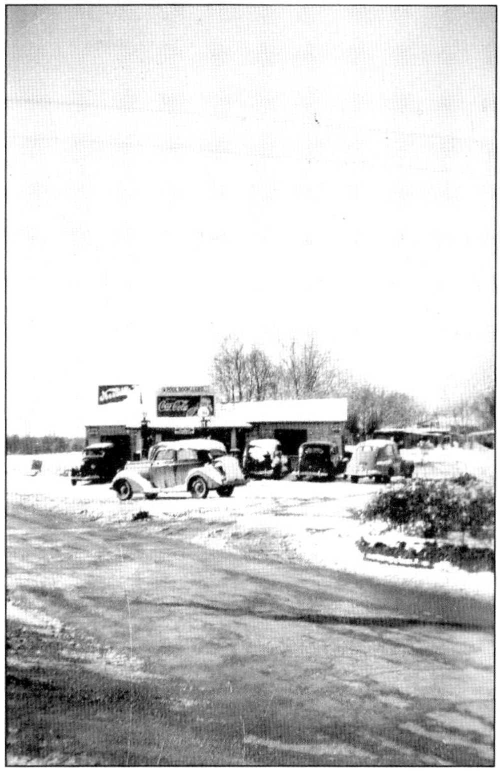

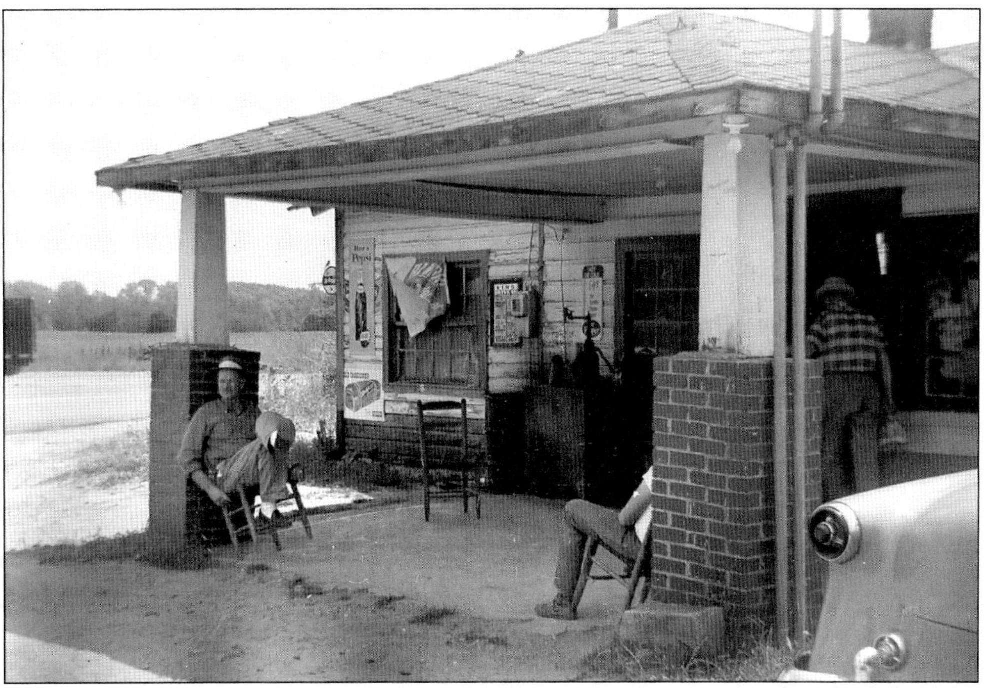

The Gilmer Newsom Store is seen here *c.* 1959. Notice the open land to the left of the store across present-day Main Street, which is today home to Colony Centre, a shopping center built in 1977. (Courtesy of Norma Newsom Cox.)

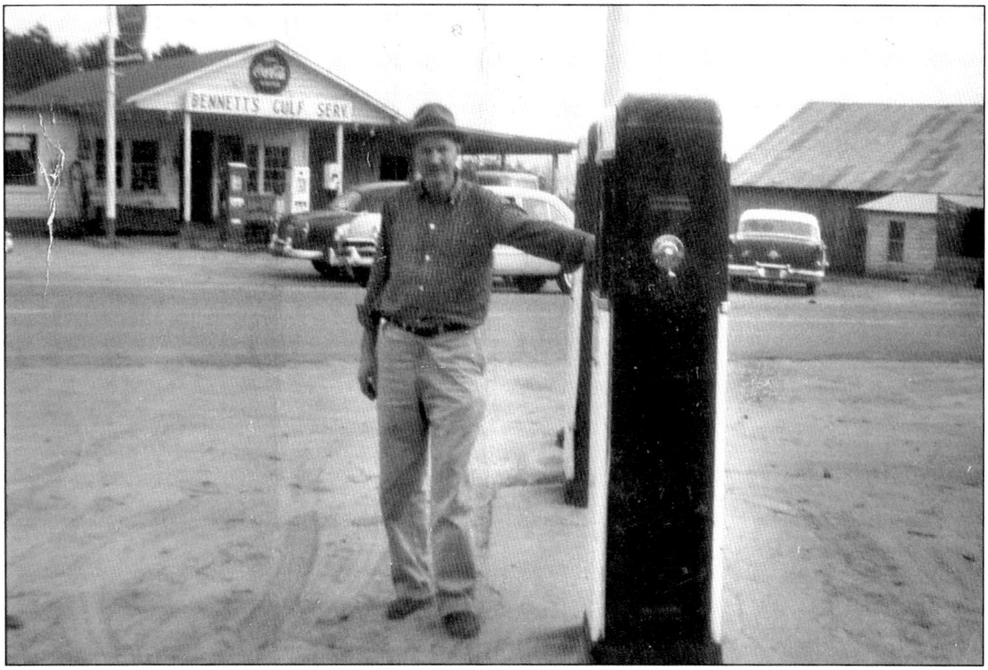

Bennetts Gulf Service Station is seen behind Gilmer Newsom and his store's gas pumps in 1958. Bennetts Gulf Service Station was located near where First Union Bank is today, at the corner of Main Street and Jefferson Church Road. (Courtesy of Norma Newsom Cox.)

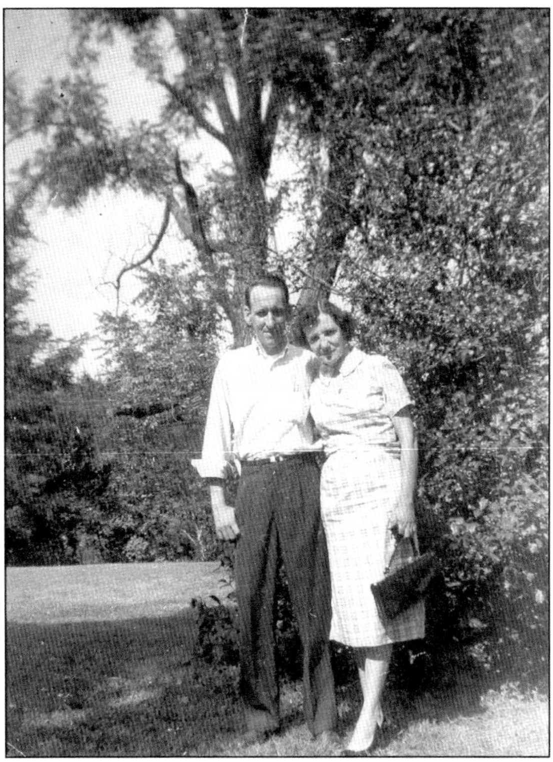

Bill and Ann Speas Boles stand at Lone Oak Farm in Five Forks. Today part of the farm is underneath Highway 52 north of the King-Tobaccoville interchange. (Courtesy of Bill Boles.)

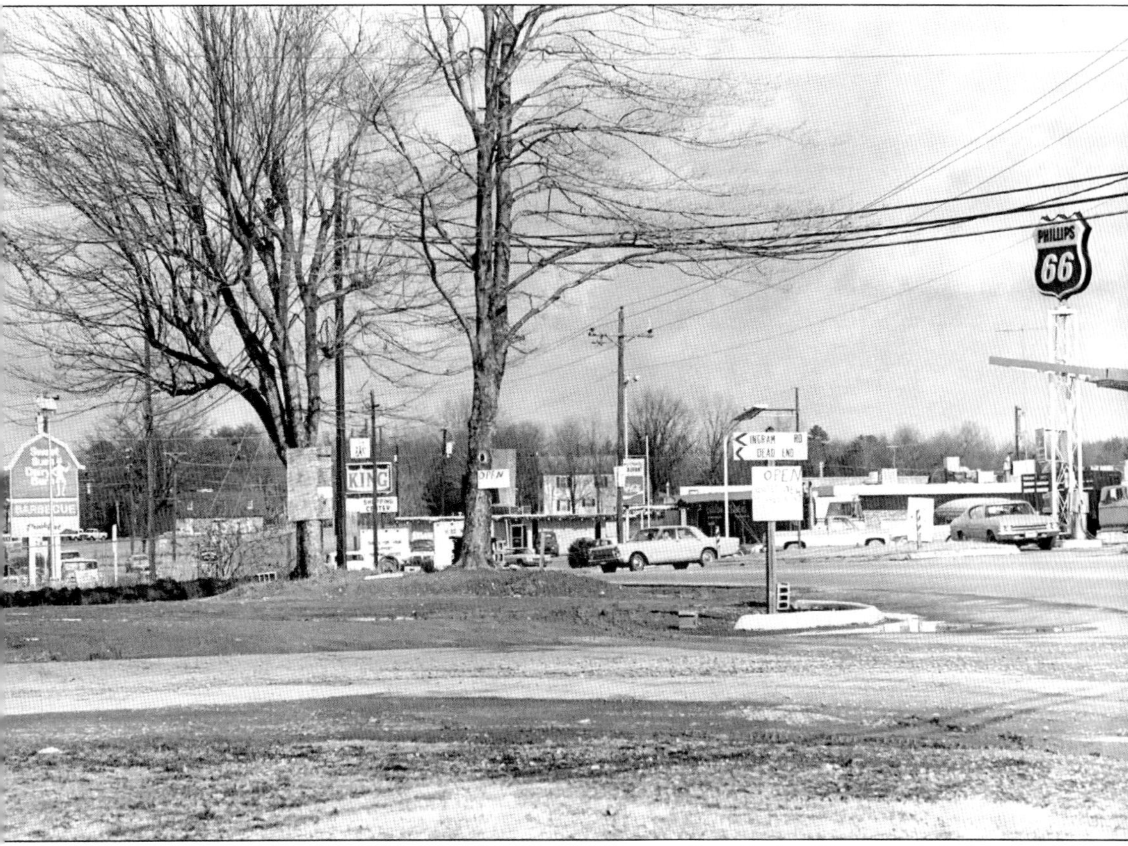

After the four-lane Highway 52 opened in the 1960s near Five Forks, King started moving toward the highway, as seen in this 1976 photograph. The photograph was taken from the corner of present-day South Main Street and Ingram Road looking north. This intersection was once the heart of the stagecoach community of Five Forks. By 1969, the King Shopping Center, seen across the street in the distance, started taking shape on the former farm of Banks Turner. At left of this photograph in the distance, Five Forks Village, a shopping center named for the once prosperous stagecoach community, would later open in 1986. (Courtesy of © 1976 *Winston-Salem Journal*/Hobart Jones.)

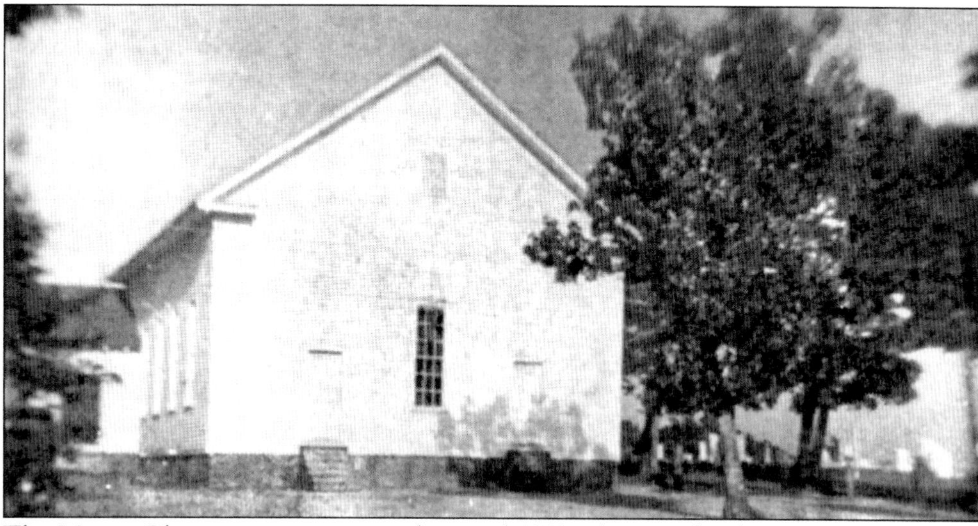

The Mount Olive community started around 1839, when a school opened, with church services possibly being held in the building that became known as the Mount Olive Meeting House. The meetinghouse was located on present-day YMCA Camp Road and is marked today by its cemetery. The church was officially organized in 1851 and moved to its present location on Highway 66 in 1889. The Ale Post Office opened in 1898 to serve Mount Olive, and it was located on Chestnut Grove Road, about a quarter-mile from the present site of Mount Olive Baptist Church. Levi Ferguson served as the first and only postmaster until it closed in 1903 to consolidate with King. The Mount Olive School opened near the church in 1910 and closed after it consolidated with King in 1928. In 1937, six Sunday school rooms were added to Mount Olive Church, as seen in the above photograph. In 1972, two years after the photograph below was captured, the congregation voted to demolish the old church and build a new brick church, which was completed in 1974. Mount Olive Baptist Church helped start Baptist churches in Brown Mountain, King, Quaker Gap, and Mountain View. (Courtesy of Mount Olive Baptist Church.)

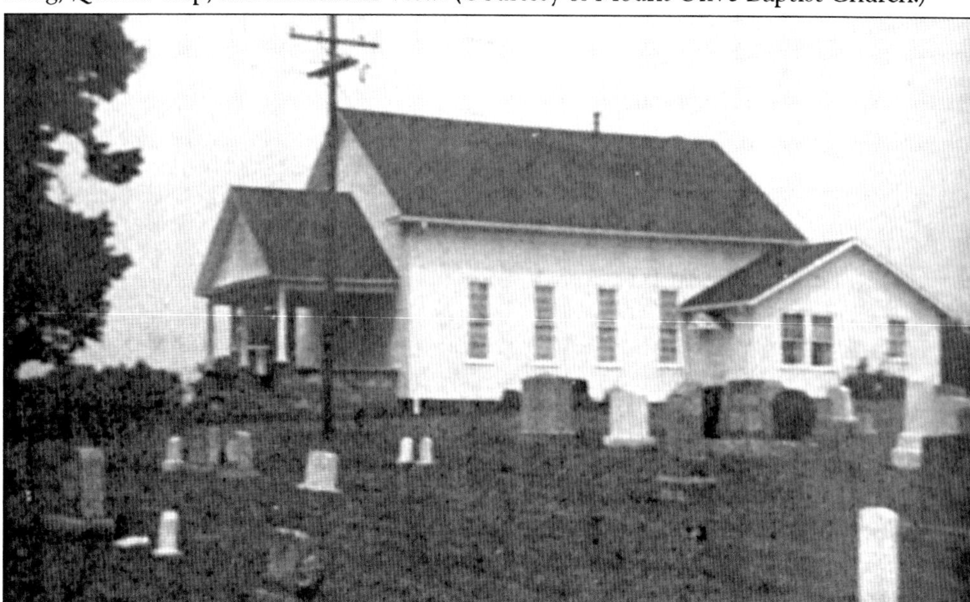

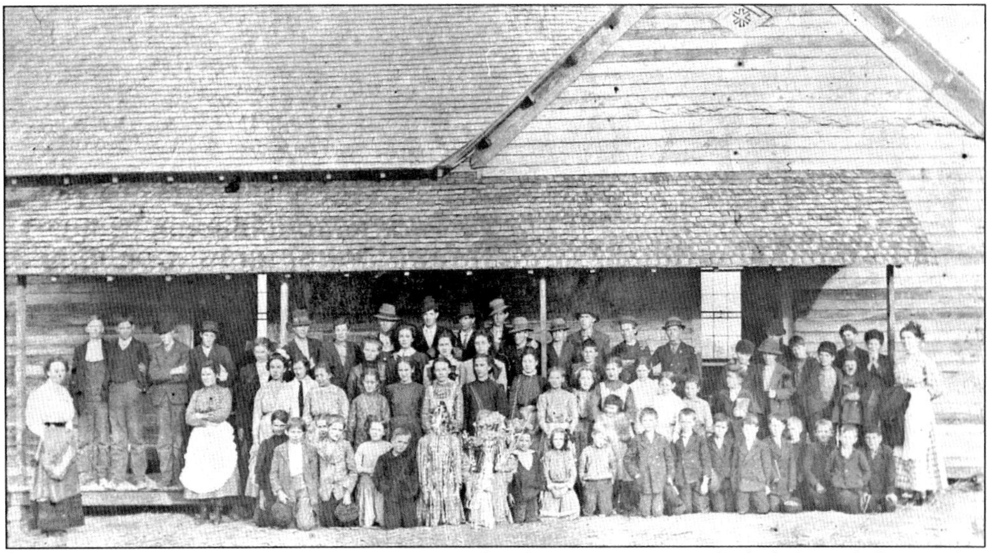

The Mount Olive School during its first school year in 1910 included, from left to right, (first row) Mary Bennett, unidentified, Daisy Boyles, Walter Bennett, Valley Boyles, Troy Jones, Ressie Fowler, Mamie Jones, William Fowler, Anna Campbell, and Herman Tuttle; (second row) unidentified, Thurman Campbell, Ed Jones, unidentified, Ott Boyles, Charlie Campbell, unidentified, Fount Moser, Hubert Tuttle, and Bob Page; (third row) teacher Dora Wall, Elsie Tuttle, Parrie Tuttle, Grace Fowler, Effie Johnson, Lillian Moser, Beulah Jones, Alice Moser, Bessie Falkenberry, Ada Campbell, Clarice Tuttle, nine unidentified boys, and teacher Clemmie Smith; (fourth row) Laura Bennett, Grace Gordon, unidentified, Mamie Falkenberry, Sada Tuttle, and Sybil Bennett; (fifth row) Herbert Jones, Floyd Long, Jessie Falkenberry, Birthel Bennett, unidentified, Paul Johnson, unidentified, Reid Jones, two unidentified students, Taylor Tuttle, Ross Fowler, Loy Campbell, Walter Moser, and Rob Gordon. (Courtesy of Robert Carroll.)

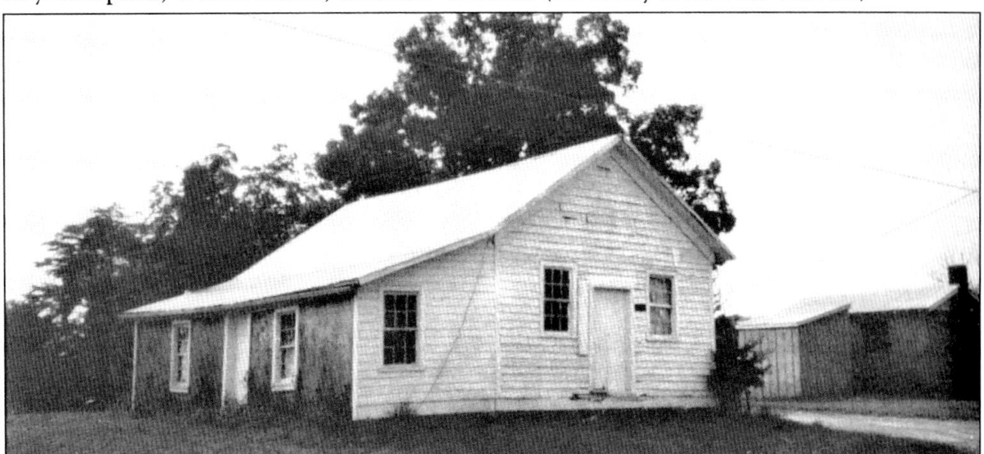

Boyles Store was built in 1871 by Albert Boyles and still stands today in Mount Olive at the intersection of Highway 66 and Denny Road. In 1886, the voting precinct moved from Centerville, near present-day Quaker Gap Baptist Church, to Boyles Store. Boyles served the community until his death in 1904; his wife, Martha Ann, continued to run the store until 1908. The Denny family bought the store, moved it a few yards, and turned it to face the road. The store closed in the 1930s. (Courtesy of Robert Carroll.)

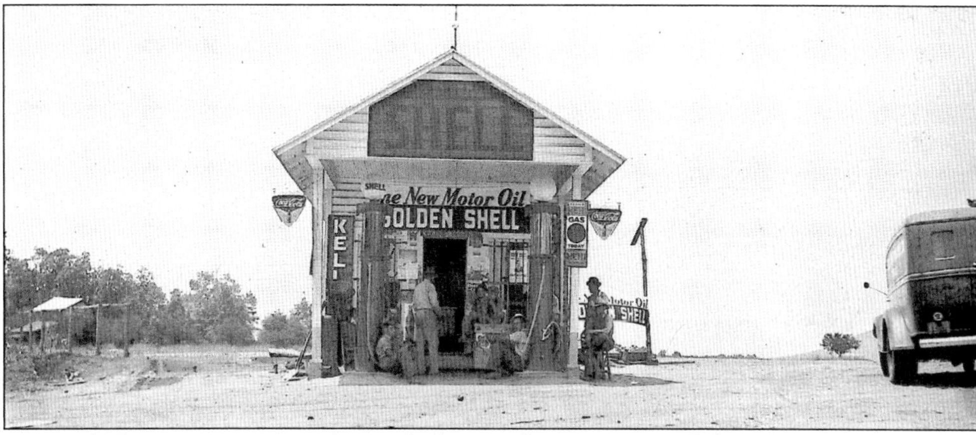

As roads became paved and people began driving automobiles, gas stations started opening. The D. D. Hall Shell Service Station stood at the corner of YMCA Camp Road and Chestnut Grove Road in the Mount Olive community. A community ball field was located behind the service station. (Courtesy of Eddie Marshall.)

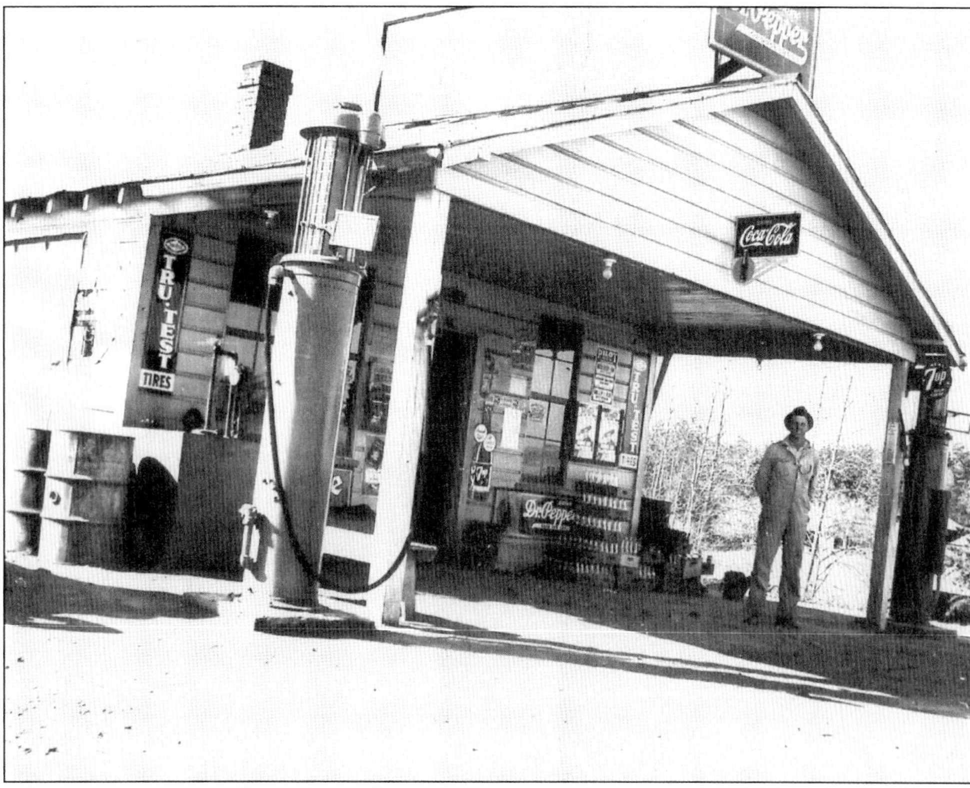

Alvin Patterson stands in front of Hatton Patterson Store c. 1941. The store was located at the corner of YMCA Camp Road and Highway 66. In 1944, Patterson moved the store south on Highway 66 next to his home at the present-day location of John Brown's Country Store. Patterson first opened his business as a garage repair shop before offering gas and groceries. (Courtesy of Jack and Annie Lou Patterson.)

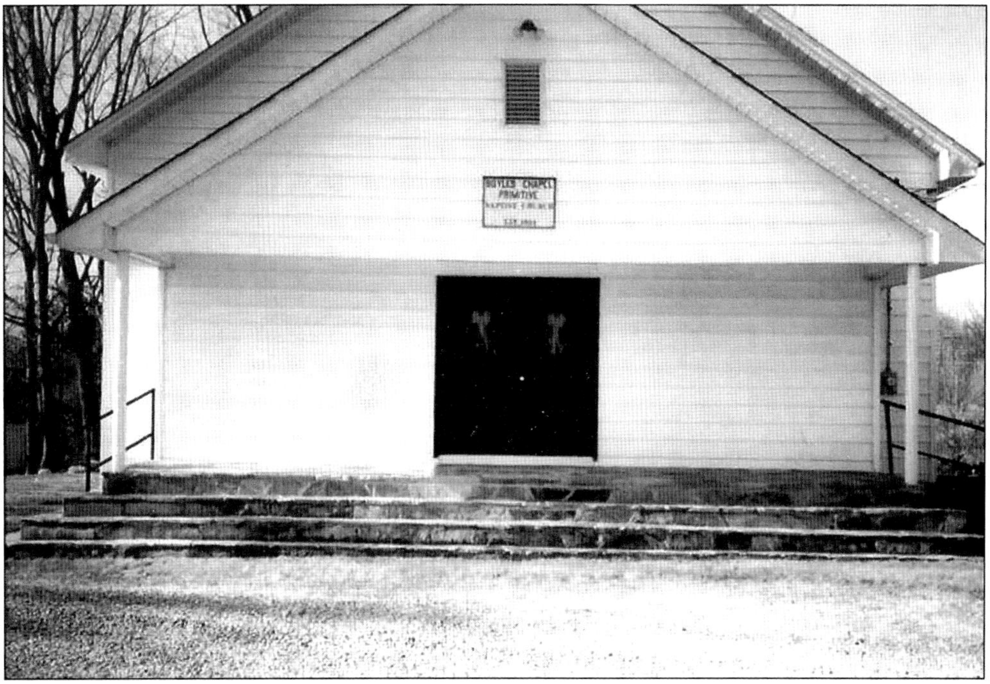

Boyles Chapel Primitive Baptist Church was established in 1924. The church, located at the corner of Highway 66 and Flynt Road, is named after John and Saluda (Selena) Boyles, who donated the land. (Courtesy of Trish Shouse.)

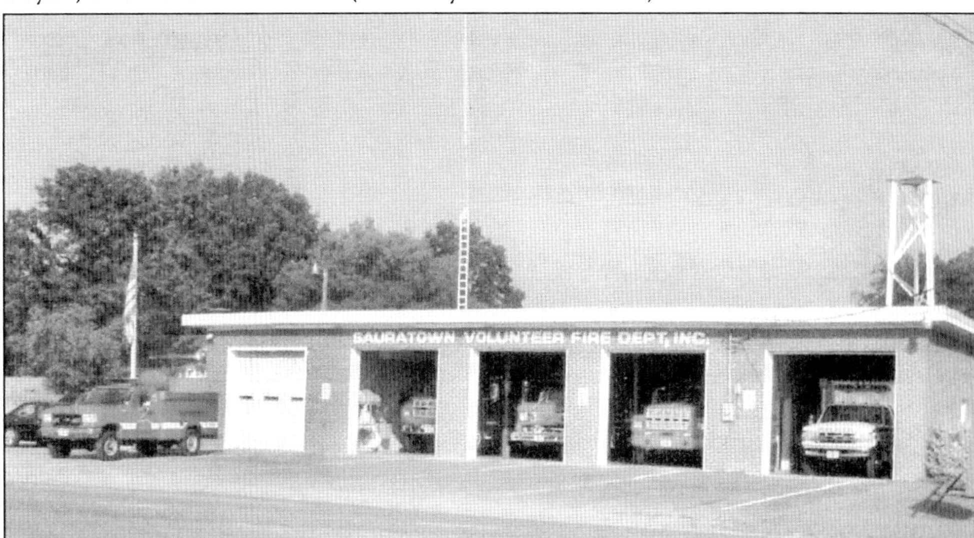

After seeing a need for fire protection in the Mount Olive–Capella community, residents formed the Sauratown Volunteer Fire Department in 1963. With land donated by Odell Ferguson and timber cut from the farm of Melvin Mabe, the fire department seen above was built on Highway 66 and served residents north of King to Danbury and Double Creek Fire District 14 and west to Walnut Cove. Forty years later, the department constructed a new, state-of-the-art fire department at the corner of Flynt Road and Highway 66. (Courtesy of Sauratown Volunteer Fire Department.)

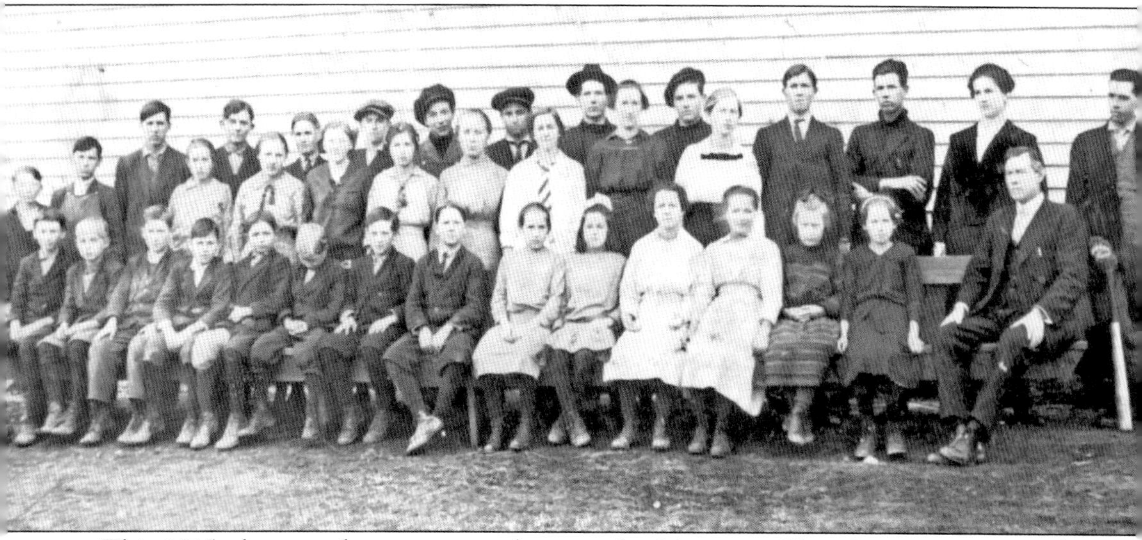

This 1915 photograph captures students at the Mountain View Institute in Mizpah. Mizpah, named for a biblical town, began in 1884, when the Mizpah Post Office opened in the home of postmaster John Slate. The Slate School, a public school on Slate Road, opened in 1880 with Samuel Rufus Slate as a teacher. The Slate School closed in 1894. In 1892, Mizpah residents formed the Mountain View Institute Company. The institute was a private school charging tuition until it consolidated with the Stokes County School System in 1920. After the institute opened, Mountain View started being used as the community name, including Mountain View Methodist Episcopal Church and later Mountain View Baptist Church. The post office kept the name Mizpah until it consolidated with the King Post Office in 1932. The community is today referred to as Mountain View, and in the early 1990s, a group of its residents met to explore incorporation. The idea failed because of lack of interest. (Courtesy of Lewis Carroll.)

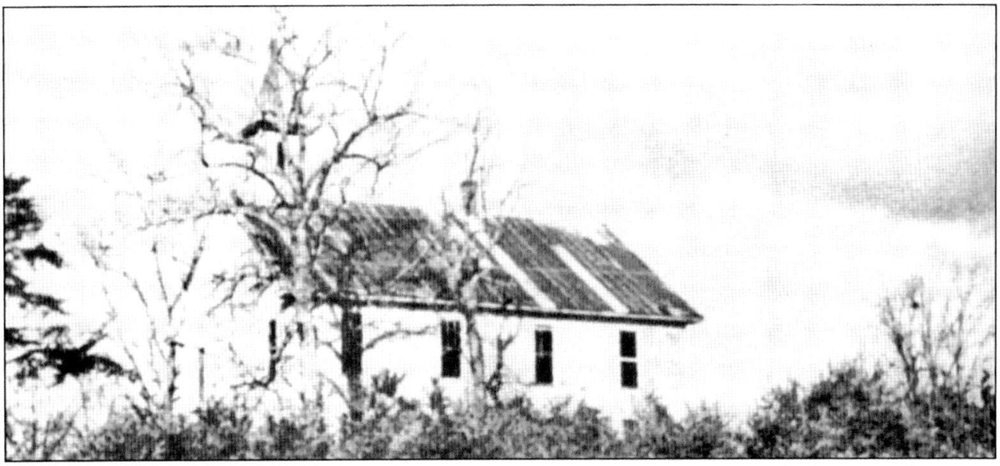

The second floor of the Mountain View Institute in Mizpah is all that can be seen in the undated photograph above. The Mountain View Baptist Church, seen below c. 1956, began in 1911. In 1900, L. S. Kiser sold a plot of land to the Mountain View Methodist Episcopal congregation to build a church. In 1910, the Methodist church dissolved and sold its property to the newly formed Mountain View Baptist Church. (Courtesy of Mountain View Baptist Church.)

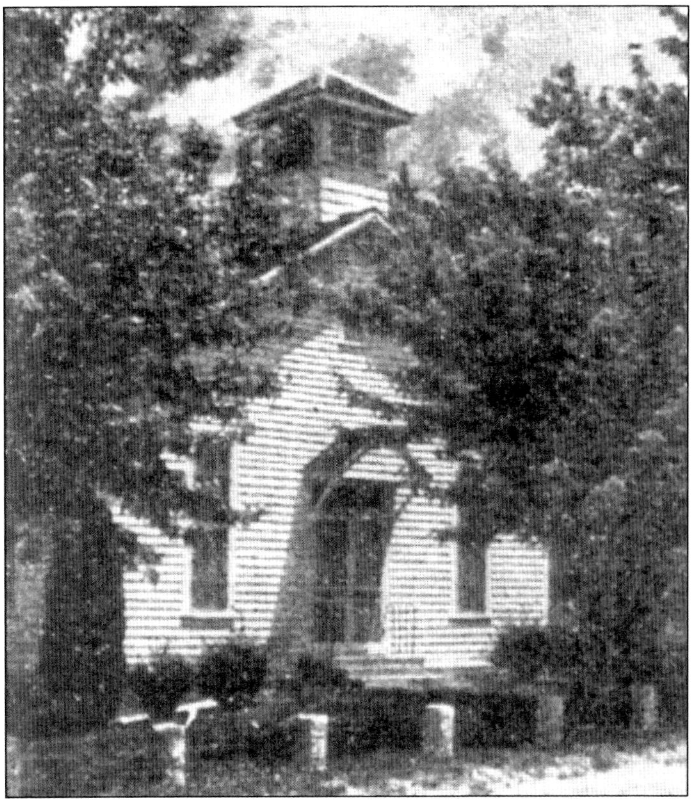

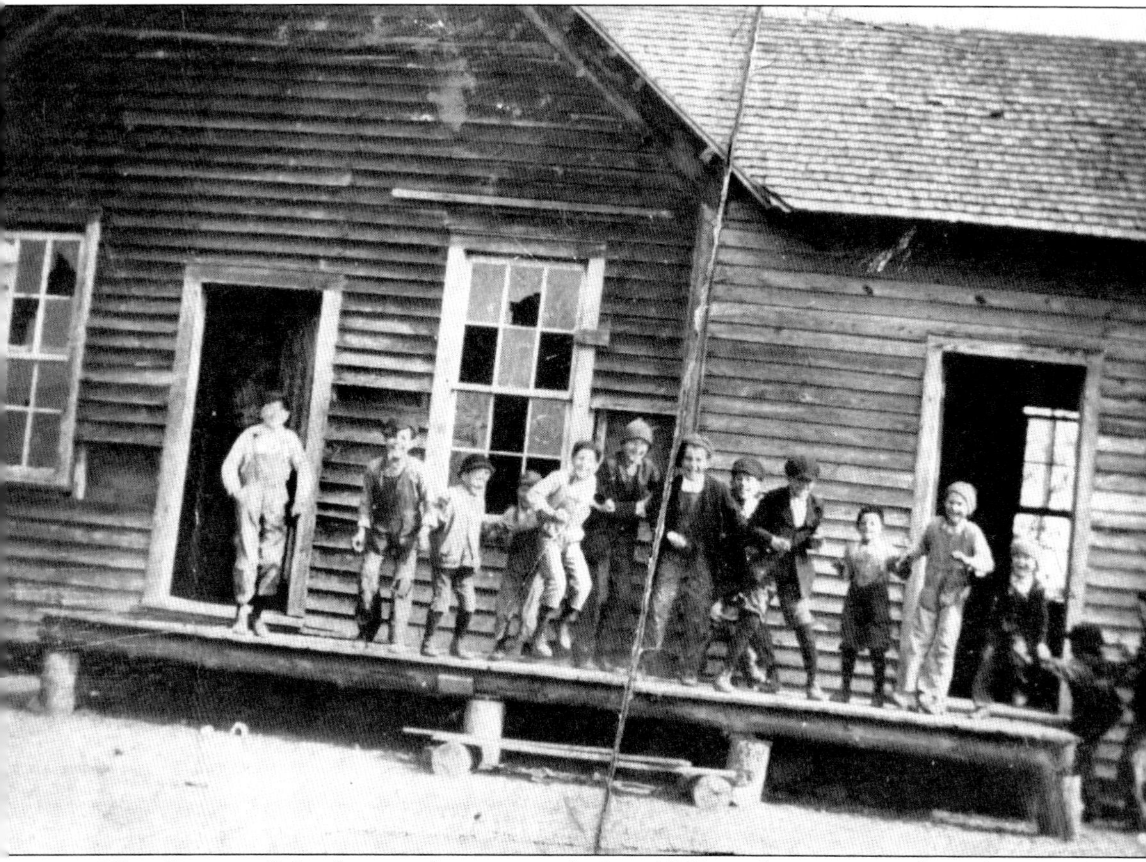

The Creason School opened sometime before 1877 in the vicinity of Quaker Road (Highway 66) and Slate Road. The school, seen above *c.* 1898, was named for James Creason, one of the school's committeemen. The community became known as Helsabeck in 1886, when the Helsabeck Post Office opened near the school with John Helsabeck as postmaster. The post office closed the following year but reopened in 1901 under the name Helsa. In the early 1890s, James Oscar Helsabeck and Robert Helsabeck began holding church services in the Creason School. The services were the foundation of Poplar Springs Church of Christ. The congregation later met under a brush arbor near its present location on Highway 66. The church takes its name from the former Poplar Springs campsite, a popular place at one time for people to stop and rest while traveling the Quaker Road. The first church building started being used in 1906. In 1904, the Helsa Post Office consolidated with the Rural Hall Post Office, which served the Poplar Springs community for several decades before the mail was delivered from King. (Courtesy of Adeline Kiser.)

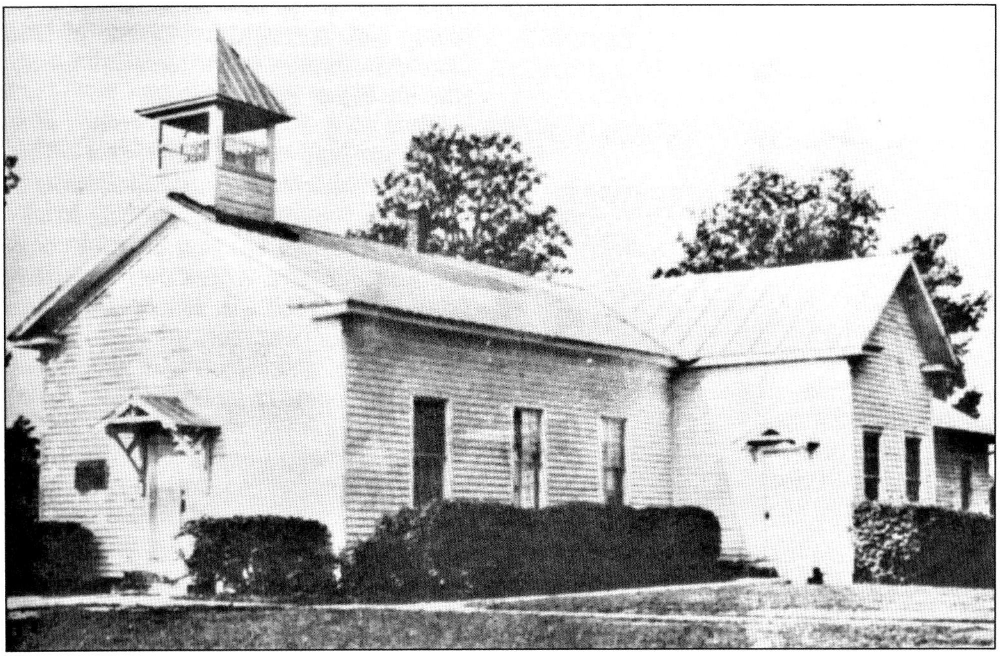

The first Poplar Springs Church of Christ building was a one-room structure. In 1917, two small Sunday school classrooms were added behind the pulpit. In 1921, a cross-wing was added to double the seating capacity. In 1934, a belfry was added, as seen above. Three years later, six Sunday school classrooms, a storage room, basement, kitchen, and social hall were added. In the early 1950s, a fund began to build a new brick structure south of the original church. In 1958, the congregation moved into the new brick building, seen below, and the old church was demolished. The church has undergone several expansions, including a family life center in 1986 and a new sanctuary in 2001. (Courtesy of Kathleen Mendenhall.)

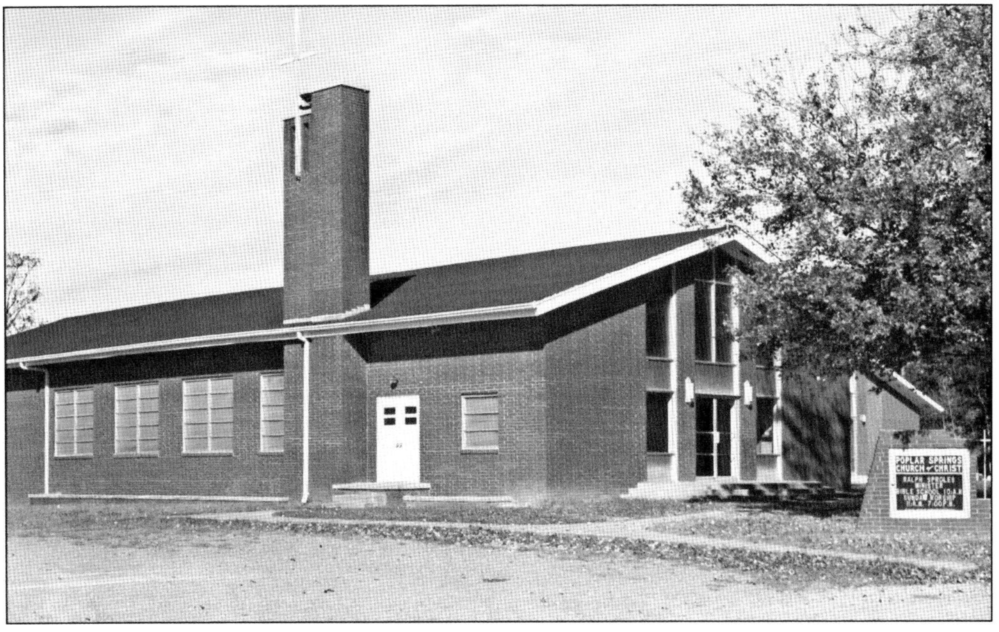

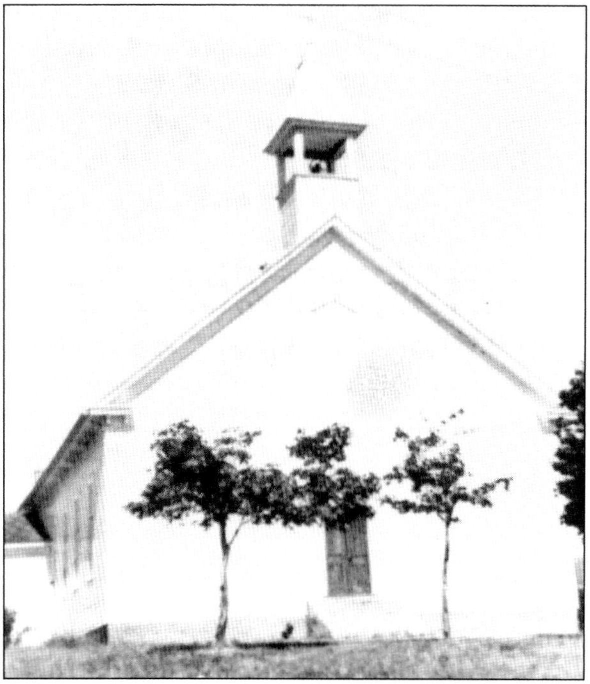

The Quaker Gap community began in 1876 when a post office opened in the home of postmaster John Caudle on present-day YMCA Camp Road. Caudle named the post office Quaker Gap because he could see Quaker Road (today Highway 66) cut through the gap of the Sauratown Mountains from his home. The post office moved closer to the area where the Quaker Gap Baptist Church, at left, would form in 1909. In 1895, the post office shortened its name to Quaker and moved to Friendship Road, where it was located until it consolidated with the Germanton Post Office in 1903. (Courtesy of Quaker Gap Baptist Church.)

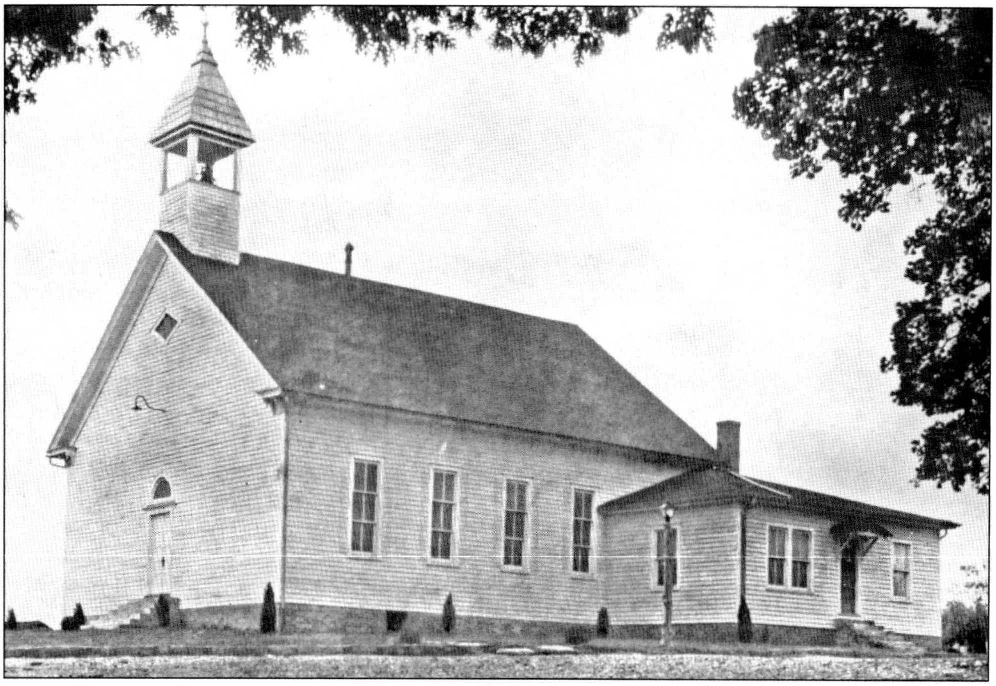

In 1909, a presbytery met at Union Hill Methodist Church to form Quaker Gap Missionary Baptist Church. The congregation continued to meet in the Union Hill Methodist Church until 1910, when they built their own church on Flat Shoals Road. The church added seven new Sunday school rooms and expanded the sanctuary in 1930. In 1960, 10 new classrooms were added, along with extensive remodeling. A new fellowship education building was added in 1988. (Courtesy of Adeline Kiser.)

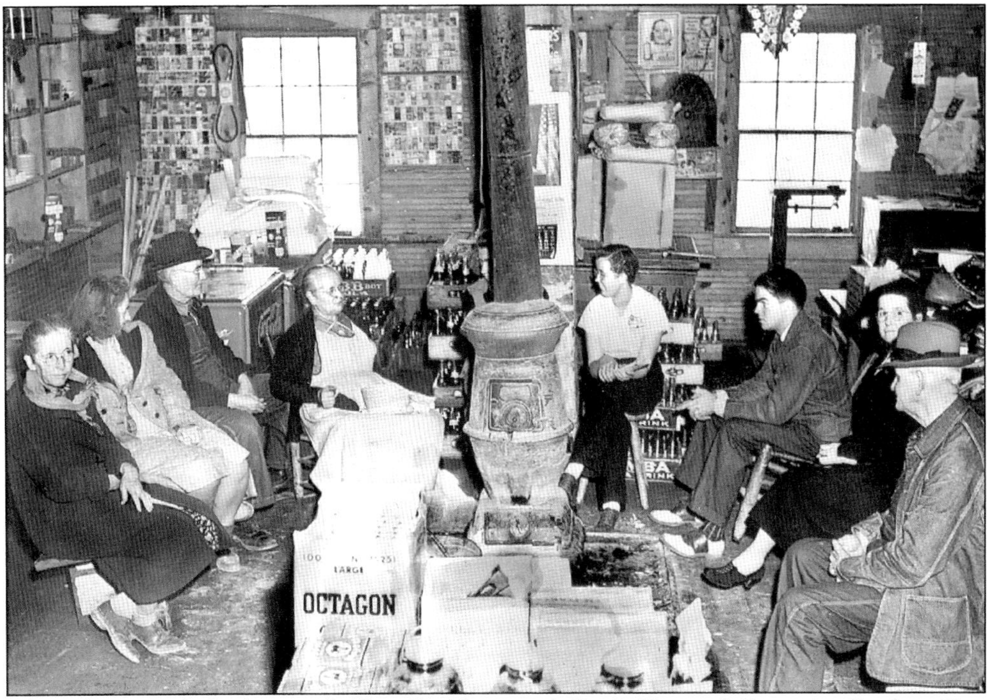

This photograph looks inside Roy Redding and Son's General Store in Quaker Gap around 1949. The store was a popular gathering place at night because it was one of the few places with electricity. Notice the collection of matchbook covers on the back wall. From left to right are Mrs. Willie Hartgrove, Mabel Hartgrove, Henry Hartgrove, Ada Hartgrove, Rheumelle Hartgrove Hall (behind the stove), Louise Southern Gibson, Wallace Carroll, Nina Carroll, and Preston Tuttle. (Courtesy of Lewis Carroll.)

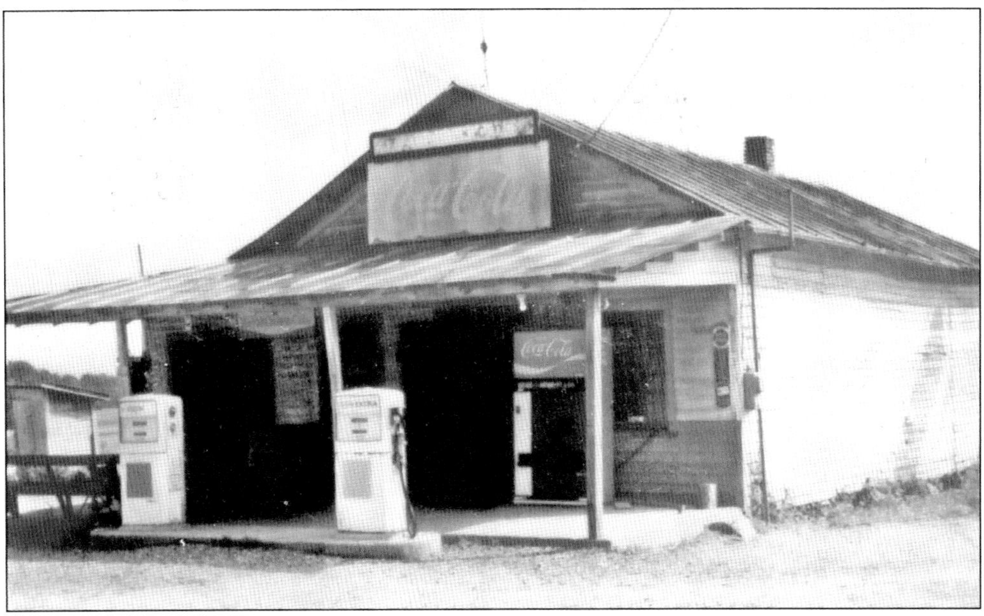

Roy Redding and Son's General Store, in Quaker Gap, was operated by Harvey "Bud" Tedder when this photograph was taken around 1960. (Courtesy of Lewis Carroll.)

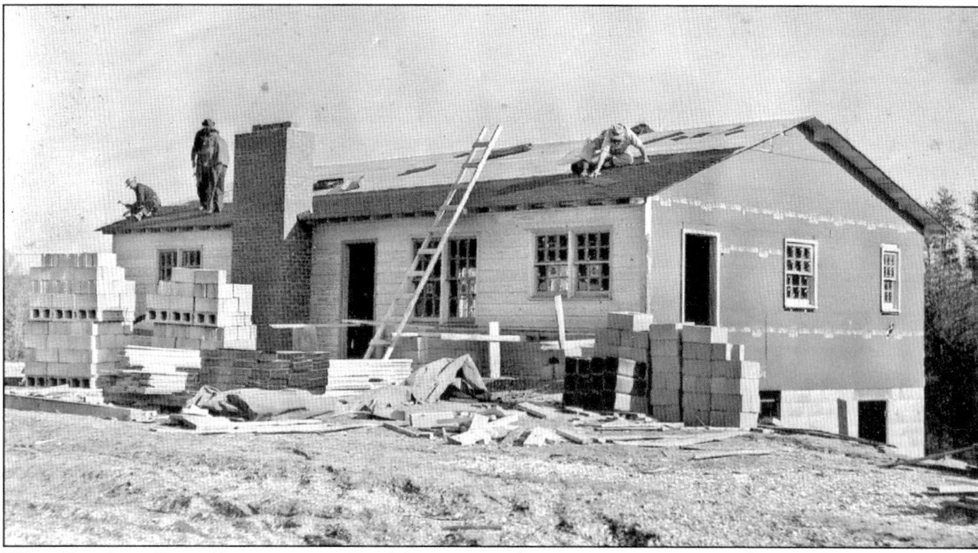

The Quaker Gap Community Building is under construction in this 1956 photograph. Buck and Nina Tedder donated the land; labor and supplies were paid for with donations and fund-raisers. The Quaker Gap Community Building provided space for Boy Scouts, 4-H Clubs, and other groups, including the Quaker Gap Community Development Association. The association became a "Blue Ribbon" community within the Northwest North Carolina Community Development Association for their work providing programs for the youth of Quaker Gap and Haw Pond areas. (Courtesy of Lewis Carroll.)

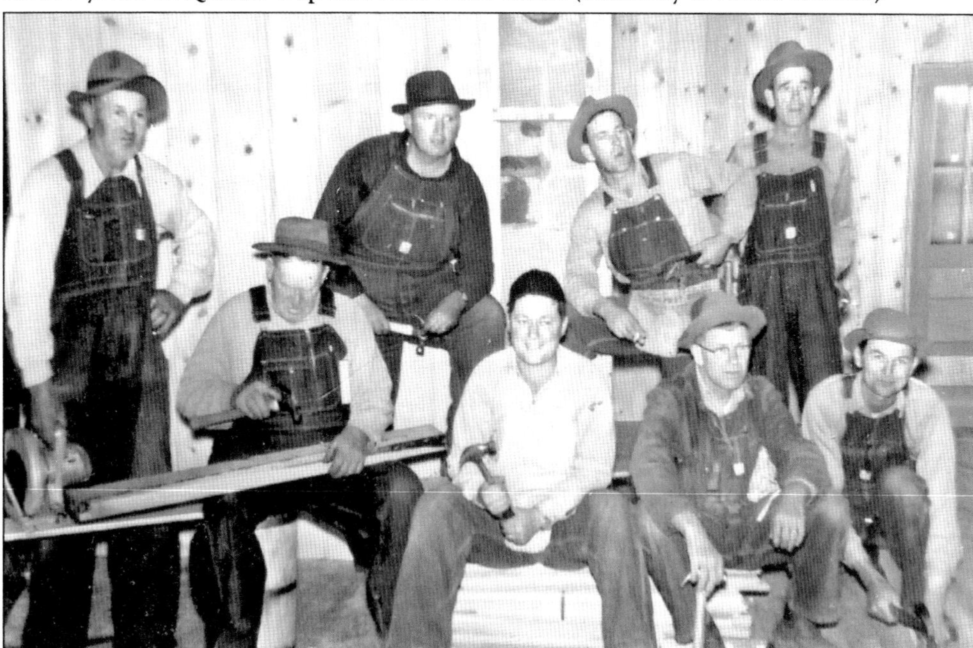

From left to right, Paul Kiser, N. O. "Numie" Tedder, Clyde Johnson, Edwin Sizemore, Otis Tedder, Newell Carroll, Homer Ferguson, and Willie Richardson take a break from working on the inside of the Quaker Gap Community Building in 1956. (Courtesy of Lewis Carroll.)

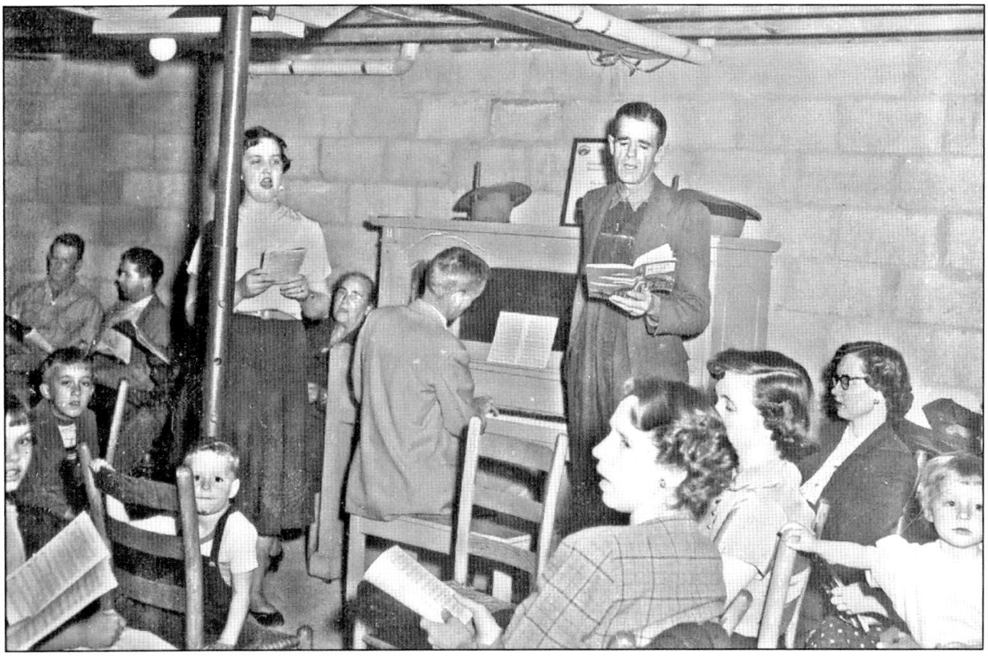

An early Quaker Gap community meeting is held in the basement of the Quaker Gap Baptist Church parsonage in 1955. Leading songs are Lanelle Johnson Watts and Homer Ferguson. Playing the piano is Bradford Nance, who at the time was a highly recognized pianist for several Southern gospel groups. (Courtesy of Lewis Carroll.)

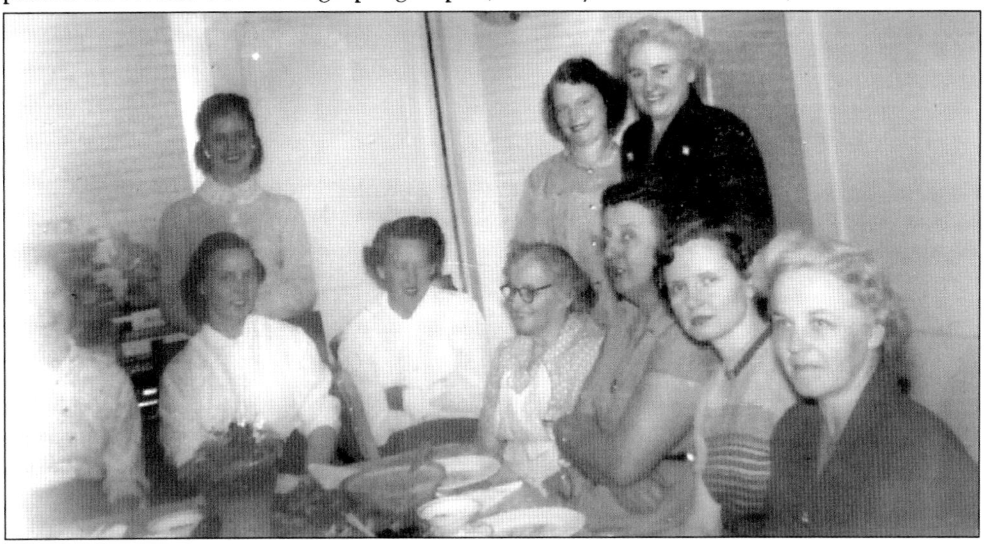

This 1953 photograph captures the meeting of the Home Demonstration Club inside the home of Minnie Redding in Quaker Gap. From left to right are (seated) Ola Sizemore, Beatrice Hall, Minnie Redding, Bessie Sizemore, Cleo Redding, and Margaret Carroll; (standing) Carolyn Oppert, Edith Ashby, and Eva Johnson. The Home Demonstration Club was developed by North Carolina State University to send agents to the rural communities and teach homemakers how to use new appliances brought on by electricity, items like pressure cookers, electric irons, and the electric stove. (Courtesy of Lewis Carroll.)

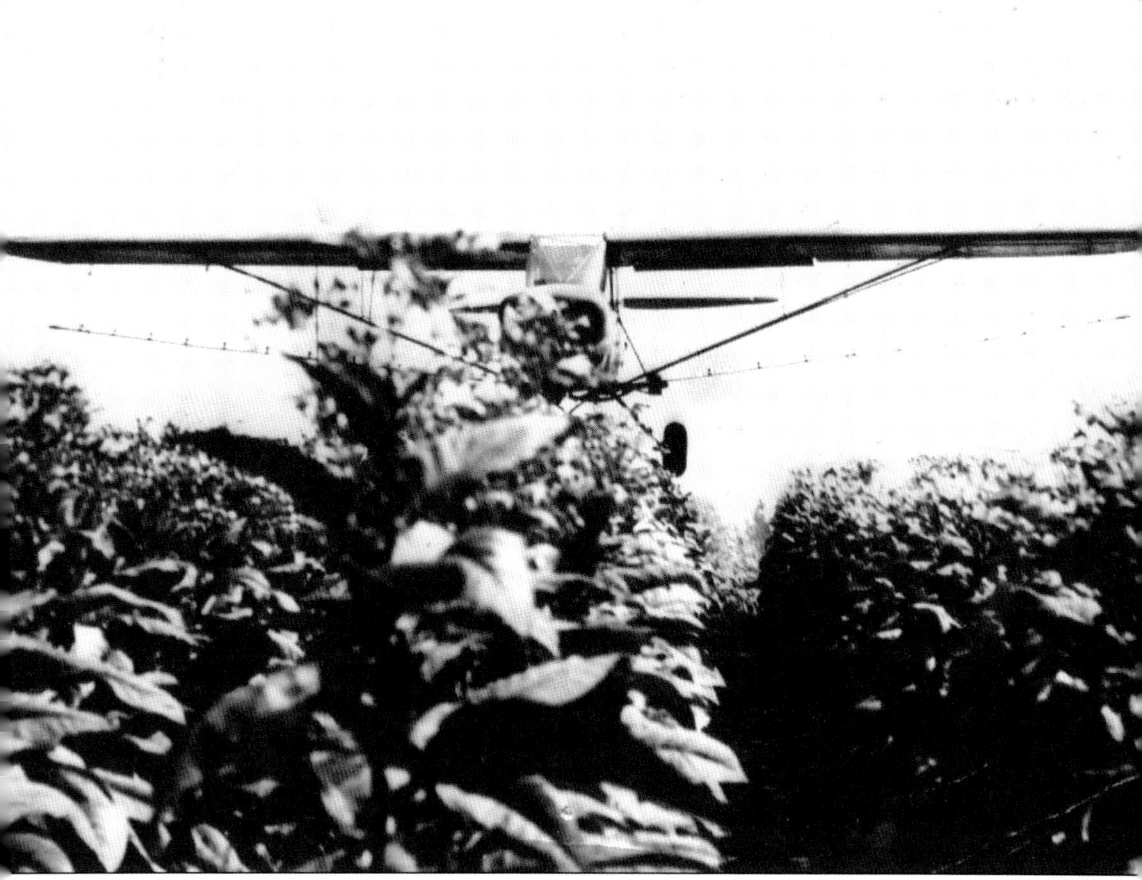

Pilot Ed Gibbs dusts crops on Quaker Gap farms in 1957. Buck Tedder introduced crop dusting to the community after meeting experienced crop dusters Ed Gibbs and Wendell Trogdon from Julian, North Carolina. Tedder arranged the service for his Quaker Gap neighbors and served as the ground crew and field spotter. The pilots used an open field in front of Tedder's parents' home for landing, refueling, refilling chemicals, and take-offs. The work expanded to a new airstrip built by Marshall Denny in the Mount Olive community, and Clyde Kiser built an airstrip in the Flat Shoals area a few years later. (Courtesy of Lewis Carroll.)

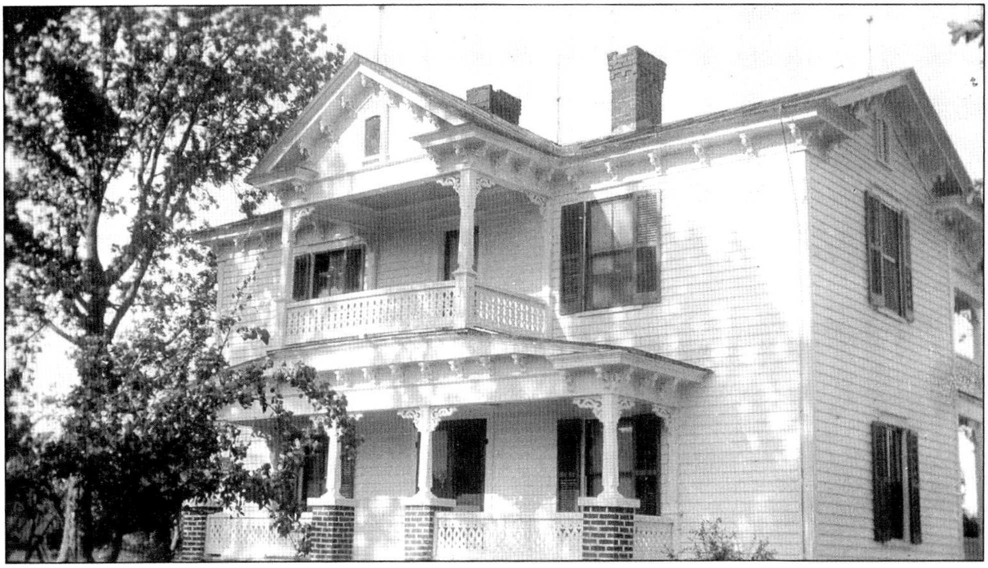

In 1884, the Slate Post Office opened in the home of postmaster William Slate, seen above, located on Gentry Farm Road near Sauratown Mountain. Slate, a Confederate veteran, operated a grain and sawmill in the community. The Oak Grove School opened nearby in 1884 to serve the community. Slate sold the home to Pinkney Bennett, who also took over the post office and became postmaster. In 1902, the post office consolidated with King, and the Gentry family bought the home five years later. The Oak Grove School consolidated with King School in 1928. (Courtesy of Hughes Gentry.)

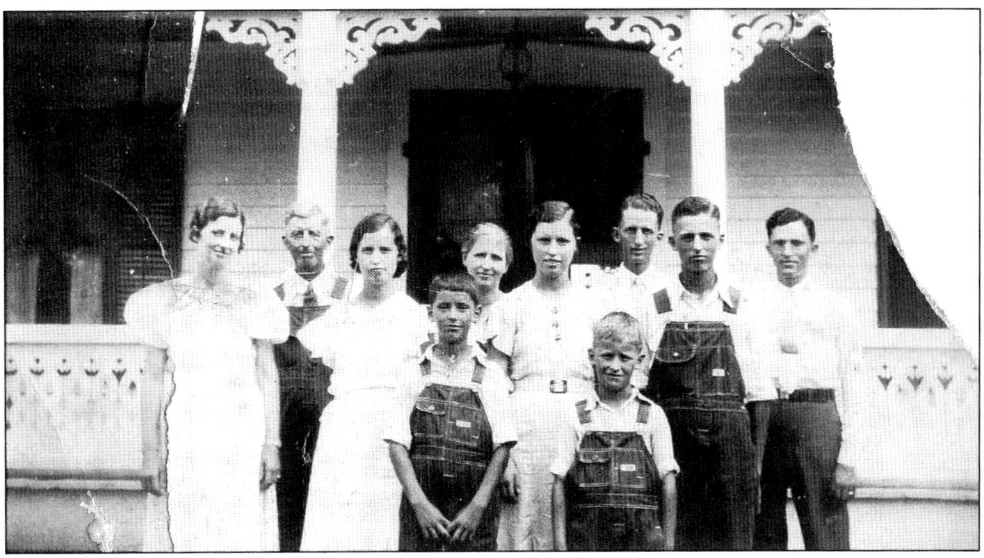

In 1907, Ira Gaston Gentry purchased Pinkney Bennett's home, where he and his wife, Mary, raised eight children. The Oak Grove School was nearby, and for many years, teachers roomed with the Gentry family. Above, the Gentry family in the mid-1930s was, from left to right (first row) Ira Gaston Gentry Jr. and William Gentry Sr.; (second row) Edith Gentry Smith, Ira Gaston Gentry Sr., Addie Gentry Harrelson, Mary Kreeger Gentry, Annie Kate Gentry, Worth Gentry, Norman Gentry, and Holton Gentry. (Courtesy of Sandra Smith.)

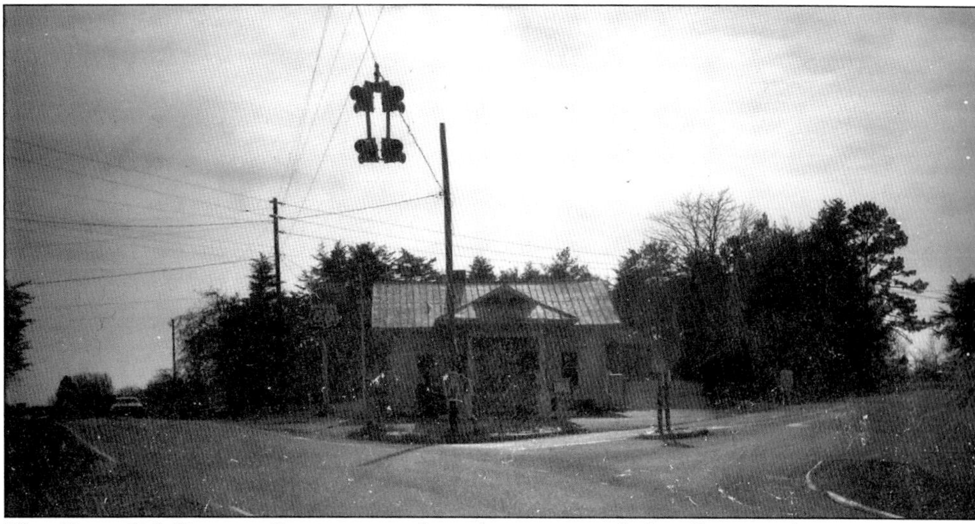

The Pure Oil Service Station stood at the corner of the Crossroads community in this 1970s photograph looking south on Highway 66 and southwest on Mountain View Road toward King. The community was first called Timmon's Crossroads after the family who originally owned the surrounding land. The Moser family owned and farmed the land for most of the 20th century, in which each corner of the crossroads became home to gas stations and convenience stores. The crossroads took on the name of a newly constructed neighborhood nearby called Timberline in the 1970s. In 2005, the descendants of Walter Moser sold 179 acres of the family farm for the development of a shopping center named Walter Ridge and a residential neighborhood called Moser Farms. (Courtesy of Jim Moser.)

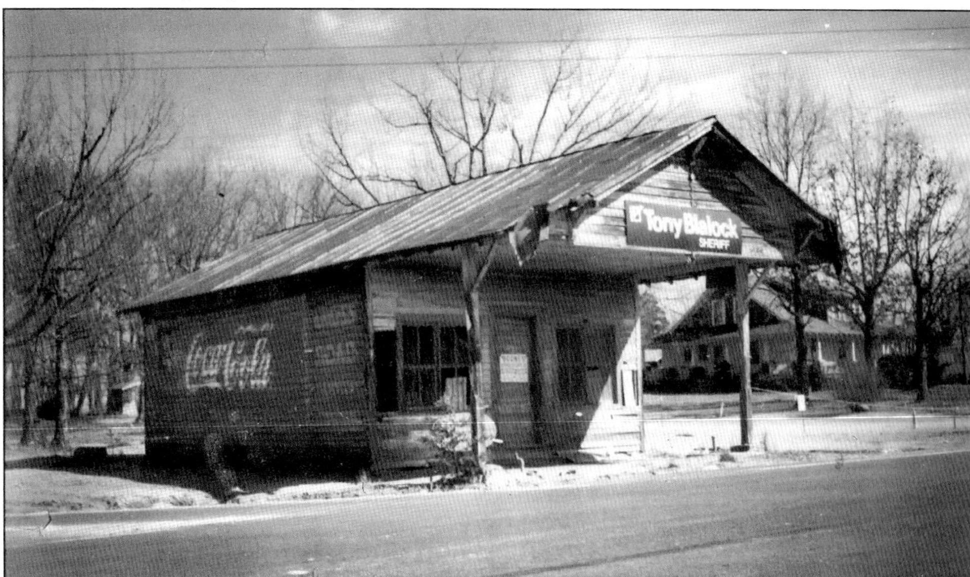

The Crossroads Service Station was built in the 1920s, when Highway 66 was a dirt road. When Highway 66 was paved, the front of the store stuck out onto the road. Because of this obstacle, some trucks hit the service station, which was torn down around 1980. (Courtesy of Jim Moser.)

Three

Summer Blessings

Some of my fondest memories growing up are from Camp Hanes.
Whether it was canoeing, horseback riding or climbing Sauratown Mountain,
it was great having such a fun place so close to home.
—North Carolina senator Richard Burr,
recalling his childhood summers at Camp Hanes

What opened in 1927 as the John W. Hanes Memorial YMCA Camp has become a place of youthful foundations built on faith and strengthened with lessons of caring, honesty, respect, and responsibility.

Since the camp opened thanks to the generosity of the children of textile magnate John W. Hanes who wanted to honor their father, thousands have created memories of table cheers, campfire songs, the Crystal Mine, cabin inspections, hikes to the White Wall, and singing "Follow the Gleam." Many activities at Camp Hanes, including swimming, volleyball, camp crafts, tennis, and story-telling, remain as they were in the 1920s, when boys loaded onto a flatbed truck at the YMCA on Spruce Street for the 25-mile journey to Camp Hanes. When the camp first opened with 10 cabins by the small man-made lake, few comforts of home were found. Swimming in the lake became the closest thing to taking a shower. Progress and amenities made their way to Camp Hanes: in the 1950s, 360 acres were added, along with a new dining hall, and in the 1960s, cabins suitable for winter stays were built, along with bathhouses. More cabins, hot water, air-conditioning, and girls eventually found their way to the camp. In 1976, Camp Hanes welcomed the first of thousands of girls, making it co-ed. Today with 400 acres and state-of-the-art facilities, such as the Baker Center Gymnasium and water park added in 2002, the camp welcomes thousands of campers year-round, 14,000 in 2005.

Some notable Americans have been blessed by summers at Camp Hanes. Basketball star Chris Paul served as a camper, counselor, and volunteer while at Wake Forest University. North Carolina senator Richard Burr was a camper in the 1960s, and while a seminary student, actor Andy Griffith served as the camp chaplain for a few summers in the 1940s.

The following collection of images captures the tranquil retreat of Camp Hanes and the spirit of life it has placed in the faces of its campers.

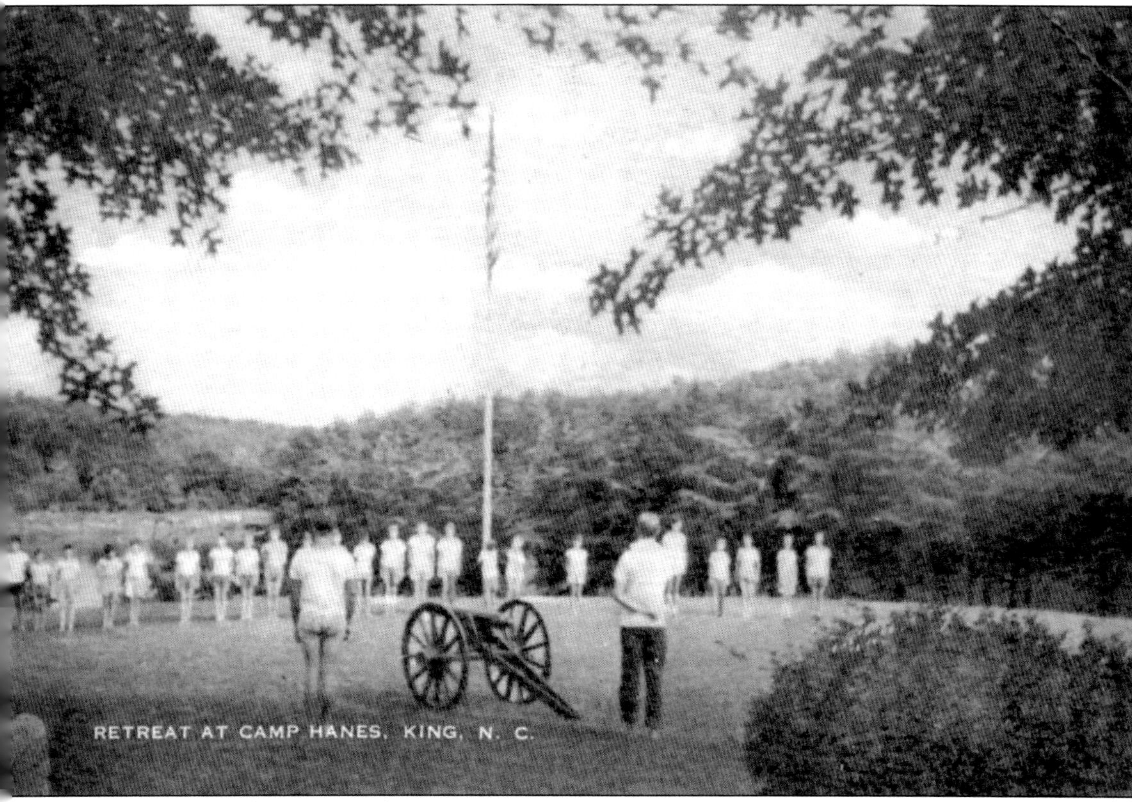

This postcard captures the morning ritual of campers standing in attendance around the flagpole at Camp Hanes about 1930.

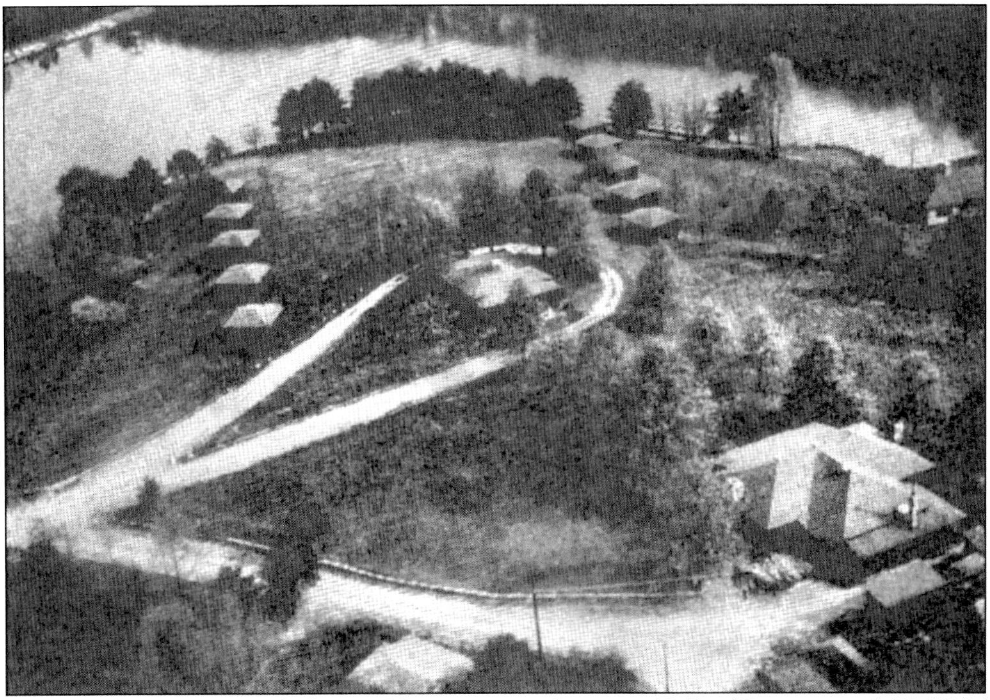

This bird's-eye view of Camp Hanes was taken in 1942. (Courtesy of YMCA/ Camp Hanes.)

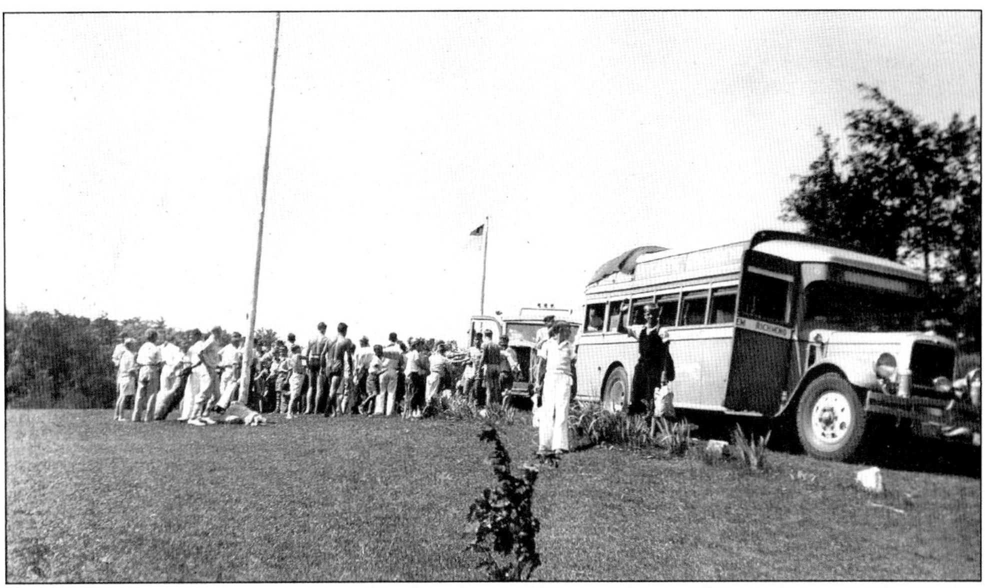

Campers arrive at Camp Hanes by Greyhound bus in this undated photograph. In the early days, campers boarded a flatbed truck at the YMCA on Spruce Street in Winston-Salem for the 25-mile trip to Camp Hanes. (Courtesy of YMCA/Camp Hanes.)

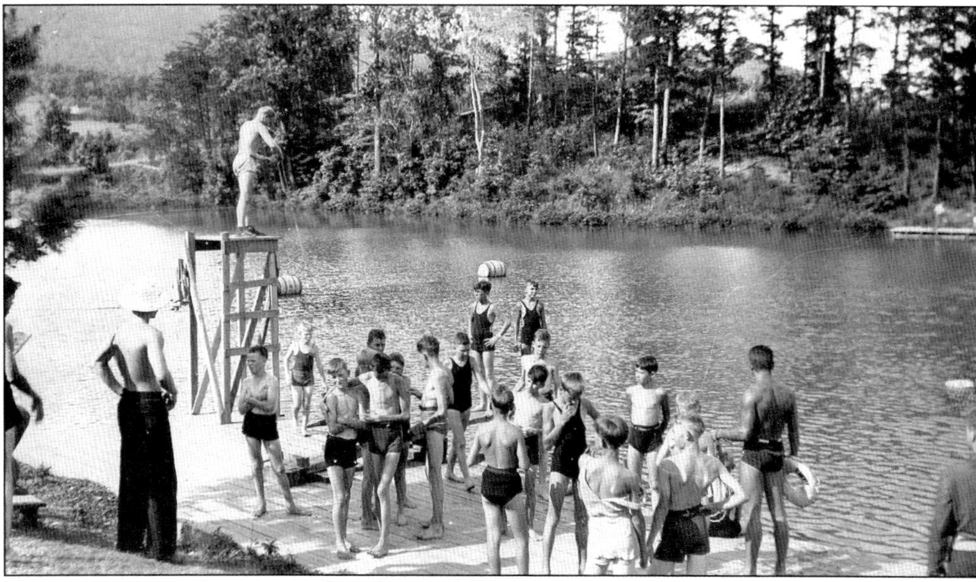

Camp Hanes is where many boys learned how to swim, as seen in this photograph taken in the summer of 1940. In the early days, the camp had no hot water, and cold water came from a faucet outside each cabin, so the closest thing to a shower was swimming. (Courtesy of YMCA/Camp Hanes.)

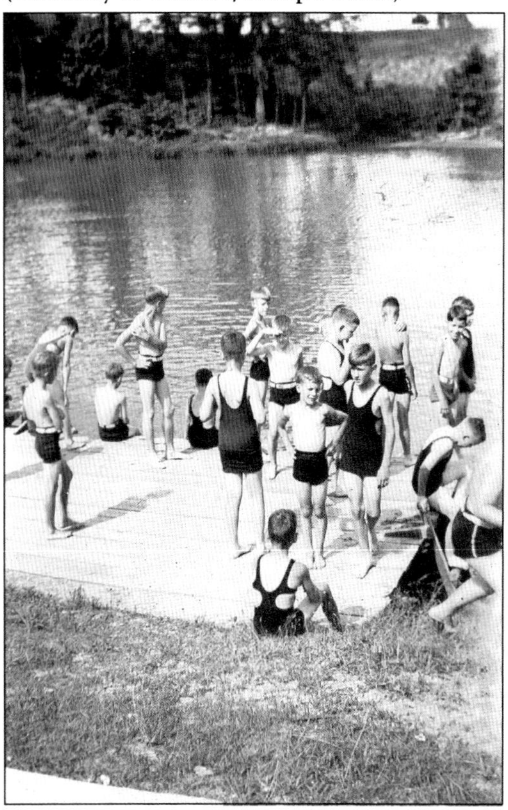

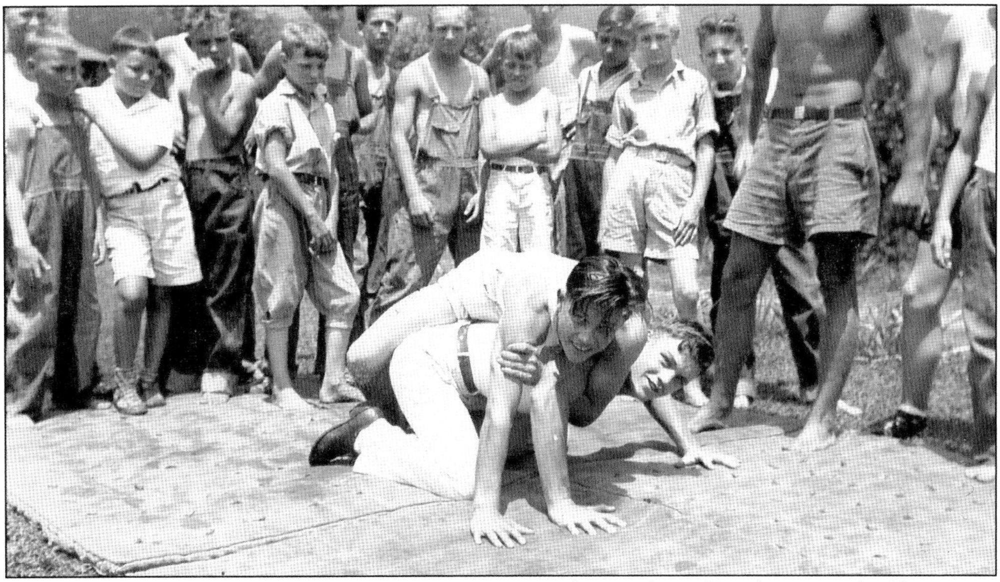

Campers are caught wrestling at Camp Hanes in this early-1950s photograph. (Courtesy of YMCA/Camp Hanes.)

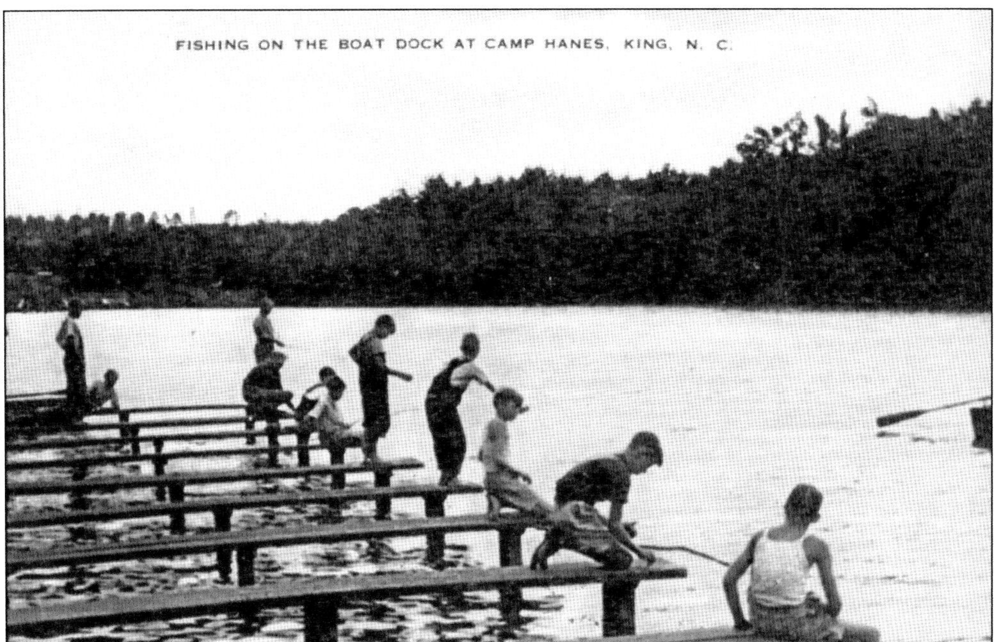

This postcard captures campers fishing on the boat dock at Camp Hanes.

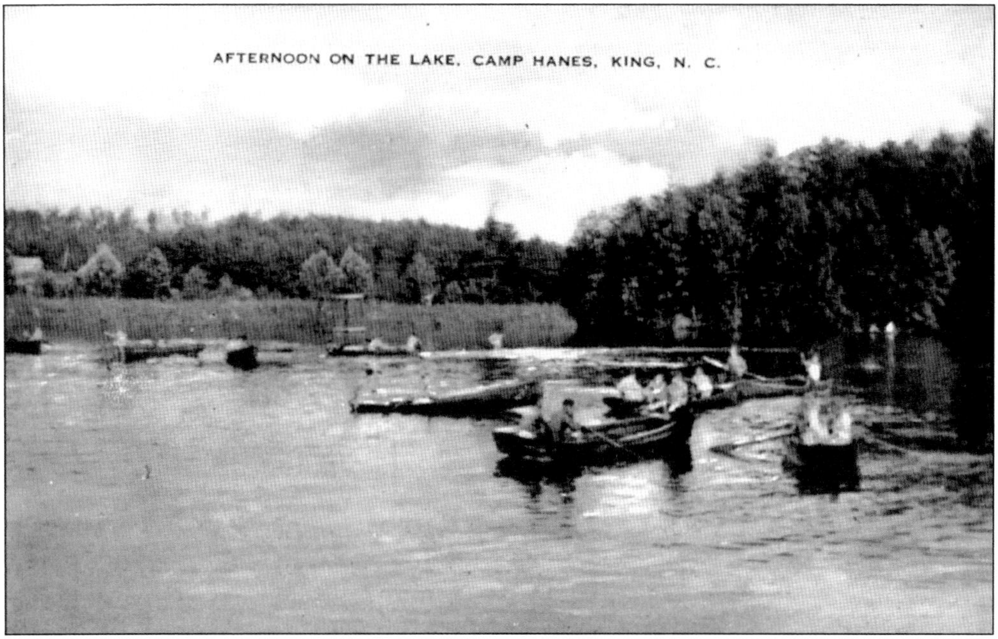

An afternoon on the lake at Camp Hanes is captured in this postcard postmarked 1947.

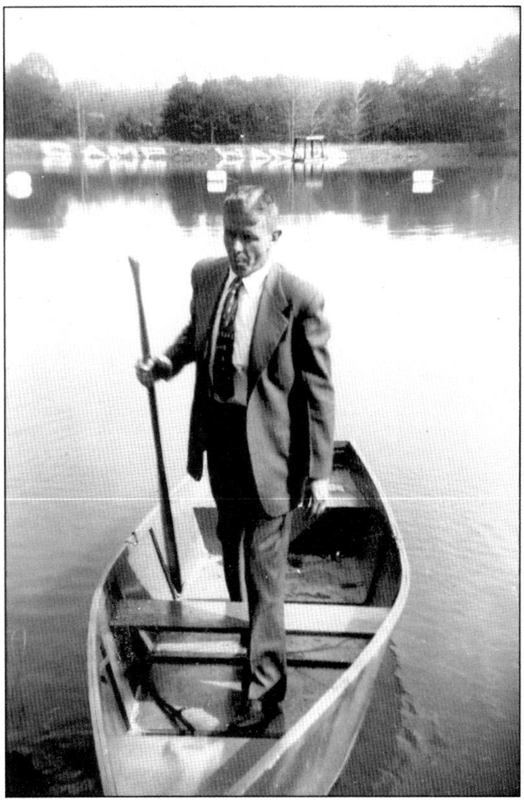

Charles Fort arrives at the docks on Camp Hanes Lake, today known as the Lower Lake. Fort served as the general secretary of the YMCA of Greater Winston-Salem, a title known today as chief executive officer. (Courtesy of YMCA/Camp Hanes.)

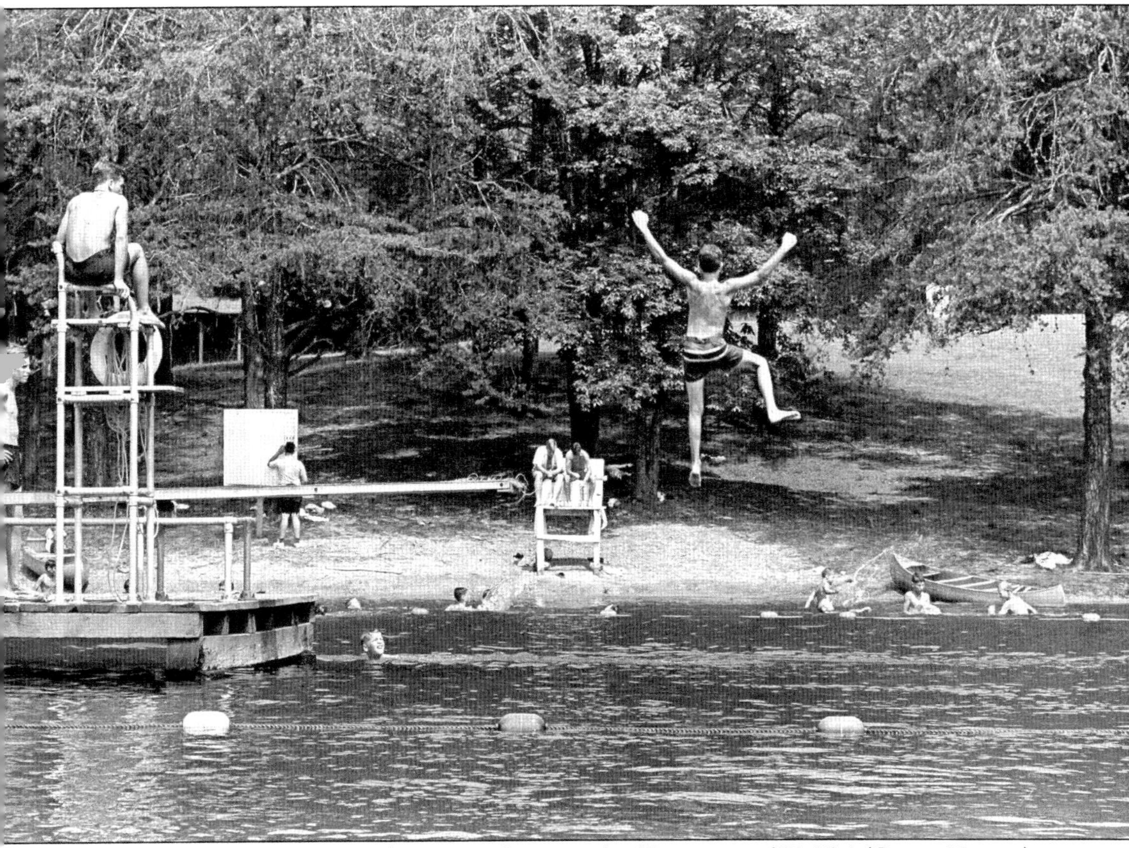

A camper takes a plunge in this 1968 photograph. (Courtesy of YMCA/Camp Hanes.)

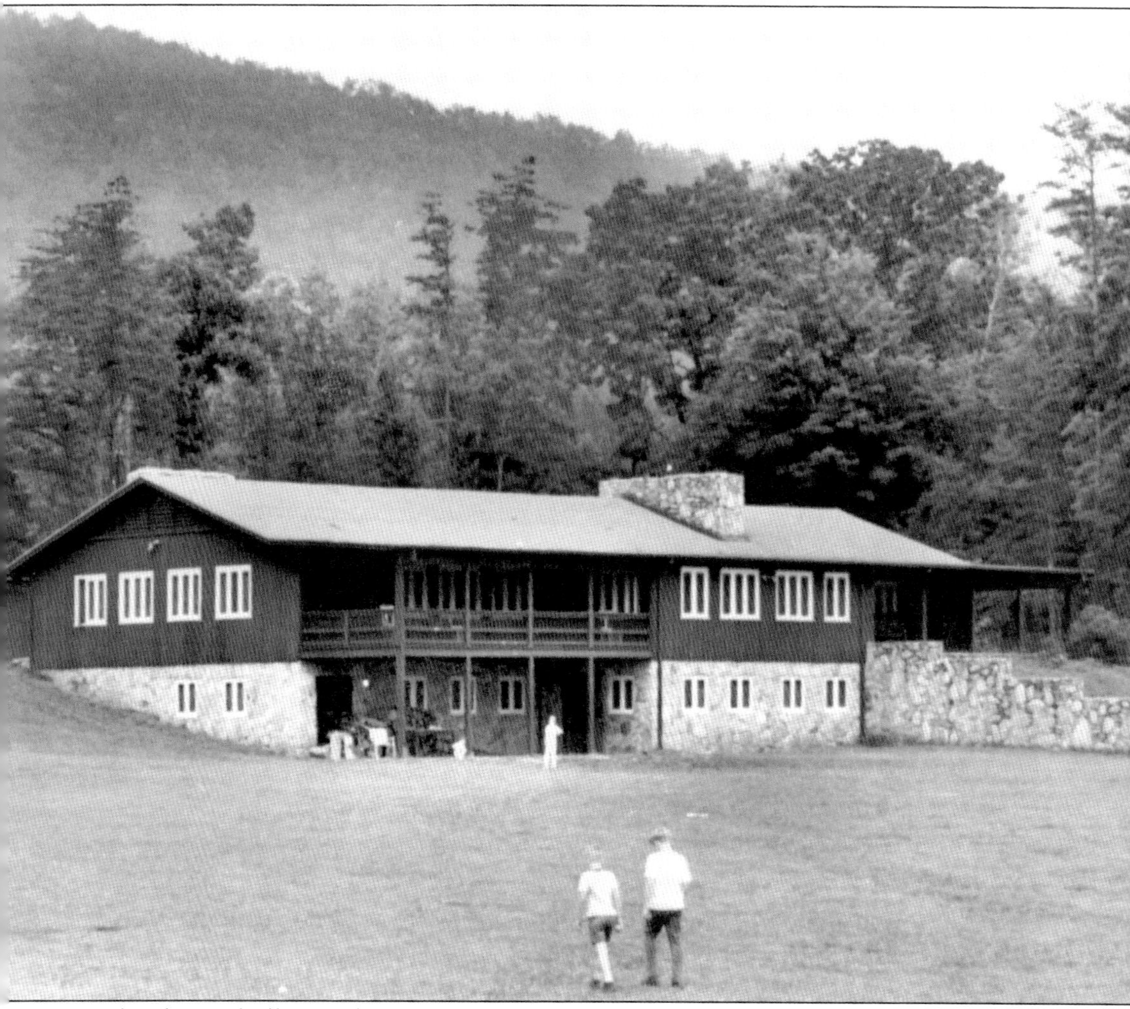

The dining hall, seen here in 1958, was built after 360 additional acres were added to the camp in the 1950s. A typical breakfast at the dining hall included pancakes and sausage, while the dinner menu held roast beef, mashed potatoes, green beans, rolls, and cobbler. (Courtesy of YMCA/Camp Hanes.)

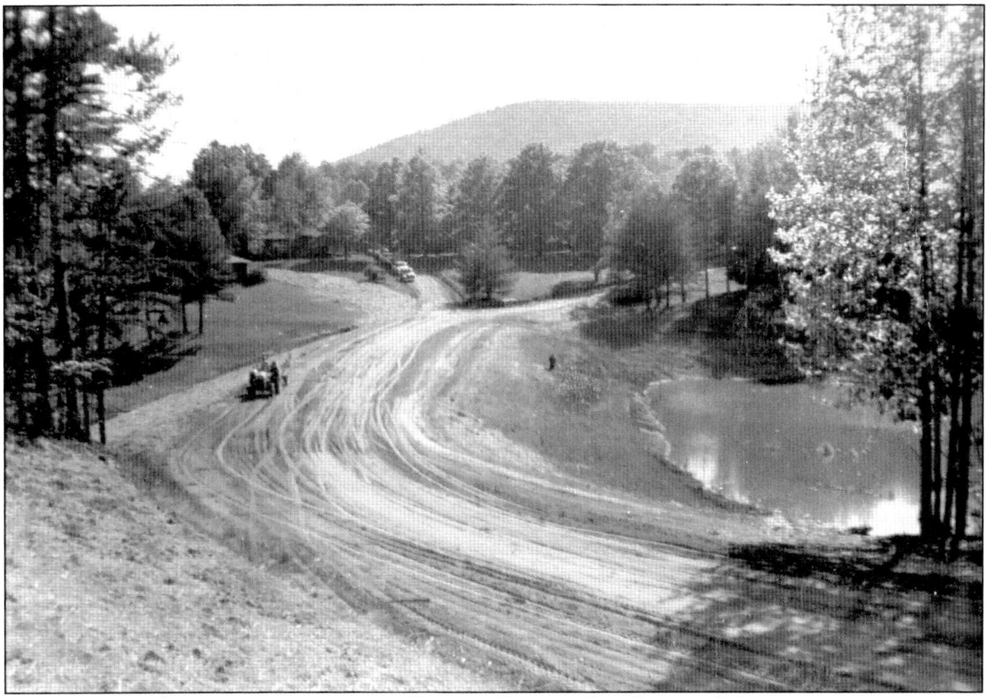

Camp Hanes began constructing a dam with a road to be used for an entrance to the camp in the 1950s photograph seen above. The construction created another lake on the other side of the dam, which became known as the Upper Lake, seen being filled in the photograph below. (Courtesy of YMCA/Camp Hanes.)

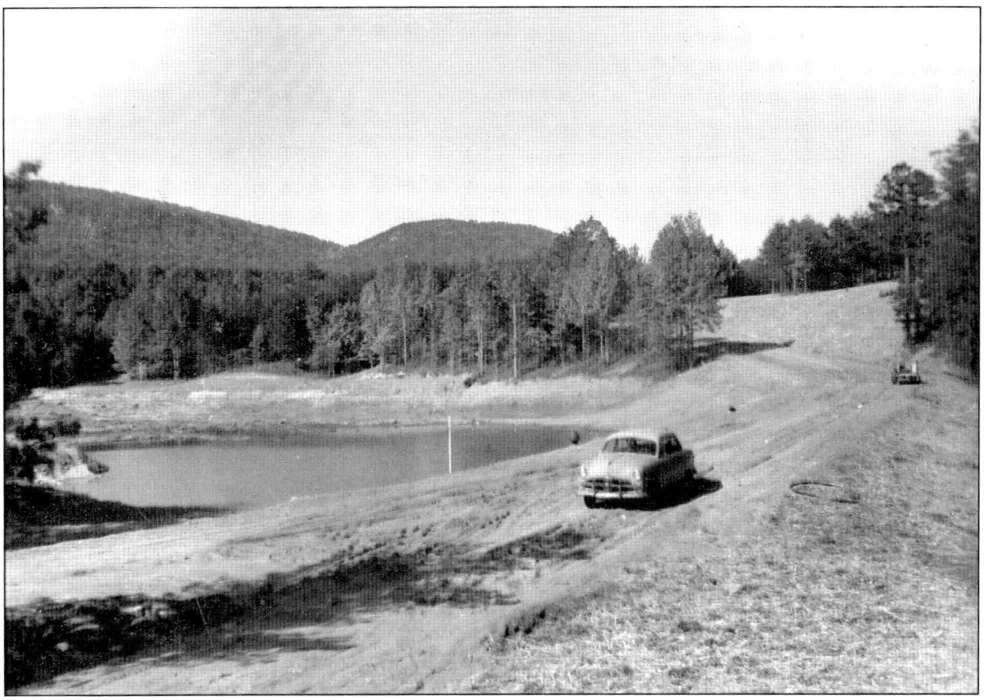

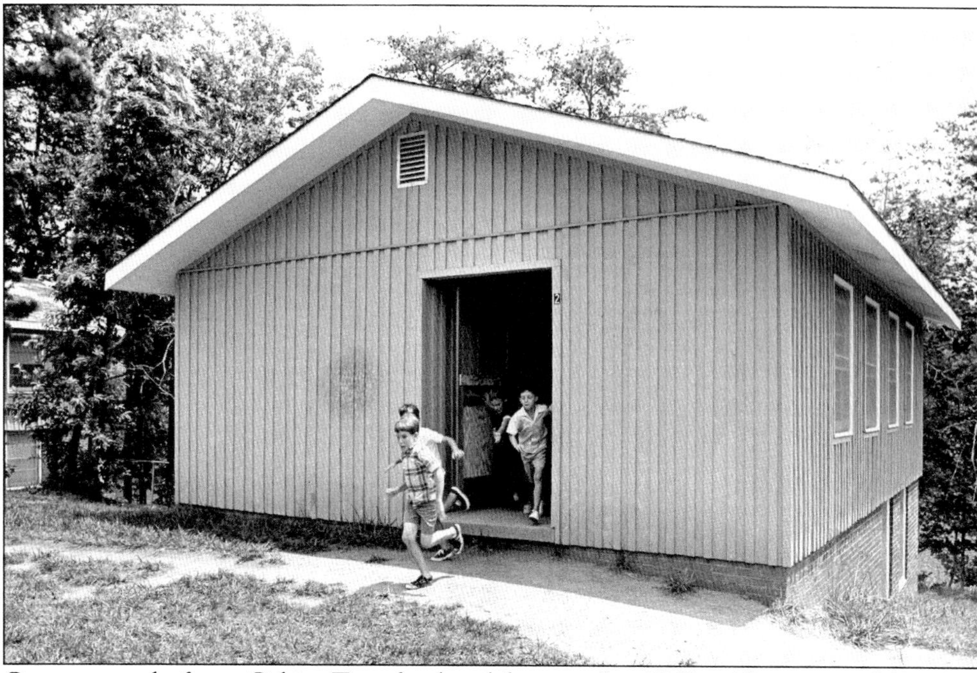

Campers rush from Cabin Two for breakfast in the 1960s. (Courtesy of YMCA/ Camp Hanes.)

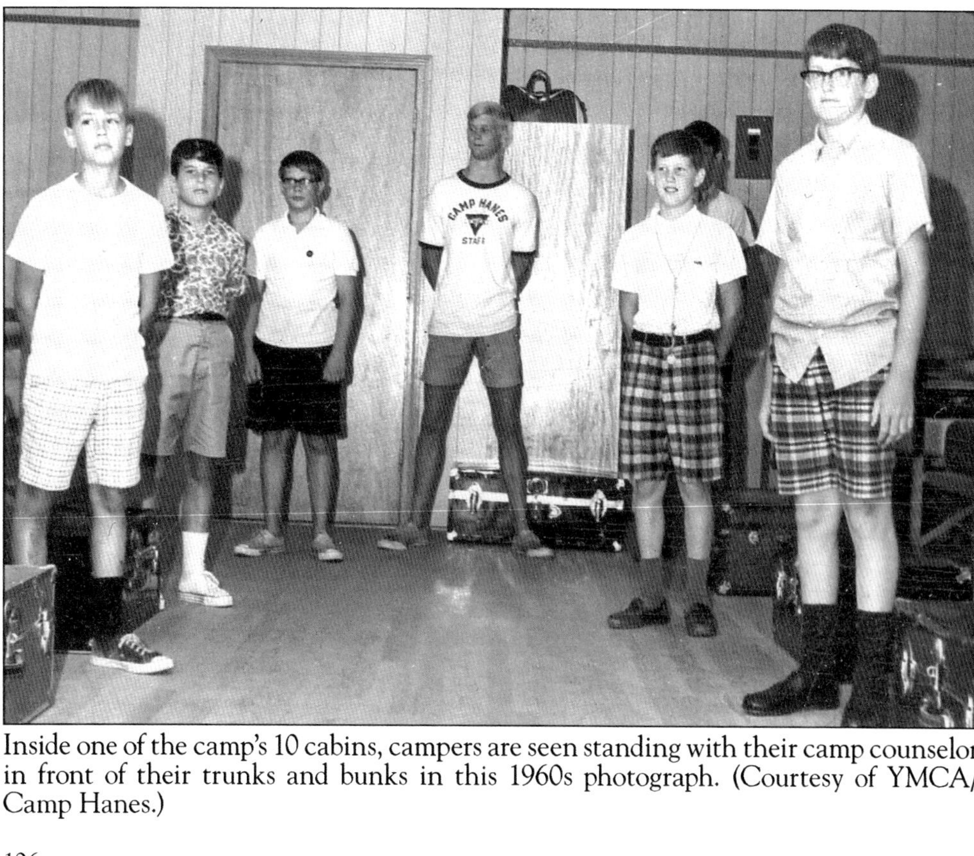

Inside one of the camp's 10 cabins, campers are seen standing with their camp counselor in front of their trunks and bunks in this 1960s photograph. (Courtesy of YMCA/ Camp Hanes.)

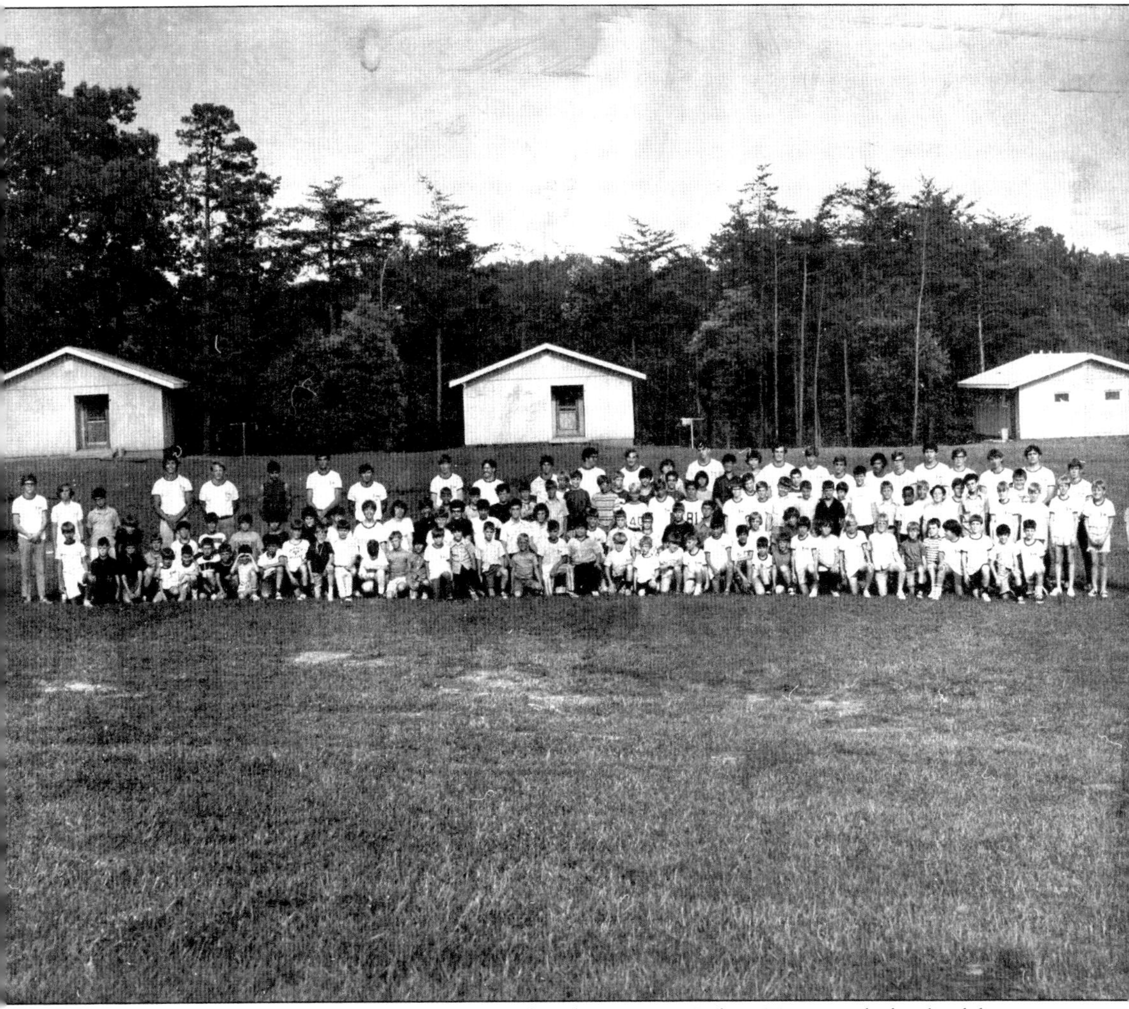

Campers and counselors pose in front of Cabin One, Cabin Two, and the bathhouse in this early-1970s photograph. The cabins were built in the 1960s, with heat allowing campers to stay in the winter. (Courtesy of YMCA/Camp Hanes.)

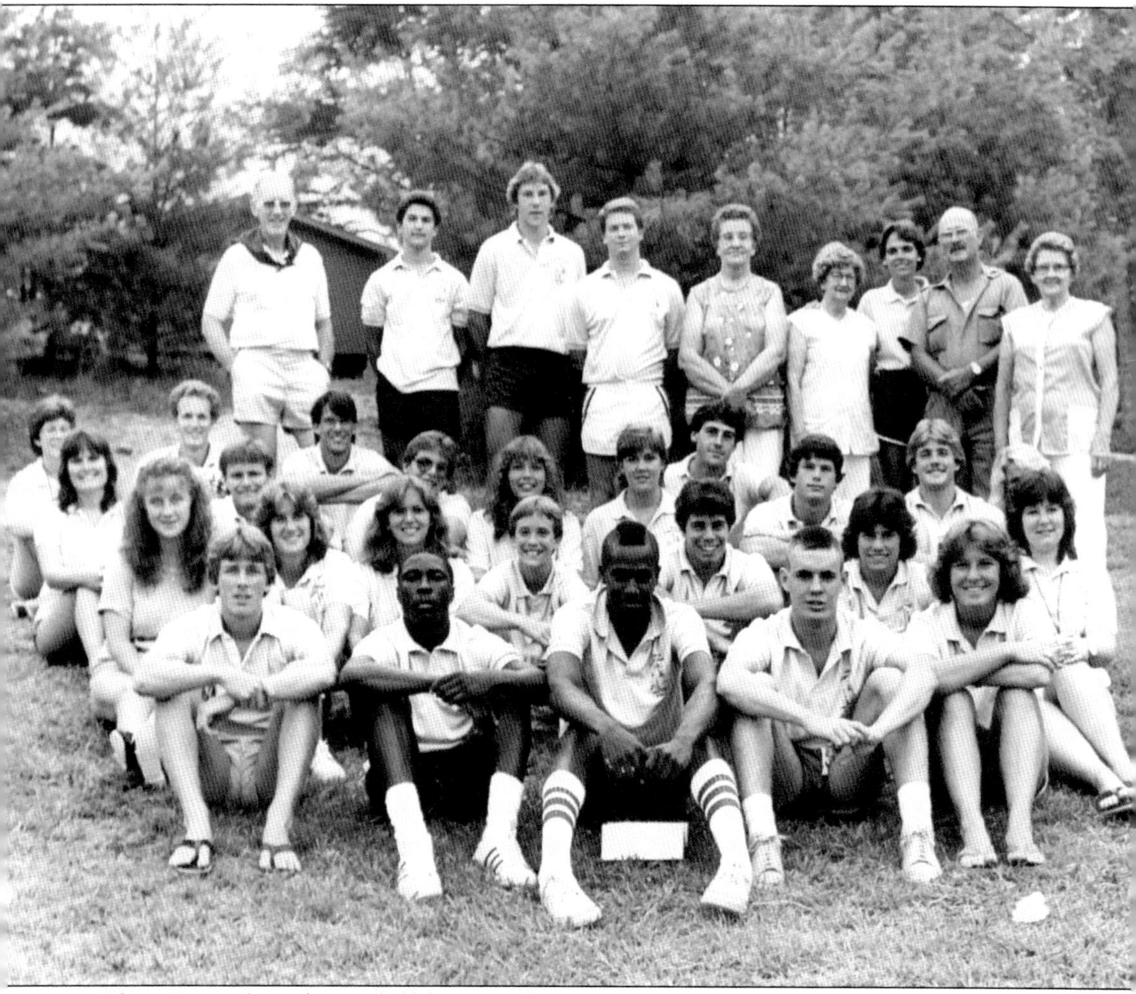

Glenn Paine (standing at left) became Camp Hanes's first full-time camp director in 1976. His first goal when he took the job was to integrate girls into the Camp Hanes program as campers and counselors, as seen in this photograph. Paine started a horseback riding program, a ropes course, and a climbing wall. (Courtesy of YMCA/Camp Hanes.)

Four

BACKDOOR NEIGHBORS

I don't care who they were, people in King pitched in to help each other, everyone helped each other regardless. It meant a lot to me to see that growing up.

—Bobby "Crow" McGee, recalling his family and neighbors growing up in King

The foundation of any community is the welcoming spirit of its people. It is a spirit seen in the faces of neighbors who welcome you through their back door, a formal entrance for those with neighborly hearts. King and its surrounding communities' strongest asset has always been people who offer their hands in times of need and lend their heart in times of sorrow. It is a quality spoken many times in action, rather than words.

The following collection of images gives a small glimpse into the large canvas of King's spirit. This glimpse is provided through photographs that capture everyday neighbors, farmers, and Boy Scout leaders. Some of our neighbors have made headlines sharing their talents with the world, from the basketball court to the *Grand Ole Opry*. From those who served our nation to the ones who won the race behind the wheel, they carried our neighborly spirit.

They are our community and our backdoor neighbors—they are each of us.

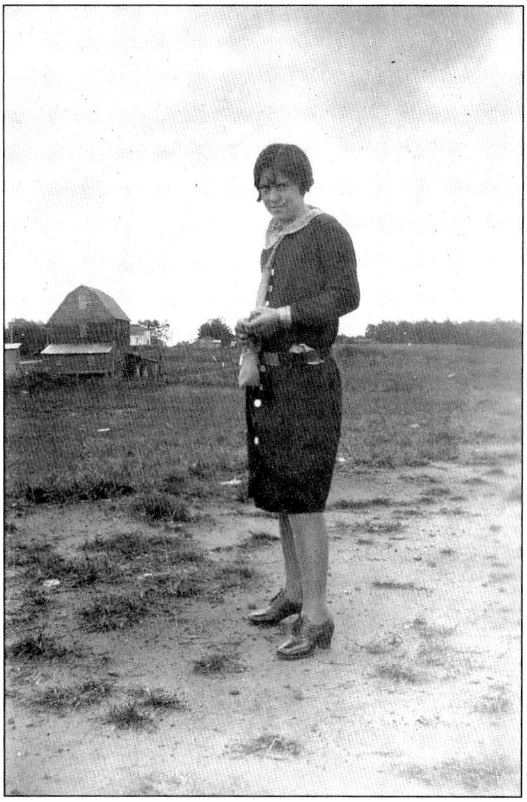

Eunice Lawson is pictured around 1923 with the King Roller Mill in the background. (Courtesy of Eunice Lawson Collection.)

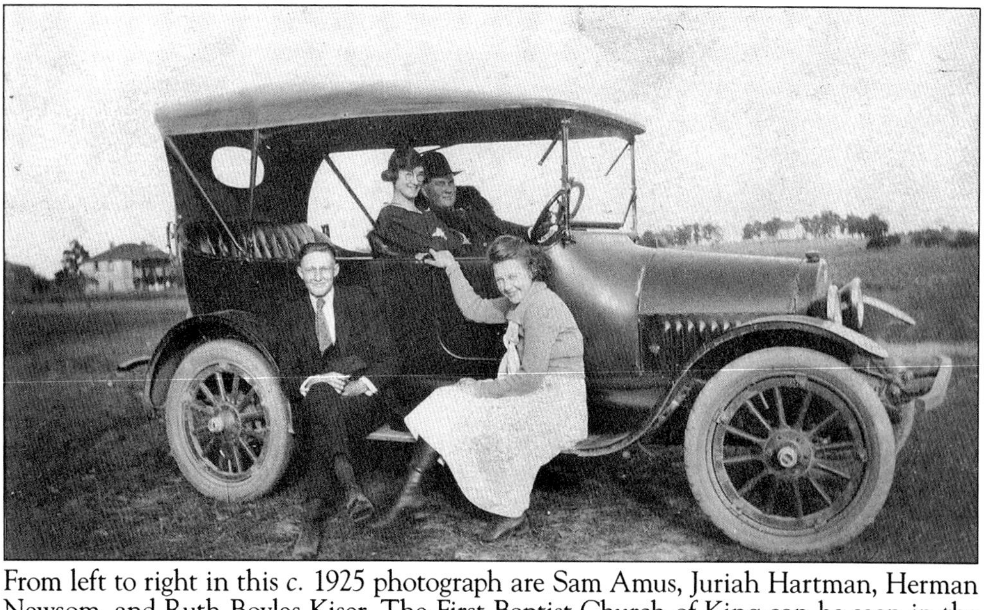

From left to right in this *c.* 1925 photograph are Sam Amus, Juriah Hartman, Herman Newsom, and Ruth Boyles Kiser. The First Baptist Church of King can be seen in the distance looking east, above the hood of the automobile. (Courtesy of Doris Rutledge and Hugh Kiser.)

Cousins Della Newsom Baker (left) and Dallas Newsom (right) are pictured with Grady Newsom in the window of the automobile around 1923. (Courtesy of Essie Spainhour.)

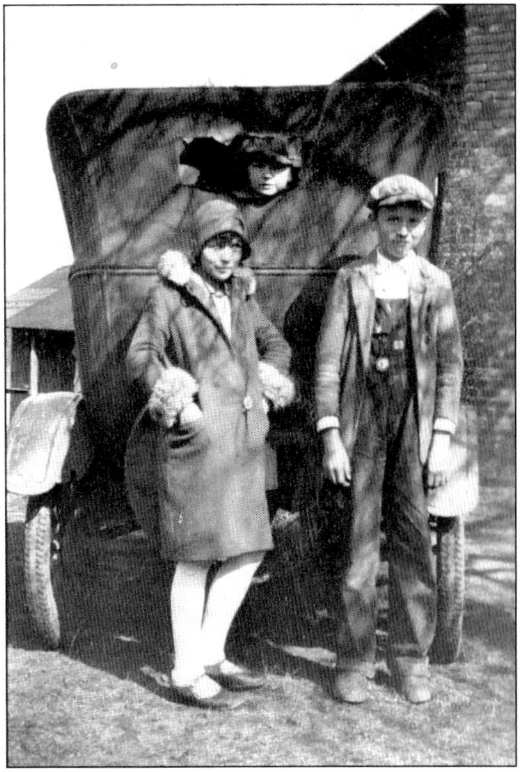

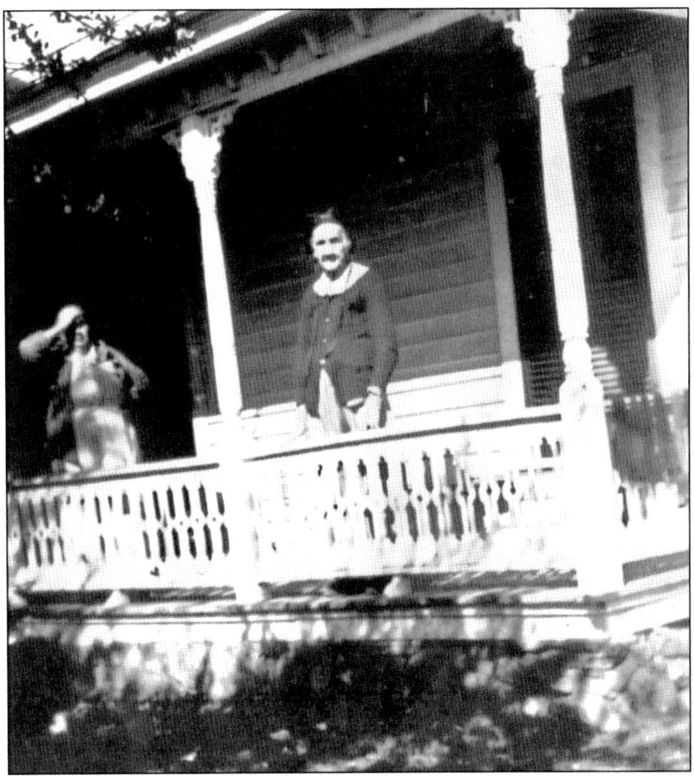

Betty King Tillotson (left) and Lucy Ann King (right) are photographed on the front porch of the Tillotson home in the Mount Olive community in the 1920s. (Courtesy of Eddy Morphies.)

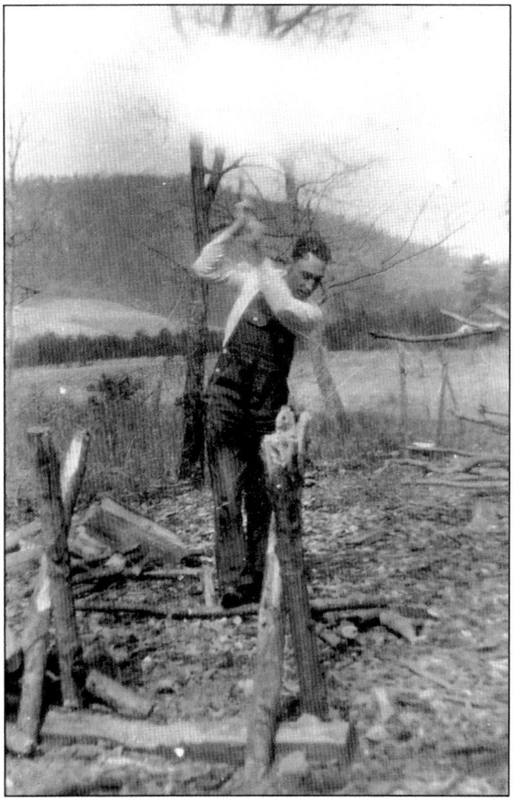

Nathan "Nate" Cardwell chops wood on his father's farm near Sauratown Mountain around 1935. (Courtesy of Betty Elliott.)

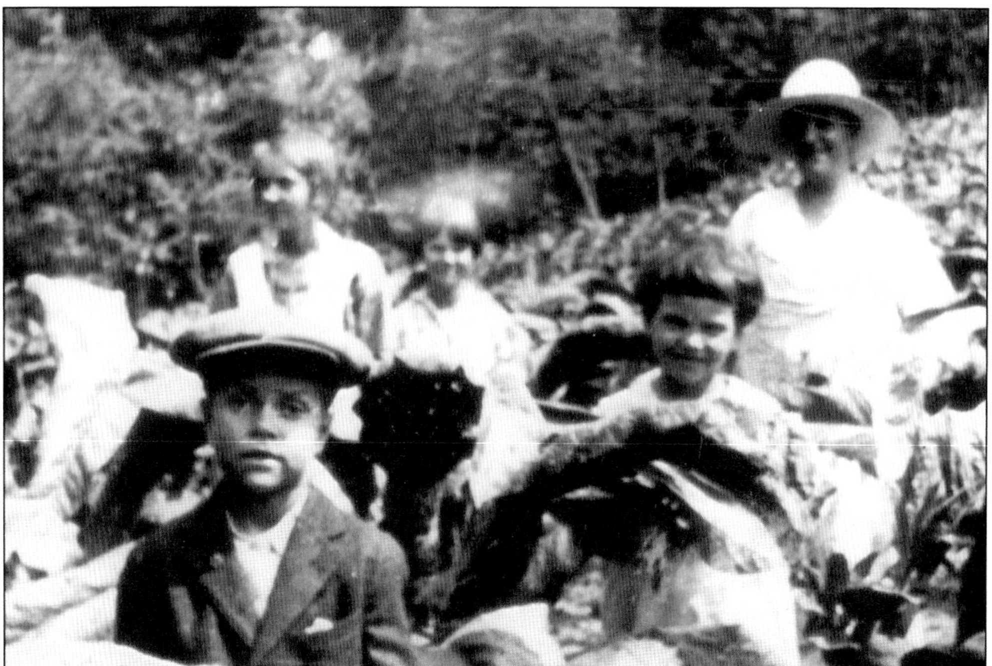

Vertie Goff Meadows works the tobacco fields with her children near King. (Courtesy of Dorothy Meadows Creed and the Bishop family.)

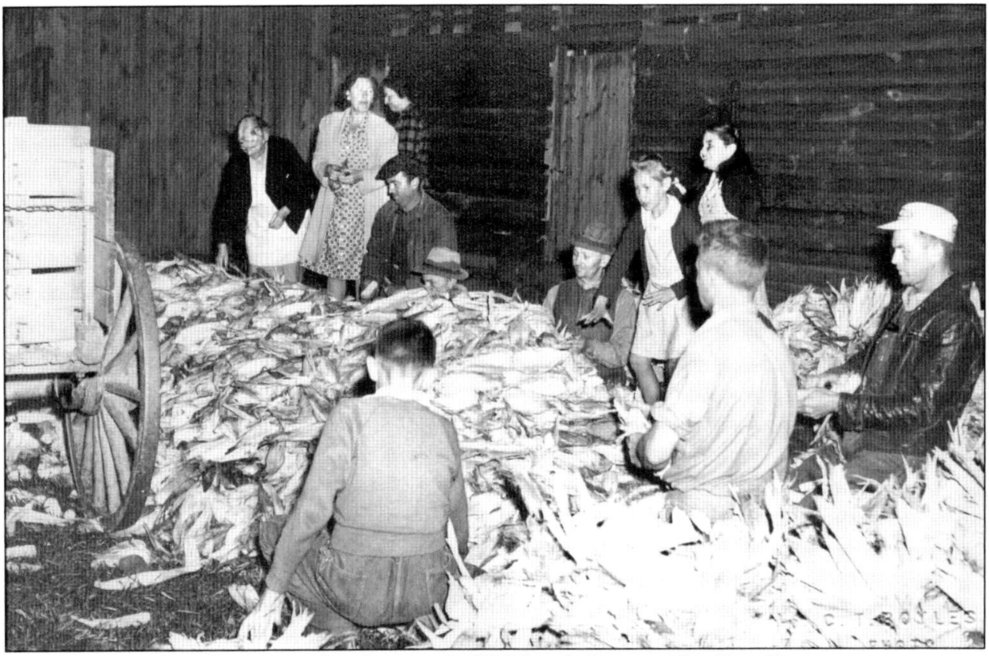

Neighbors gather for a corn shucking at J. W. Kiser's farm in the Dry Springs community near King in the late 1930s. Included here are Decie Boyles, Ruth Kiser, Effie Napier, George Stanley, Dwaft Tuttle, Doris Kiser, Marie Smith, Dewey Rierson, and Grant Smith. (Courtesy of Doris Rutledge and Hugh Kiser.)

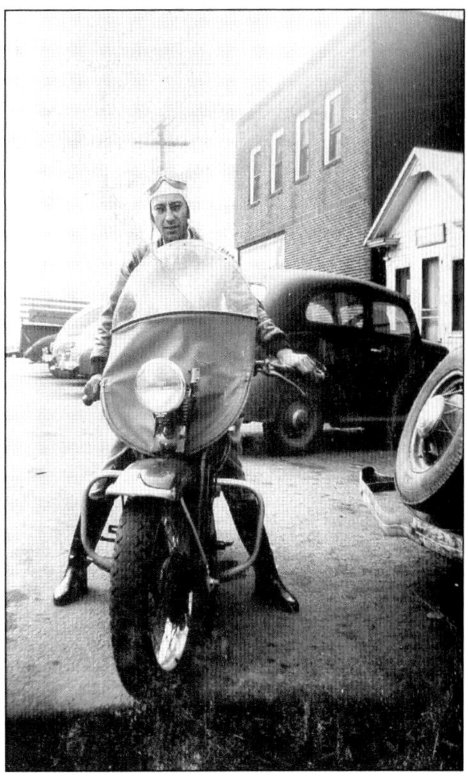

Renard Griffin is pictured on his motorcycle in downtown King in 1946. (Courtesy of Annie Sue Griffin.)

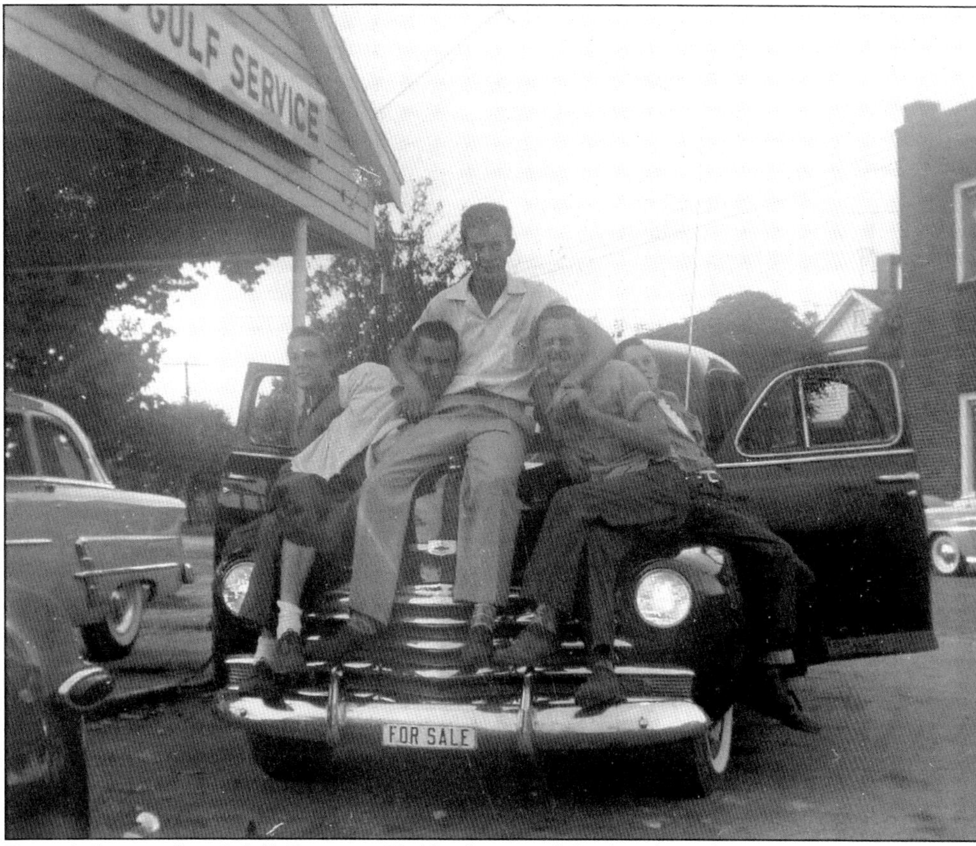

From left to right, Odell Cromer, Teddy Cox, and Richard Mickey pose on the hood of a car at King Gulf Service Station in downtown King around 1955. (Courtesy of Norma Newsom Cox.)

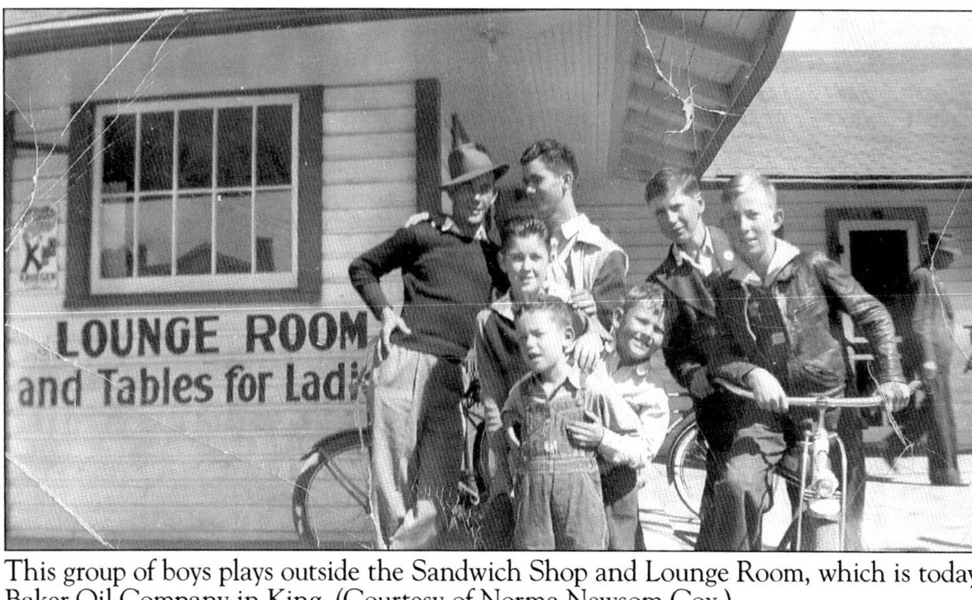

This group of boys plays outside the Sandwich Shop and Lounge Room, which is today Baker Oil Company in King. (Courtesy of Norma Newsom Cox.)

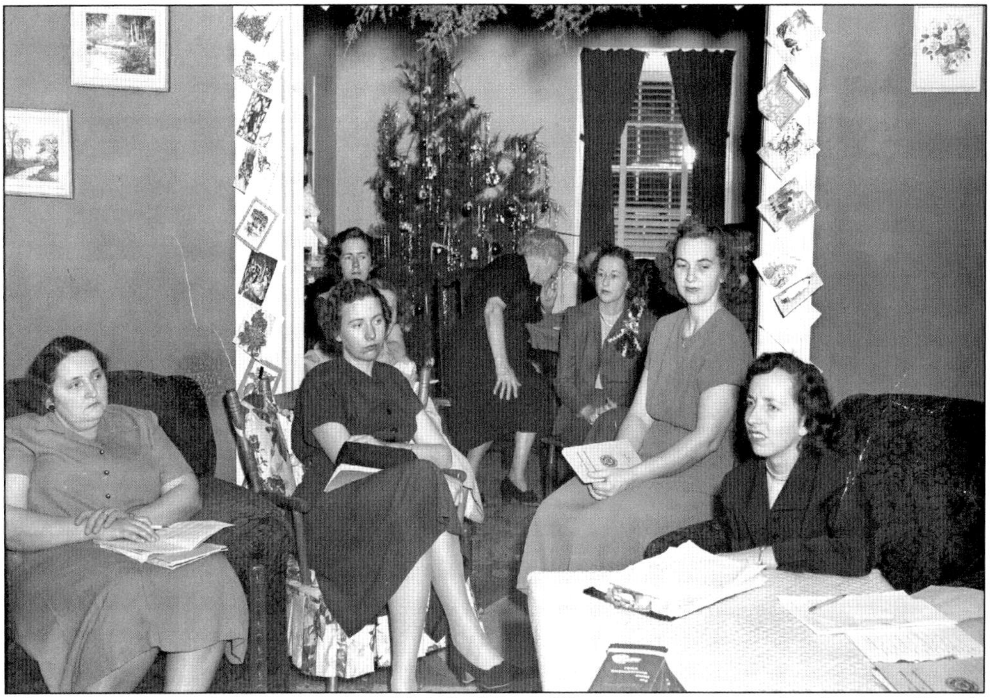

The King Home Demonstration Club held its Christmas party at the home of Ruth Kiser in 1952. From left to right are Madeline Long, Christine Gentry, Edith Keiger, Decie Boyles, Alma Barr, Ruth Kiser, Hessie Barr, Annie Sue Griffin, and agent Jane Bledsoe. (Courtesy of Annie Sue Griffin.)

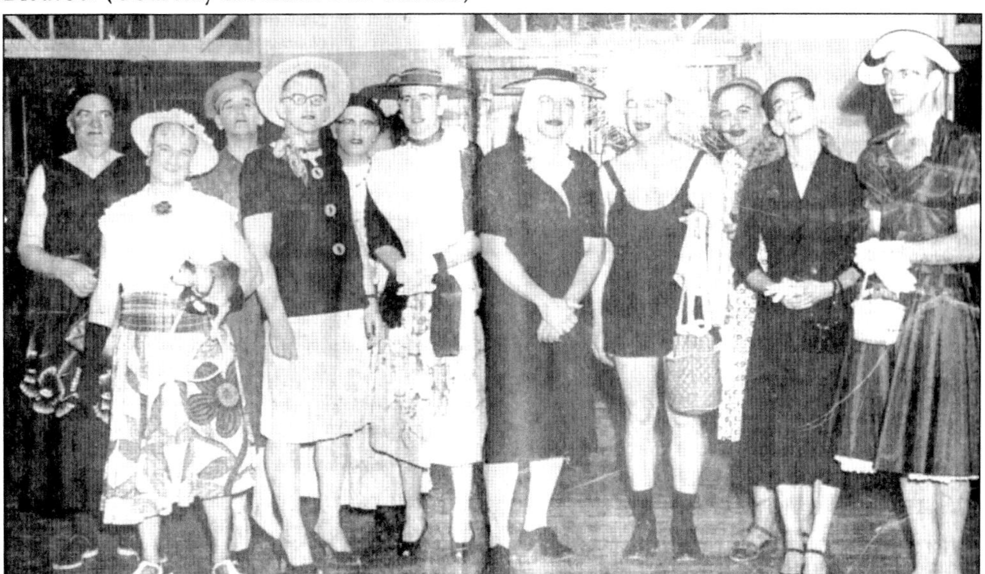

The King Lions Club dressed to the nines during a fund-raiser in the 1950s. From left to right are C. T. McGee, Isaac Booe, S. B. Brandon, Worth Gentry, Holton Gentry, Howell Patterson, Bill Helsabeck, Frank Pulliam, "Snip" Hutchens, Frank Rains, and Thomas McGee. (Courtesy of Trish Shouse.)

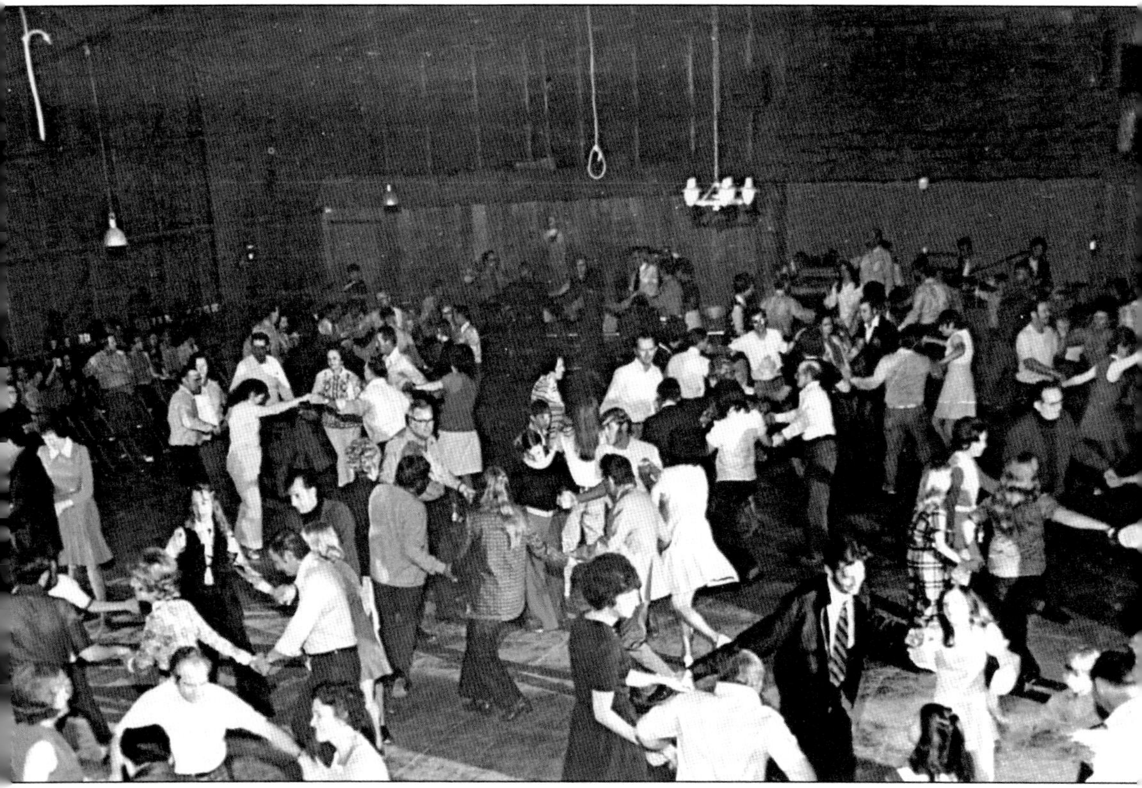

The King Barn Dance, seen above, opened in the late 1960s inside a former airplane hanger on Meadowbrook Drive. In the late 1970s, after a change in ownership, this favorite dance spot for folks in King became known as the Music Palace. In 1988, a new owner changed the name to the Carolina Opry, and since 1990, it has been known as the Country Corral.

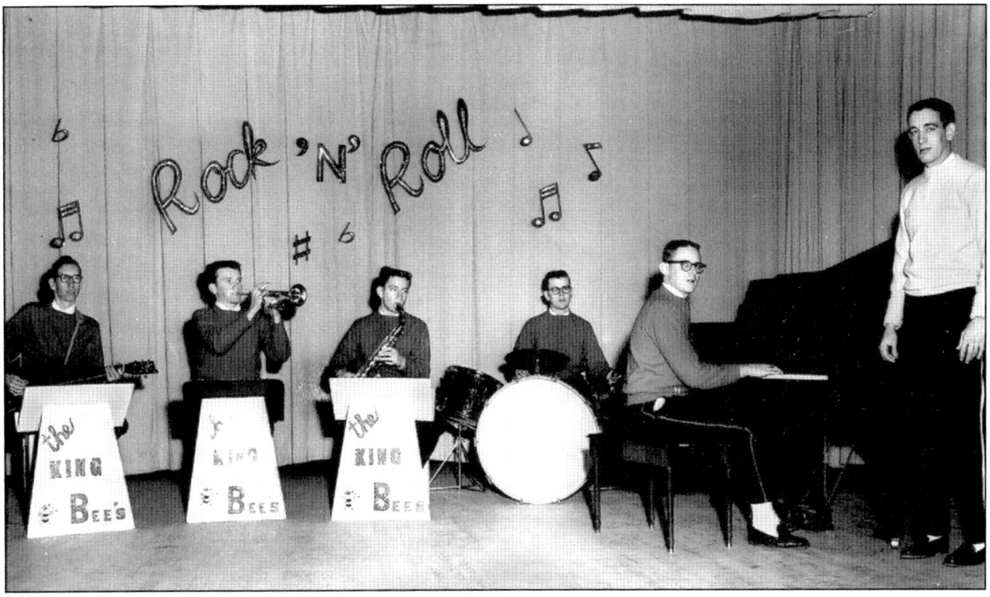

The King Bees, here *c.* 1958, were originally formed in 1956 from a group of King High School band students who were going to the Beta Club State Convention in Raleigh. Their club adviser, Audrey Kirby, encouraged them to form a combo and compete in a talent contest. The original group, whose name was the King-B's, referring to the Beta Club, consisted of Billy Long on saxophone, Robert Slate on clarinet, Lenwood Lawson on trombone, Lewis Carroll on drums, Daphne "Pat" Tuttle on piano, and vocalist Pat Newsome Kapp. They won the talent contest and became an instant hit in the community. At the end of 1956, four members graduated and left the band. In the above photograph, the King Bees are, from left to right, Harvey Mabe on guitar, Tony Newsome on trumpet, Billy Long on saxophone, Lewis Carroll on drums, Dale Boyles on piano, and vocalist Wayne Lee Smith. (Courtesy of Lewis Carroll.)

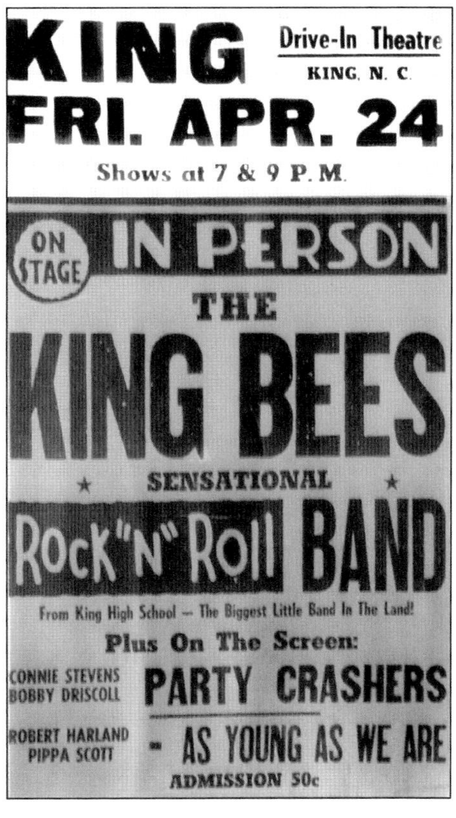

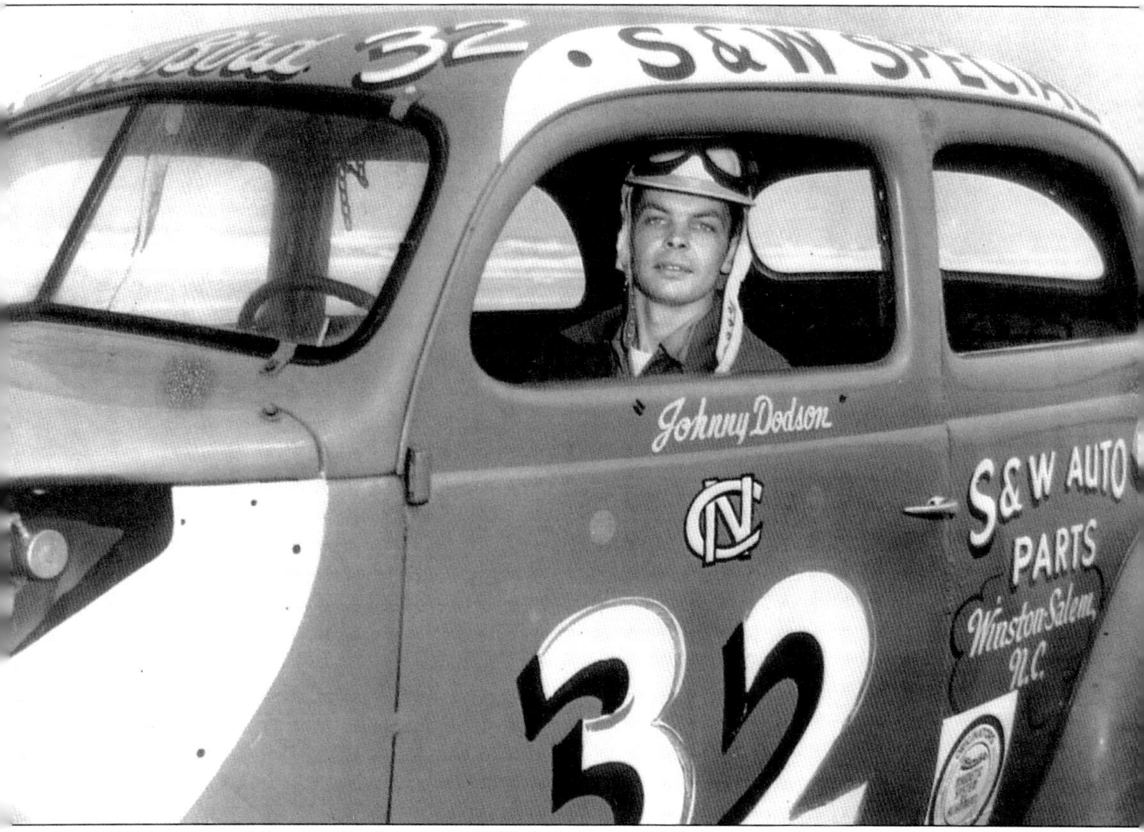

King native Johnny Dodson, c. 1950, became widely known for his talent as a racecar driver during the 1950s. He had numerous successes at Bowman Gray Stadium in Winston-Salem, winning the Tobacco Bowl 100 and winning at tracks in Charlotte, Greensboro, and Raleigh. He raced in several states in the Grand National Series, which later became known as the Winston Cup Series of NASCAR. He drove for Lee Petty in the Convertible Series in 1958. He drove seven races for the Pettys, including on the beach track of Daytona, and had four top-10 finishes. His talents and skills were passed on to his children. Four sons—Brad, Bruce, Barry, and John Dodson—continued his love of racing, working for Petty Enterprises. Brad's career began with Rusty Wallace's Blue Max Team, and he has become known as one of NASCAR's best in fabricating sheet metal for several Busch Series teams. Bruce is now in trucking. Barry became the crew chief for Rusty Wallace and was there when Wallace won his only Winston Cup Championship in 1989. John is a technical director for NASCAR Technical Institute in Mooresville, North Carolina. Johnny Dodson died in April 2004. (Courtesy of Lewis Carroll.)

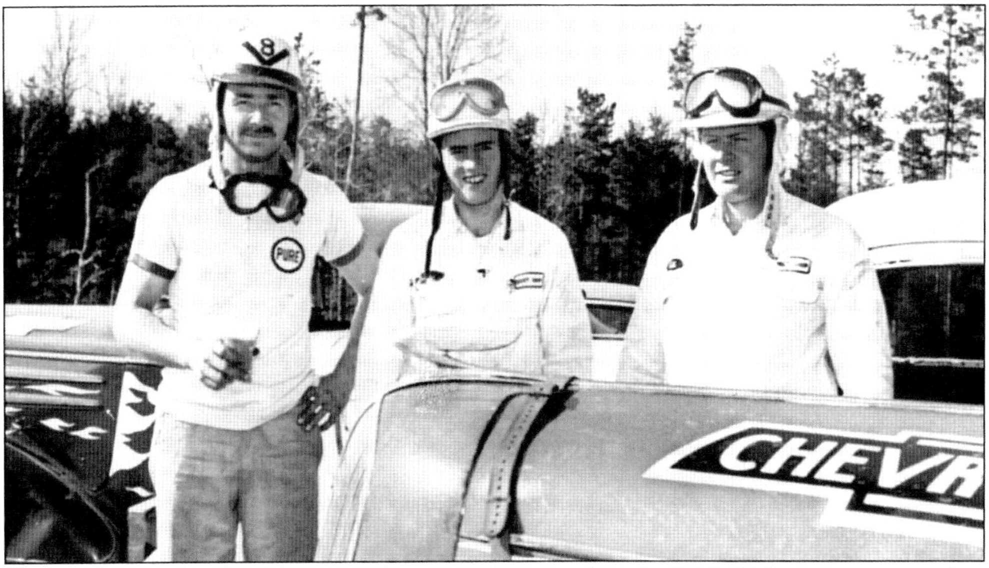

From left to right, Carl Burris, "Fuzzy" Clifton, and E. B. "Eb" Clifton are pictured c. 1956. Brothers Fuzzy and Eb Clifton made a name for themselves racing and building engines. In the early 1950s, Eb built the first Chevrolet to run in NASCAR. In 1969, Eb built a Dodge driven by Jimmy Pardue. Eb's grandson won six championships in the modified division at Bowman Gray Stadium. In 2002 and 2003, Eb's car, driven by Rik Newsome, finished second in points in the Legends series, and in 2004, Eb won the series championship. (Courtesy of Lewis Carroll.)

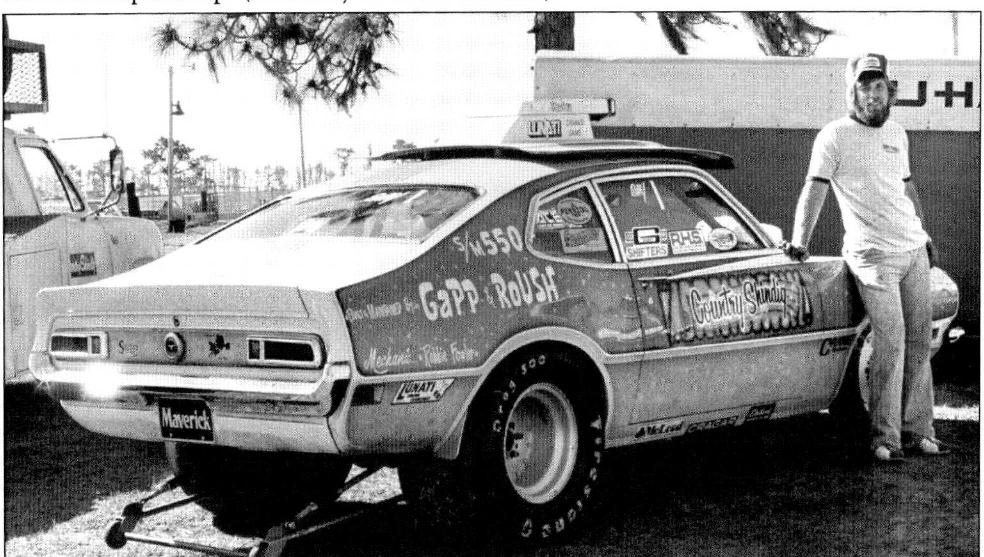

King's Rickie Smith, in 1976, is synonymous with professional stockcar racing in the Southeast. Smith won the International Hot Rod Association (IHRA) Pro Stock World Championship in 1982 and 1986 and was the first driver to breach the seven-second barrier in a Pro Stock racecar. He is the only competitor to have won IHRA National Championships in both professional and sportsman categories. Smith is credited with the quickest elapsed time in Pro Stock history, a 7.17-second clocking at the 1987 IHRA Winter Nationals. (Courtesy of Rickie Smith Racing.)

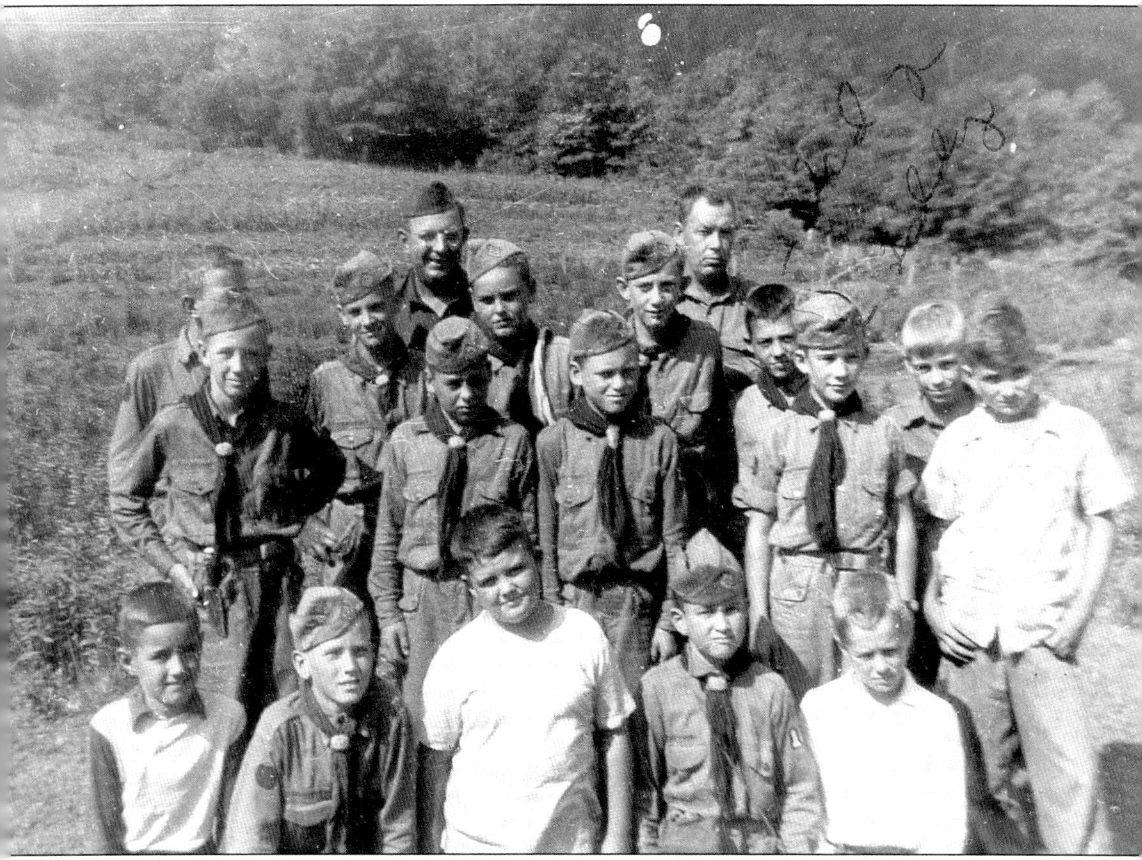

The King Boy Scouts are pictured in the late 1940s. (Courtesy of Norma Newsom Cox.)

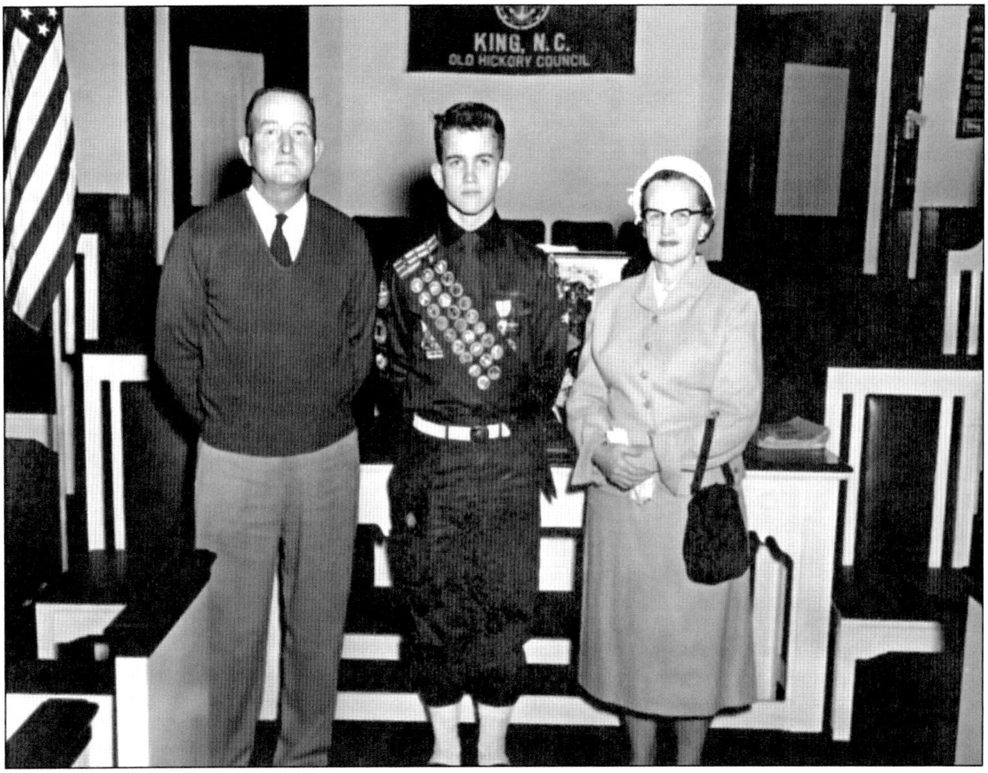

In 1959, Wayne Southern received Stokes County's first Silver Award in the Explorer division of the Boy Scouts of America. He is seen here with his father, Lynn Southern, and mother, Ethel. (Courtesy of Lewis Carroll.)

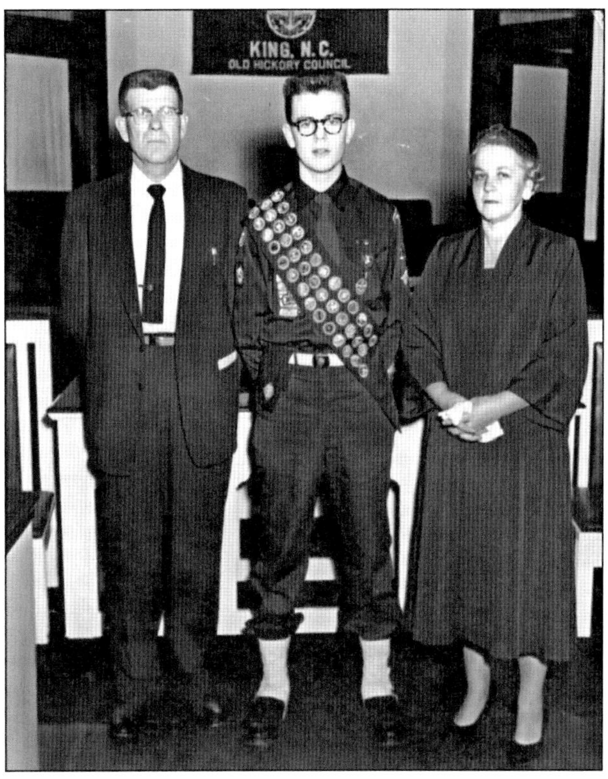

Lewis Carroll became Stokes County's first Eagle Scout in 1959, receiving his award from his father, Newell "Newt" Carroll, and mother, Margaret. (Courtesy of Lewis Carroll.)

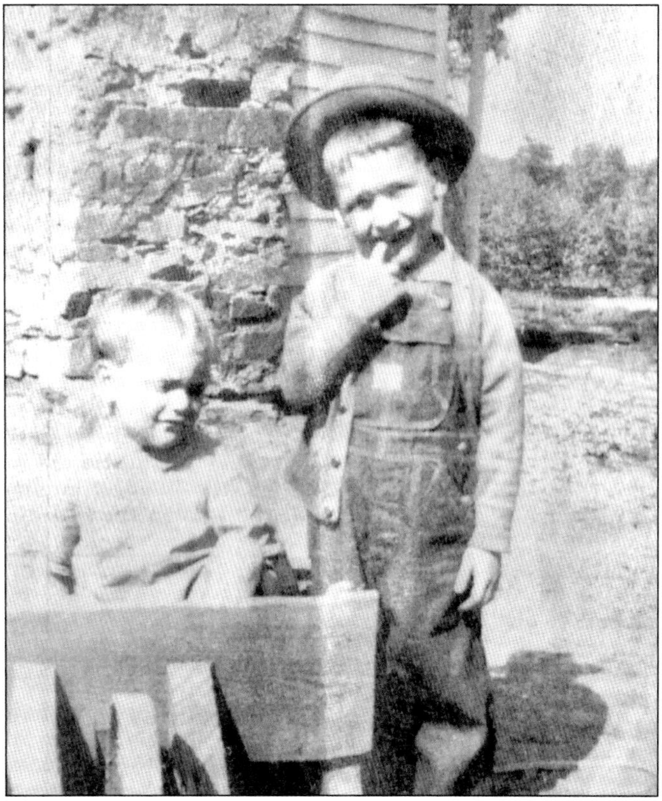

Standing is Billy Boles with his brother, Donald "Bubba," in the Mount Olive community. Billy Boles went on to North Carolina State University and served an illustrious career in the U.S. Air Force, becoming a four-star general. He retired from Randolph Air Force Base in Texas. On March 1, 1997, King honored him with Gen. Billy Boles Day. (Courtesy of Bobby "Crow" McGee.)

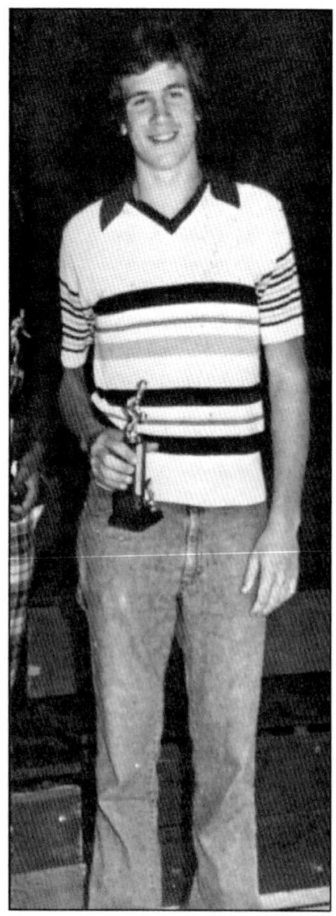

Kenny Dennard is photographed being honored with All-Conference Varsity Basketball at South Stokes High School in May 1976. Dennard grew up in King, and after high school, he went on to play basketball for Duke University and two NBA teams: Kansas City from 1981 to 1983 and Denver from 1983 to 1984. (Courtesy of South Stokes High School Archives.)

Country singer Joe Nichols spent a few years of his youth in King attending Chestnut Grove Junior High School and South Stokes High School. At right is his 10th-grade class picture. Born in Rogers, Arkansas, he lived in King with his father, Mike Nichols. Joe credits his father with inspiring him to become a musician. After a few years in King, Nichols returned to Arkansas, where his mother lived. His father passed away in King in 2002, just as Joe celebrated the rise of his debut single, "The Impossible," which earned him three Grammy nominations. (Courtesy of South Stokes High School Archives.)

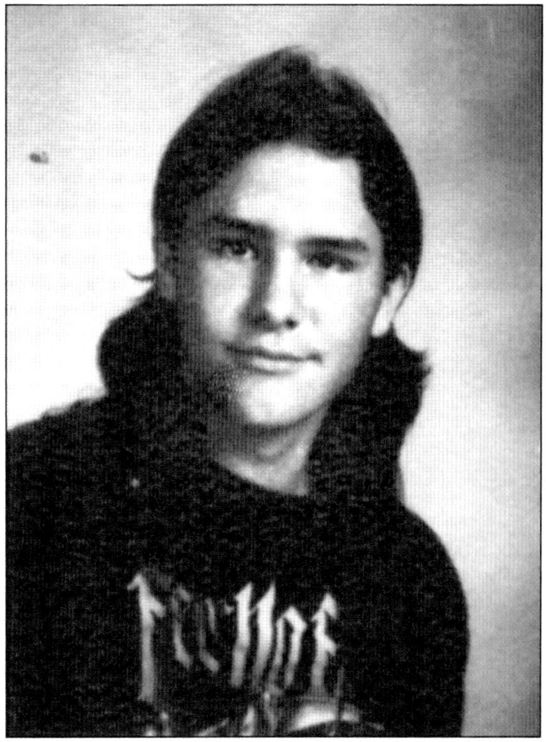

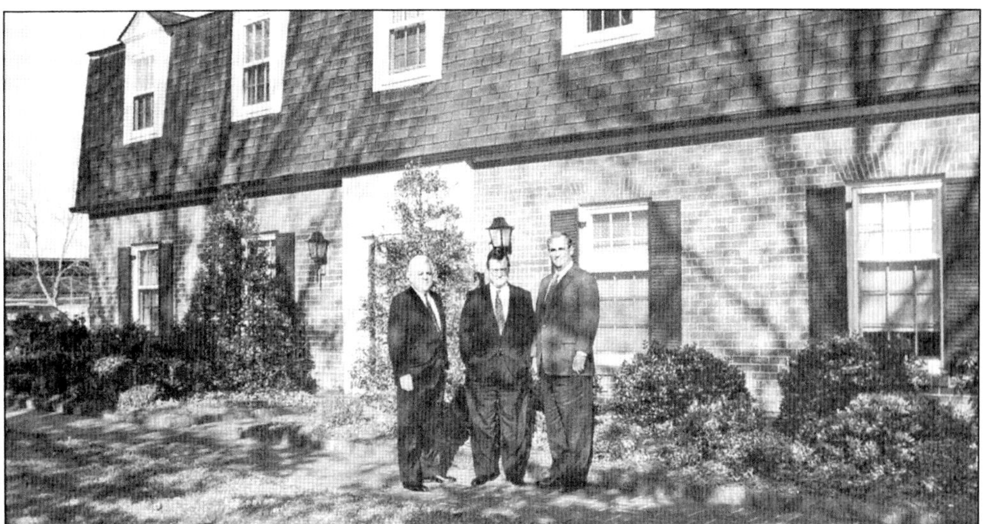

Charles (left) and Ed Shelton (center) are pictured with their friend and former business partner Marvin Gentry in front of Fortis Enterprises in the fall of 1993. In 1962, the Shelton brothers moved from Mount Airy to King and founded Fortis Enterprises, which became the state's largest builder of subdivisions. The company, which was purchased by Daniels International in 1971, built 12 residential subdivisions in King by 1983, helping it turn from a rural agriculture community to a bustling suburb. The brothers gave generously to King churches, schools, and its library. They continue to prosper with Shelton Vineyards, an award-winning winery and the state's largest, near Dobson. (Courtesy of Charles and Edwin Shelton.)

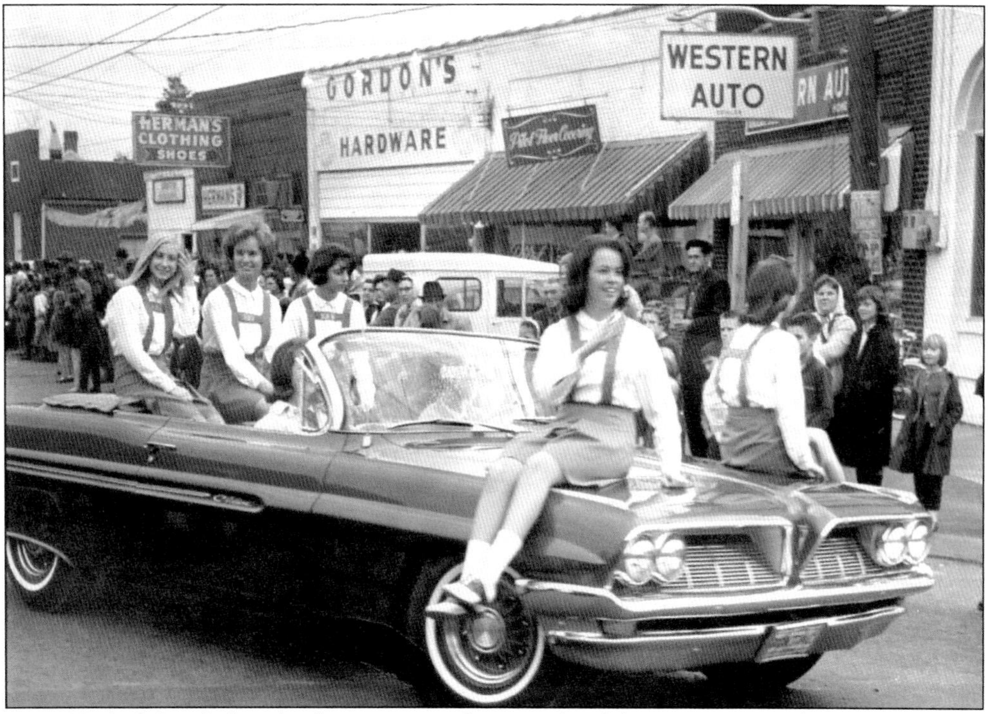

King High School cheerleaders wave to the crowds of the 1963 King Christmas Parade. (Courtesy of Hughes Gentry.)

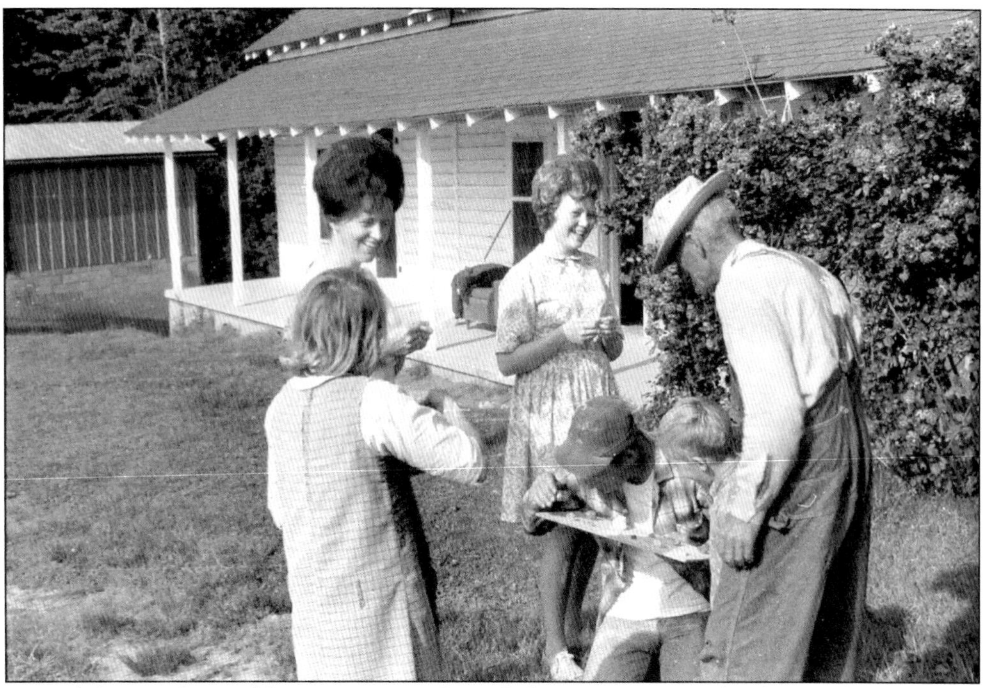

From left to right, Debbie, Vina Lee, Sue, Calvin, Ronnie, and John Tucker laugh as Calvin looks at his son Ronnie's rock collection at their home in the Mount Olive–Capella community in the 1960s.

BIBLIOGRAPHY

BOOKS

Carroll, Robert. *One Hundred Years of King History.* Winston-Salem: Sara Lee Graphics, 1988.
Carroll, Robert. *The History of Mount Olive Baptist Church 1851–1976.* King: Robert Carroll, n.d.
Covington, Howard E. Jr., and Marion A. Ellis. *Working Together, The Sheltons of North Carolina.* Charlotte: The Shelton Cos., 1994.
Covington, T.J. *Walnut Cove and Stokes County,* booklet. Farm Bureau, 1912.
Duncan, Wade, and the Stokes County Historical Society. *The Heritage of Stokes County, North Carolina.* Vol. 2. Charlotte: Delmar Printing and Publishing, 1990.
Hunter, Rixie. *Stokes County, North Carolina,* booklet. Winston-Salem: Pepper Printing Company, c. 1960.
Woodard, John R., ed., and the Stokes County Historical Society. *The Heritage of Stokes County, North Carolina.* Vol. 1. Winston-Salem: Hunter Publishing, 1981.

Images in this collection without a courtesy are from the personal collection of the author.

INTERVIEWS

Boyles, Jim. Interviewed by author. Pinnacle, NC, September 2005.
Carroll, Robert. Interviewed by author. Winston-Salem, NC, February 2004, August–October 2005.
Cox, Norma. Interviewed by author. King, NC, October 2005.
Engelhardt, Linda. Interviewed by telephone. Silex, MO, October 2005.
Griffin, Annie Sue. Interviewed by author. King, NC, August 2005.
Johnston, Margaret. Interviewed by author. Dalton, NC, September 2005.
McClanahan, Margaret. Interviewed by author. King, NC, August 2005.
McGee, Bobby. Interviewed by author. King, NC, October 2005.
Moser, Becky. Interviewed by author. King, NC, March 2004.
Moser, Ralph. Interviewed by author. King, NC, September 2005.
Petree, Susan. Interviewed by author. Tobaccoville, NC, September 2005.
Spainhour, Sallie. Interviewed by author. King, NC, February 2004.

NEWSPAPERS

Danbury Reporter
King Times-News
Winston-Salem Journal

INDEX

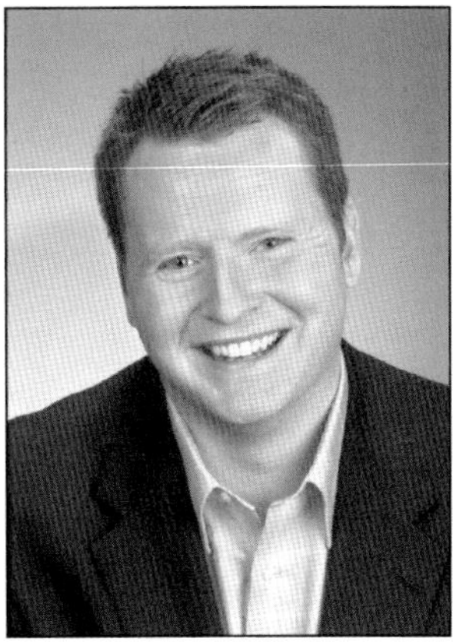

Television journalist Chad Tucker has worked across North Carolina as a news producer, reporter, and anchor. He began in radio at the age of 12 at WKTE AM in King. Chad holds a bachelor's and master's degree from East Carolina University and has been honored for his work by the North Carolina Associated Press and, along with his colleagues, the Edward R. Murrow Award for coverage of Hurricane Floyd and the floods that followed in 1999. A reporter for Fox affiliate WGHP TV, Chad grew up in the Mount Olive–Capella community of King, where his family roots run deep. He is a fifth-great-nephew of Charles King, whose home, King's Cabin, became the namesake of the city of King. Chad is also author of Images of America: *Stokes County*. (Photographed by Megan Morr.)